Contents

Preface to the third edition

The object of this book is to provide an introduction to the soils of the world and to give the widest possible readership a better understanding of their nature, properties and distribution. Environmentalists have vociferously drawn attention to the possible damage which can be caused by pollution of the atmosphere, the oceans, the rivers and aquifers, but all too often the effects of human actions on soils are overlooked. Very little publicity ever reaches the media about soils; they are not newsworthy and regrettably are regarded as unimportant by many people.

This is a pity because soils are some of the most interesting natural features on the Earth's surface. They are an essential part of natural ecosystems and are necessary for the growth of human food, animal fodder, fibre and timber crops. Soils underpin all natural and human-modified ecosystems to which they provide moisture, nutrients and support. It is just as important to have knowledge of and to care for our soils, as it is to study and be aware of the problems mankind faces if air and water supplies are abused.

Environmental awareness was raised by the 1992 United Nations Conference on Environment and Development (UNCED), even though those who prepared the documentation for this important conference scarcely mentioned soils; they did, however, refer to land and the concerns there are about the loss of agricultural production through land degradation, which is occurring throughout the world. Soil is a major component of land and, as such, the general public, administrators, planners and governments must be made aware of its importance. A significant outcome of UNCED was the idea of the sustainable use of the land. For soil scientists, soil conservation is not a new idea, but it must now be taken in a wider context embodied in the holistic approach introduced in Chapter 1. Whilst it is possible to dismiss this as simply a new way of looking at an old problem, soil scientists are keen to take the initiative in determining the most appropriate ways in which our soils are used.

Chapters 2, 3, and 4 follow the pattern of the previous edition of *World Soils*, describing the components of soil, the factors and processes which determine soil formation. Chapter 5, on soil classification,

discusses some of the concepts behind classification systems and introduces the following seven chapters, which deal with the major soils of the world. Soils dominated by the nature of the parent materials are the subject of Chapter 6, and soils with moderately formed profiles are considered in Chapter 7. The increased importance of human modification of soils is reflected by an extensive review of Anthrosols in Chapter 8. The dominant soils of the cool, temperate, arid and humid tropical parts of the world are considered in Chapters 9, 10, 11 and 12 respectively.

The final two chapters are devoted to soil mapping and use of soil information. The skill and industry of soil scientists during the 20th century has produced soil maps of virtually all corners of the Earth and a wealth of knowledge and experience has been accumulated about the nature and properties of soils. Soil scientists wish to share this knowledge for the benefit of all human beings. Local, national and global environmental issues all require an input of basic soil knowledge and, with the encouragement of the International Society of Soil Science, and national soil science societies, this expertise is being made more widely available.

Education of future generations about the value of soils is particularly important, and consequently it is essential that the teaching profession is kept well-informed about soils. Soils can provide many interesting and different examples of investigative techniques for teachers who are involved with teaching basic science. Soil development and distribution have many intriguing aspects for geographical and environmental studies. Thus, the third edition of *World Soils* is a contribution to broadening the understanding of soils and raising public awareness of their importance. Many advances have been made during the past 15 years, so this edition has been completely rewritten to take into account the current understanding of our most basic resource.

E. M. Bridges,
International Soil Reference and Information Centre,
Wageningen, The Netherlands

Acknowledgements

The author wishes to acknowledge the help and encouragement given by many friends and colleagues during the compilation of this edition. In the first place I wish to thank the Director and Staff of the International Soil Reference and Information Centre (ISRIC) at Wageningen for providing facilities for me to complete the revision of the text for this third edition. I am also indebted to ISRIC for the use of illustrative material from their worldwide collection of soils. A special word of thanks is reserved for my colleagues Dik Creutzberg and Hans van Baren who have both made constructive comments on draft chapters as they have been written. Their extensive knowledge of soils and wide experience have been of great help to me in presenting a picture of the soils of the world. I am also indebted to Otto Spaargaren, Sjef Kauffman, Albert Bos and Wouter Bomer for suggestions and help with the soil descriptions, analytical details and photographs of soils from their own collections and the ISRIC Soil Information System.

It is with great pleasure that I acknowledge the help of my former colleague Guy Lewis, of the Cartographic Unit at the University of Wales, Swansea, who has made rough sketches and vague ideas into the line diagrams which illustrate the text. The majority of the diagrams in this edition have been completely redrawn, but where close similarities exist to already published material, an acknowledgement is made in the figure caption.

A sincere word of thanks must be made to the many authors of books and scientific papers whose work has been consulted in the preparation of this edition; without their arduous field work and meticulous recording, a book such as this would not be possible. The inspiration of others is frequently responsible for triggering a chain reaction of ideas, and readers are strongly recommended to go back to the original sources whenever the subject interests them.

A short further reading list is presented at the end of each chapter, but reference has not been made to every factual detail used. As a very wide range of literature, together with considerable personal experience of soils on all five continents, has been used in preparing this edition, to fully reference each fact would make too many interruptions in the text and obstruct the presentation. As with the illustrative material, if a colleague finds a close similarity with some of his or her own concepts or ideas, I hope this general word of acknowledgement and thanks will be acceptable.

Lastly, and most importantly, I must acknowledge the support of my wife, who has endured many long absences whilst I have had the invaluable experience of working in different countries and gaining the background necessary for writing about the soils of the world.

1 Introduction

Soil is an important basic natural resource upon which we all depend. Farmers, horticulturalists and gardeners till it, providing human beings with food and beautiful flowering plants, foresters plant trees in it, engineers move it about in Juggernaut-like machines, small boys dig in it, and mothers abhor it as being dirty.

It is most unfortunate that soil, for many people, is simply trampled underfoot and is synonymous with dirt. They should know better, for soil plays a vital and important role in both the natural world and the life of human beings. It is one of the most undervalued of our natural resources, as virtually all human food is obtained from crops grown in soil, or from animals which graze on grass and other fodder crops also grown in the soil. Natural fibres such as cotton and flax, which provide us with clothing, are grown in the soil and soil materials can be used to make bricks, aluminium and glass. For many people throughout the world, charcoal and wood are the only sources of heat for cooking and comfort, and timber from trees is widely used for building purposes. Soils and soil products play an important part in our lives.

As Sir John Russell has written, 'a clod of earth seems at first sight to be the embodiment of the stillness of death'; however, he goes on to show that it is in fact a highly organized, physical, chemical and biological complex on which all of us are dependent. As the support for vegetable life, the soil plays the most fundamental role in providing sustenance for all animals and human beings, irrevocably linking the living world to the inanimate rocks and minerals.

The position of soil in the whole biotic complex can be illustrated diagrammatically (Fig. 1.1). It can be seen that the climate influences plants, animals and soils directly. However, plants influence the soil in which they grow, the animals which live in and on them as well as the climate near the ground.

The animals, too, play a considerable role in soil development and often the nature of the soil in turn influences the animals which are present in it. Animals often exercise considerable control over the plants growing in the soil, and human beings may be responsible for the maintenance of the soil's fertility or its degradation. Finally, climate, through weathering, causes breakdown of the rocks, which in time become part of the soil as they are first weathered and later acted upon by the soil-forming processes.

The study of soils is of interest to many environmental scientists and in particular is the focus of study for the soil scientist. Soil science has several specialist branches, including the study of soil through physics, chemistry and biology. However, the aspect of soil science which brings all these points of view together is known as **pedology**. The pedologist studies soil as a natural

Fig. 1.1 The position of soil in the environment. The arrows indicate the various interactions and suggest the strength of the different influences.

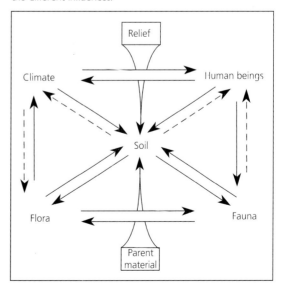

1

phenomenon in its own right, and is interested in the appearance, the mode of formation, the distribution and the classification of soils wherever they occur.

In this respect, pedology makes use of a large number of branches of scientific knowledge, and as an integrative science resembles the role of physical geography. Chemistry, physics and biology have important contributions to make to the study of soils, as have studies in agriculture, forestry, history, geology, geography and archaeology. From all these subjects the information can be obtained for synthesis into a scientific discipline and natural philosophy separate from, and yet closely related to, many other branches of natural science.

Pedology may be studied as a pure science in which investigations into soil-forming processes, soil distribution and classification form an important part of the subject in their own right. However, the results obtained can be applied to practical problems in agriculture, horticulture, forestry, engineering, and more generally in planning the future use of the land. In this respect pedology, which draws from so many different disciplines, already has had to adopt a broad approach and so can claim to be both a pure and an applied science.

In all branches of science, one of the main reasons for investigation is to obtain information which can be applied for the benefit of mankind. Although in the past much interesting scientific work on soils has been accomplished, its results have not always been applied, nor have they provided the benefits which were anticipated. One reason for this is that soil is a much more complicated entity than can be dealt with by the scientific approach alone: there are also political, social, economic, financial and legal implications to be considered. It may be taken out of its natural context for study, but research into its problems and the advice given to land-users cannot take place in a scientific vacuum. These ideas have resulted in recent proposals to adopt a holistic approach for future studies in soil science. This approach recognizes that soils are used within a social and economic framework which cannot be ignored when framing scientific policy, or when providing advice to farmers, foresters or other users of the land.

The emergence of soil science

It is recorded that, about 4000 years ago, attempts were made in China to recognize different types of soils and to arrange them in a sort of land classification. In Europe, 2000 years ago, the Greeks and Romans followed a similar approach. The best-known Roman book on agriculture was that of Columella, in which good soils were distinguished from those which were poor for plant growth. This sort of practical knowledge was passed on by medieval scholars, who repeatedly copied what was known already without improving upon it. By the late 18th and early 19th centuries a scientific interest in the natural world had emerged from the alchemy of earlier years, and this eventually gave rise to the branches of science recognized today.

Present-day soil science emerged just over 100 years ago from two different schools of thought, one chemical, the other geological. The German scientist Liebig (1803–1873) was probably the most renowned of the early exponents of the chemical view of the soil, but even before Liebig, in 1803, a Swedish scientist, Berzelius, described soil as a chemical laboratory of nature in whose bosom various chemical decomposition and synthesis reactions took place in a hidden manner.

Early pedologists with a geological background considered soil to be comminuted rock with a certain amount of organic matter added from the decomposition of plants. As late as 1917, a German scientist, Ramann (1851–1926), described soil as 'rocks that have been reduced to small fragments and have been more or less changed chemically, together with the remains of plants or animals that live in it or on it'. Even today it is still possible to hear people use terms of convenience such as 'limestone' soils or 'granite' soils, but the soils which overlie these parent materials are very different from the rocks in almost all respects.

The origin of current definitions of soil results mainly from the work of two men: in Russia, Dokuchaev, and in the United States, Hilgard. In the 1880s, it was Dokuchaev (1846–1903) who first enunciated the concept of the soil as an independent natural body, but separately both men noted that soils could be described in broad geographical zones which, with the state of knowledge at the time and at the scale of world maps, could be correlated with climate zones and also with the associated belts of natural vegetation. Although we now know this to be only partly true, it did serve to direct attention to the environmental relationships of the soil cover of our planet.

In the USA, Hilgard (1832–1916) noted that soils in the state of Mississippi were distributed in broad belts associated with surface geology, but when he subsequently moved to work in California, he realized that climate also had an important influence, for instance on the accumulations of carbonates and other salts present in the soils of drier regions.

Definition of soil

Soil may be defined broadly as *the unconsolidated mineral or organic material at the surface of the Earth capable of supporting plant growth*. This is in line with a simple definition used in an agricultural context, which describes soil as *the stuff in which plants grow*. Such definitions are sufficient for many practical purposes, but for the soil scientist a definition of a more explanatory nature is preferable.

The definition propounded by Joffe (1949) has the advantage that it brings together the physical character, as well as the chemical and biological constituents, and throws the right amount of weight on the morphology of the soil: *The soil is a natural body of animal, mineral and organic constituents differentiated into horizons of variable depth which differ from the material below in morphology, physical make-up, chemical properties and composition and biological characteristics.*

Another definition describes soils as *the collection of natural bodies, formed on the Earth's surface containing living matter and supporting or capable of supporting plants*. The action of various chemical, physical and biological processes on the original geological materials produces features which we recognize as soils. These changes, which affect the upper part of the weathered rocks (or regolith), can be seen as a sequence of layers, technically called **horizons**, having different colours, composition and structure in a sequence known as the **soil profile**.

The soil profile

A soil profile comprises the natural horizons of the soil as revealed in a vertical section, from the organic material at the surface, through the horizons of the mineral soil, to the parent material or other layers beneath, which influence the genesis or behaviour of the soil (Fig. 1.2).

Fig. 1.2 An area of land with its soil shown as a pedon (left) and as a profile (right).

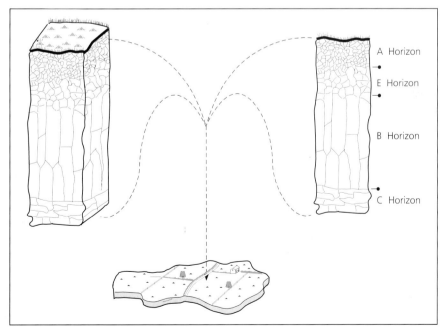

A Horizon

E Horizon

B Horizon

C Horizon

3

This concept of the soil profile is a simple view of the soil in a vertical direction, whereas soils are in fact three-dimensional features, extending over the landscape. Thus, for the purpose of classification and mapping, pedologists have adopted the idea of a soil volume, a three-dimensional body of soil called a **pedon**. A pedon is described as the minimal amount of material which can be logically called 'a soil', and it may range in size from 1 to 10 m². As soil is rather variable in composition and appearance, a range in characteristics is encompassed by allowing a number of pedons to be grouped together as a **polypedon**, which is a recognizable, geographic area of closely related soils. For practical purposes, most pedons described in the literature are of the soil revealed in a profile pit, the lateral dimensions of which are approximately 1 by 1.5 m, and its depth is governed by the depth of the soil. It is only in extended sections, such as road cuts or pipeline trenches, that the true picture of lateral variability of soils can be appreciated.

Soil horizons and their designations

A soil horizon is a layer of soil, revealed in a soil profile, lying approximately parallel to the Earth's surface, which possesses pedological characteristics.

The horizons of a soil profile are the morphological expression of the processes which have formed the soil. These processes will be discussed in Chapter 3. Horizons can be distinguished one from another by their physical make-up, chemical properties and composition, and biological characteristics. The vertical and horizontal limits of horizons occur where these attributes are significantly different in appearance or amount.

Certain soil horizons possess specific characteristics resulting from their mode of formation which, through experience, pedologists think are significant. These horizons can usually be readily identified in the field and they bring a sense of order to the description of the soil profile and permit the identification of the horizons present.

Early in the development of pedology, Dokuchaev began a system of labelling the horizons which he observed in the soil profiles he was describing. At first he used either letters (ABC) or numbers (123) as ciphers simply to label the horizons, but by the beginning of the 20th century these letters had acquired a special genetic significance. These horizon designations are still in use today. Over the years their purpose has been questioned and their role redefined, but whatever their detractors say, horizon designations are of great use in soil description, interpretation, in discussion and even in classification of soils.

Two systems of horizon designation, which are very similar and in wide usage, are those of the Food and Agriculture Organization of the United Nations (FAO) and the United States Department of Agriculture (USDA). As this book is concerned with a review of world soils, the FAO system will be presented here. Seven capital letters, O, H, A, E, B, C, and R, are used to represent the most significant horizons, called **master horizons**. Subordinate characteristics within the master horizons are designated by a lower-case letter following the master horizon letter. Each country with a soil survey organization may use these letters in a slightly different way, and give the letters their own particular meaning.

A summary of the master horizons and the main subdivisions of the FAO system is given in Table 1.1.

The O and H horizons are often replaced by the letters **L** for litter, **F** for fermentation and **H** for humus horizons, but the other master horizon designations are now in standard use in virtually all parts of the world. These designations will be used throughout this book and will be shown by the symbols depicted in Fig. 1.3.

The changing paradigm of soil

Unlike an animal or a plant, a soil is not a separate organism. Its lateral boundaries to other soils are not usually abrupt, but zones of transition. Although it is possible to see without difficulty the upper surface of a soil, the lower boundary between soil and 'non-soil' material is rather vaguely defined. In the preceding discussion of the soil profile, it was stated that the simple section or soil profile was an inadequate way of looking at the soil and that pedologists had adopted a three-dimensional approach. A well-known American pedologist has written that 'the success of a teacher

O An organic horizon at the soil surface, normally not saturated with water.

H An organic horizon at the soil surface normally saturated with water, characteristic of peaty deposits.

A A mineral horizon formed at or near the surface, characterized by the incorporation of humified organic matter intimately associated with mineral materials. Subdivisions include:

    Ah for an uncultivated horizon; accumulation of humus;
    Ap for a cultivated (ploughed) horizon;
    Ag for a poorly drained surface horizon.

E A mineral horizon, just below the soil surface, which has lost clay, organic matter or iron by downward movement. Subdivisions include:

    Eg for poorly drained horizons.

B A subsurface mineral horizon resulting from the change *in situ* of soil material or the washing in of material from overlying horizons. Subdivisions include:

    Bg for poorly drained;
    Bh for accumulation of humus;
    Bs for an illuvial accumulation of iron or aluminium sesquioxides;
    Bt for increase of clay;
    Bw for changes of colour or structure;
    Bx for compact brittle horizon known as a fragipan;
    By for accumulation of gypsum;
    Bz for accumulation of salts more soluble than gypsum.

C An unconsolidated or weakly consolidated mineral horizon which retains evidence of rock structure and lacks the properties diagnostic of the overlying A, E or B horizons. Subdivisions include:

    Cg for poorly drained;
    Ck for enrichment with calcium carbonate;
    Cm for cemented material;
    Cx for compact brittle material known as a fragipan;
    Cy for enrichment with gypsum;
    Cz for accumulation of salts more soluble than gypsum.

R Continuous hard or very hard bedrock.

Table 1.1 *Soil horizon designations*

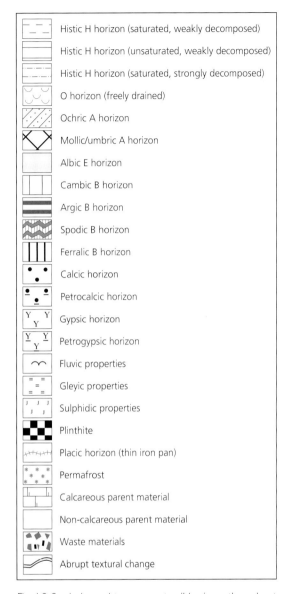

Fig. 1.3 Symbols used to represent soil horizons throughout this book.

depends to a high degree upon his ability to create in the minds of his students an integrated model of his subject as a whole'. Throughout this book a conscious attempt is made to provide the reader with such a model of the different major soils of the world and how they are related to each other.

From their studies of soils on the Russian plain, the Russian pioneers of modern soil science adopted the soil profile as the first 'model' of soil. As the effect of relief in Russia played only a small role in soil formation, the two-dimensional model sufficed, with the horizons developing parallel to the soil surface and only a small amount of lateral variation of soil characteristics. It was from an idea originally put forward by Dokuchaev that the first real conceptual model of soil formation was proposed by Jenny and published in 1941 in his book *Factors of Soil Formation*. This model, which will be discussed more fully in Chapter 3, was the most widely used model of soil development for almost 40 years. Another important general 'model' for soil development, proposed by Simonson in 1959, allowed a systems approach, with feedback for certain stabilizing functions which help to maintain the status quo. Many other models developed in recent years have permitted the estimation of certain unknown parameters from known measurements.

The widespread adoption of electronic methods of data storage in the last two decades has revealed shortcomings inherent in previous methods of soil survey, which gathered data for presentation in book and map format. These were usually a mixture of qualitative and quantitative data, providing information on the attributes of typical examples of soils from an area; they did not provide information on the continuous variability within soil mapping units. The nature of the data collected, in terms of classification units with abrupt boundaries, is not very suitable for input into data files for use in geographical information systems. It is argued by some authors that forms of continuous classification systems using 'fuzzy' mathematical methods should be used instead, but the fact remains that most available data were not collected for input into databases or computer models, and new data are either not available, or are very expensive to obtain.

Already, computerization of data has introduced a greater degree of standardization in the gathering of soil information worldwide. In recent times, many different models have been suggested which simulate processes operating in soils. The lead has been taken by studies of the influence of the physical characteristics of soils on the movement of water, plant nutrients and pollutants through the soil, their availability and effects on plants. However, extrapolation from these detailed site-specific data to regional or global systems can be fraught with many difficulties.

It will be obvious that soil is regarded in different ways by different people; attention was drawn to this in the opening paragraph of this chapter.

Soil scientists are no exception to the public at large, and individuals hold different points of view. Views of the soil have also changed with time as new ideas have emerged and new facts have been discovered. Changes are constantly taking place in the way soil scientists regard the soil. Stimulated by the challenges provided by the United Nations Conference on Environment and Development (UNCED), held in Rio de Janeiro in 1992, ideas of soil resilience to some uses and the vulnerability to damage by other land-use practices have led to concepts of sustainable use of the land. In order that successive generations can have the means to grow crops, it is necessary to ensure that our current use of the soil will not detract from the future use of the land.

The realization that widespread damage has already occurred to the soils of the world, and that the warnings given by responsible soil scientists, amongst others, have not been heeded, has led to the suggestion that a wider, more comprehensive approach to soil conservation should be adopted, involving the users of soil in a closer understanding and collaboration with other scientists. This **holistic** approach may be defined as *the task of all people concerned with the soil to direct their interest, not just towards the physical, chemical and biological aspects, but also to those environmental economic, social, legal and technical aspects that affect soil use.* In the past, the results of research in soil science have not been effectively communicated to those who work the land, those who plan its future or those who administer the legal and financial framework within which soils must be conserved. This situation must be changed.

Land, with its cover of soil, has always been an important element in the environment of the human race; it has supplied food, fibre and forestry products. These crops also provide a renewable source of energy. The soil is a biological factory for waste purification; it has a rich diversity of flora and fauna which can convert most organic compounds into simple recyclable elements; the same flora and fauna help soil to maintain clean, fresh water supplies both on the surface and in the deep aquifers. Soils, through their carbon content, can influence the atmospheric concentration of 'greenhouse gases' such as carbon dioxide, methane and nitrous oxide. Soil is also the surface upon which almost all human activity takes place. Soil is clearly one of the most important components of the terrestrial environment.

Further reading

AFES, 1992. *Référential pédologique: principaux sols d'Europe.* INRA, Paris.

Avery, B.W., 1980. *Soil Classification for England and Wales.* Technical Monograph No. 14. Soil Survey of England and Wales, Harpenden.

Bridges, E.M., 1990. *Soil Horizon Designations.* Technical Paper No. 19. International Soil Reference and Information Centre, Wageningen.

Bridges, E.M. and Catizzone, M. 1996. Soil science in a holistic framework: dicussion of an improved integrated approach. *Geoderma* **71**:275–87.

Cline, M.J., 1961. The changing model of soils. *Proceedings of the Soil Science Society of America* **25**:442–6.

FAO, 1990. *Guidelines for Soil Profile Description.* 3rd edition, FAO, Rome.

Jenny, H., 1994. *Factors of Soil Formation. A System of Quantitative Pedology.* Dover Publications, New York.

Joffe, J.S., 1949. *Pedology.* Pedology Publications, New Brunswick, New Jersey.

McDonald, P., 1994. *The Literature of Soil Science.* Cornell University Press, Ithaca.

Ruellan, A. and Dosso, M., 1993. *Regards sur le sol.* Universités francophones, Foucher, Paris.

Russell, E.J., 1957. *The World of the Soil.* New Naturalist Series, Collins, London.

Simonson, R.W., 1959. Outline of a generalized theory of soil genesis. *Proceedings of the Soil Science Society of America* **23**:152–6.

Simonson, R.W., 1968. Concept of soil. *Advances in Agronomy* **20**:1–47.

Strzemski, M., 1975. *Ideas Underlying Soil Systematics.* National Centre for Scientific, Technological and Economic Information, Warsaw.

Wild, A., 1989. Soil scientists as members of the scientific community. *Journal of Soil Science* **40**:209–21.

2 Composition of soils

There are four main constituents of soil: mineral matter, organic matter, air and water (Fig. 2.1). These will be considered in turn in this chapter. The mineral matter includes two main groups of materials. First, there are the resistant minerals weathered from the rocks and which persist to form the parent material; these are often referred to as primary minerals. Secondly, there are those minerals which have been formed in the soil by recombination from substances in the soil solution. The former are often coarse-grained, the latter fine-grained. The presence of sand, silt and clay particles in different proportions determines the texture of the soil.

Organic matter is derived mostly from decaying vegetable matter which is broken down and decomposed by the action of the many different life forms which inhabit the soil. Composed mainly of cellulose, starch and lignin in various states of decomposition, the organic matter of soils takes on several distinctive forms.

Except for loose sands and a few other soils which are described as structureless, the mineral and organic components of soil are aggregated in

Fig. 2.1 Volume composition of a typical topsoil: amounts are approximate as the percentage of certain constituents (e.g. air and water) is constantly changing.

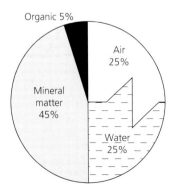

discrete structural units, termed peds, which are surrounded by spaces. These spaces between the peds, and spaces between individual sand grains and organic soil constituents, are referred to collectively as pores. Normally, both air and water occupy these spaces between the mineral aggregates, but if the soil is saturated most of the air is driven out. In a soil which is freely drained, some water is still present as thin films around the mineral particles, leaving the pores open for gases to diffuse in and out of the soil.

Mineral matter

The mineral portion of the soil is derived mainly from the geological substratum by processes of *in situ* weathering. However, in some locations, the mineral material from which the soil is formed has been transported by a river and laid down as alluvium, or it has moved downslope by creep as colluvium. In addition, a variable contribution comes from fine aeolian dust. The mineral part of soils consists of particles with a range of sizes, from very small clay particles up to sand-size particles. This part of the soil is known as the **fine earth** and it is upon this fraction of the mineral material that the **texture** of the soil is based. Particles larger than 2mm, stones or gravel, also occur, but except for their physical presence and bulk they contribute little to the soil.

The fine earth, which most people think of as soil, is composed of three fractions, sand, silt and clay, determined according to the size of the particles. In an internationally agreed logarithmic scale, sand particles have a diameter of between 0.02 and 2.0mm, silt has a size range of between 0.02 and 0.002mm, and clay is the material of less than 0.002mm in diameter. By taking a soil sample, moistening it and then estimating the proportions of sand, silt and clay present, it is possible to relate the soil to a texture class, as shown on the triangular diagram (Fig. 2.2). Descriptions of the twelve different classes of soil texture in common use are given in Table 2.1.

The particle-size classes are used for the description of texture of each horizon within a profile, but sometimes there is a need for broader groupings of soil texture for use when describing the whole profile or groups of profiles of similar soils. These textural groupings are:

Clayey	very fine
	fine
Silty	fine
	coarse
Loamy	fine
	coarse

Sandy

The relationship of the twelve texture classes to these broader groupings can be seen in the triangular diagram (Fig. 2.2b). These broad groupings cut across several of the textural classes as they are based on slightly different particle-size ranges. This has occurred because of the need for closer co-operation between engineers and soil scientists, which has resulted in the pedological size grades being modified.

In turn this needed some modification of the texture classes to conform with different size grades. The scheme adopted by the Soil Survey of England and Wales is given in the third triangular diagram (Fig. 2.2c). Where stony material amounts to more than 35 per cent of the volume of a soil horizon it is indicated by the term **skeletal** (where rock fragments exceed 90 per cent the word **fragmental** is used by American pedologists) in association with the appropriate textural grouping.

These different soil textures reflect properties which influence the management and economic use of the soil such as permeability, water-holding capacity and aeration. Coarse-textured, sandy soils are usually freely drained, and in a dry summer may suffer drought, but cultivation is relatively easy. Frequently, clay soils are poorly drained, and the expense of installing a drainage system can be large. Clay soils are more retentive of plant nutrients, but cultivations are always likely to be difficult, although in a dry year these soils may produce

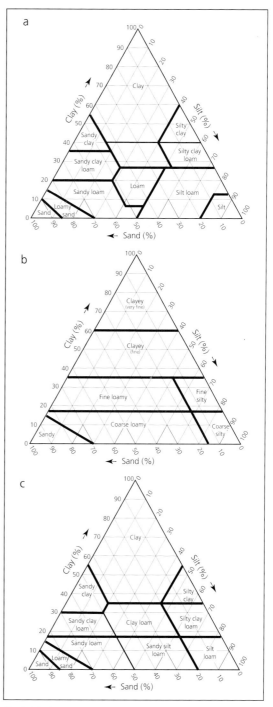

Fig. 2.2 Soil texture classes. The three sides of the triangle are base lines for sand, silt and clay with the opposite apex representing 100%. (a) USDA; (b) broad texture groupings, USDA; (c) soil texture classes, Soil Survey of England and Wales.

9

Sand. Soil consisting mostly of coarse and fine sand, and containing so little silt and clay that it is loose when dry and not sticky when wet. When rubbed it leaves no film on the fingers.

Loamy sand. Soil consisting mostly of sand but with sufficient clay and silt to give slight plasticity and cohesion when very moist. Leaves a slight film of fine material on the fingers when rubbed.

Sandy loam. Soil in which the sand fraction is still obvious, which can be moulded readily when sufficiently moist, but in most cases does not stick appreciably to the fingers. Threads do not form easily.

Loam. Soil in which the fractions are so blended that it moulds readily when sufficiently moist, and sticks to the fingers to some extent. It can with difficulty be moulded into threads but will not bend into a small ring.

Silt loam. Soil that is moderately plastic without being very sticky and in which the smooth soapy feel of the silt is dominant.

Sandy clay loam. Soil containing sufficient clay to be distinctly sticky when moist, but in which the sand fraction is still an obvious feature.

Clay loam. The soil is distinctly sticky when sufficiently moist and the presence of sand fractions can only be detected with care.

Silty clay loam. Soil that contains very small amounts of sand, but sufficient silt to confer something of a soapy feel. It is less sticky than silty clay or clay loam.

Silt. Soil in which the smooth soapy feel of silt is dominant.

Sandy clay. The soil is plastic and sticky when moistened sufficiently but the sand fraction is still an obvious feature. Clay and sand are dominant and the intermediate grades of silt and fine sand are less apparent.

Silty clay. Soil which is composed almost entirely of very fine material but in which the smooth soapy feel of the silt modifies to some extent the stickiness of the clay.

Clay. The soil is plastic and sticky when moistened sufficiently and gives a polished surface on rubbing. When moist, the soil can be rolled into threads, is capable of being moulded into any shape and takes clear fingerprints.

Table 2.1 *Soil texture class descriptions*

better crops than a coarser-textured soil. Silty soils may also be troublesome as they must be cultivated within certain moisture limits, otherwise they become cloddy and the preparation of a seed bed is made difficult. Also, the effect of heavy rain on silts can cause surface sealing which inhibits seedling emergence and encourages erosion.

Soil mineralogy

The minerals present in the soil belong to two completely different groups, based on their origin. **Primary minerals** are those derived from the parent material and **secondary minerals** are the product of chemical weathering and have been formed in the soil itself. The primary minerals present in a soil have usually been through at least one cycle of weathering, so that only the more resistant ones remain. In the soils of the humid temperate climate zone, the sand fraction is composed largely of quartz grains, but it may also contain some grains of feldspar, mica, and a few of the rarer persistent minerals such as zircon, tourmaline or glauconite (Fig. 2.3). These minerals can sometimes be used to determine the origin of the soil parent material and also to determine quantitatively the path of weathering from rock to soil. Quartz grains often constitute between 90 and 95 per cent of all the sand and silt particles of soils derived from sedimentary rocks.

In soils developed in the humid tropical environment, most weatherable primary minerals such as feldspars and mica are normally absent and the soil is composed largely of quartz and secondary clay minerals. The clay mineral kaolinite together with iron and aluminium hydroxides constitute the clay fraction. The amount of quartz sand is variable but silt-sized material is proportionately low.

The **clay minerals** are the most important of the mineral constituents of soils; they consist of fine (<2 μm), platy-shaped mineral grains which can be identified only indirectly, or by an electron microscope. Clay minerals are characterized by a layered, crystalline structure, and chemically they are hydrous silicates of aluminium. There are three main members of this group of minerals: kaolinite, smectite and the hydrous micas, although transitional forms occur between each group. All clay

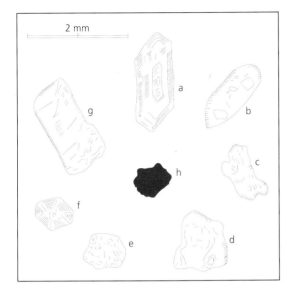

Fig. 2.3 Some of the less common (heavy) minerals present in the soil: (a,b) zircon, (c) glauconite, (d,e) garnet, (f,g) tourmaline, (h) magnetite.

minerals are constructed from layers of silica and aluminium atoms and their attendant oxygen and hydroxyl groups (Fig. 2.4). The silicon and aluminium layers are held together by shared chemical bonds. Kaolinite has one layer of silicon atoms and one layer of aluminium atoms in a 1:1 structure (Fig. 2.5). Smectite minerals have three layers with the aluminium atoms lying between two layers of silicon atoms in a 2:1 structure, sharing the valencies of their oxygen atoms.

Many soil minerals are derived directly from the parent material, but clay minerals are formed in the soil itself; these are referred to as secondary minerals. Weathering releases elements that pass into the soil solution from which recrystallization takes

Fig. 2.4 Silicon tetrahedron and aluminium octahedron: the building blocks for silicate clay minerals (after Brady, 1984).

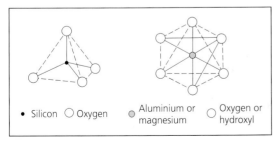

- Silicon ○ Oxygen

⬤ Aluminium or magnesium ○ Oxygen or hydroxyl

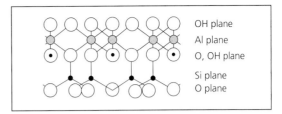

OH plane
Al plane
O, OH plane
Si plane
O plane

Fig. 2.5 The structure of kaolinite: sheets of silicon tetrahedra and aluminium octahedra are linked by shared oxygen atoms. It is a 1:1 mineral (after Brady, 1984).

place to form a completely new mineral. Hence kaolinite, $Al_4Si_4O_{10}(OH)_8$, can be formed in this way from soil solutions rich in aluminium and silicon; where base-rich conditions prevail the mineral montmorillonite, $NaMgAl_5Si_{12}O_{10}(OH)_6$ (smectite group), may be formed (Fig. 2.6). Clay minerals can also be formed in the soil by simple alteration of primary minerals.

Other secondary minerals can accumulate in the soil. Where oxidation and reduction are prevalent, iron and manganese oxides precipitate as scattered concentrations throughout the horizons of poorly drained soils as the minerals goethite or lepidocrocite. These concentrations grow by the addition of concentric layers of iron and manganese compounds. Where warm summer temperatures occur, the iron minerals may dehydrate to bright red hematite. Concretions of calcium carbonate or gypsum are unusual in the soils of humid regions because leaching prevents their formation, but they are common in the soils of seasonal and dry climates, such as on the steppes or in desert and semi-desert areas.

Because the clay mineral particles are so small in size, the minute electrical forces of the molecules at the surface of the clay become dominant and confer upon the clay particles a **colloidal state**. A colloidal state occurs when particles of less than one micron (<0.001 mm) are dispersed evenly throughout another medium. (Two familiar examples of colloids are milk, in which tiny solid particles are dispersed throughout a liquid, and cloud, where water droplets are dispersed in air.) The properties which the colloidal state confers upon soil materials are plasticity, cohesion, shrinkage, swelling, flocculation and dispersion, all of which are significant for the physical properties of a soil (Fig. 2.7).

Fig. 2.6 Structure of montmorillonite (smectite): it is built of two sheets of silicon tetrahedra and one sheet of aluminium octahedra, linked by shared oxygen atoms. It is a 2:1 mineral (after Brady, 1984).

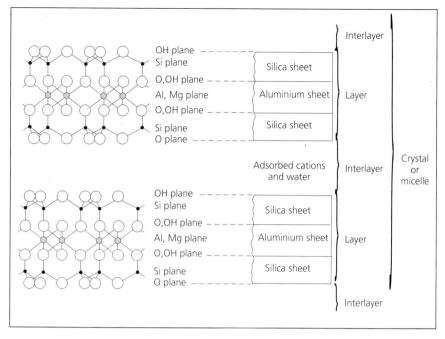

Clay minerals (and organic matter) have electrical charges associated with their surfaces. These charges enable clays to attract, hold and exchange cations and anions. The most important property of the clay minerals is the **cation exchange capacity** (CEC), measured in centimoles of positive charge per kilogram of soil. Kaolinite has a low CEC, 8 $cmol_c\ kg^{-1}$, but clays of the smectite group are higher, up to 100 $cmol_c\ kg^{-1}$; other clay minerals have an intermediate CEC.

Organic matter

Soil organic matter can be present in several forms: it may be intimately mixed with the mineral matter of the surface horizon, it may be present in an illuvial B horizon, or it may form discrete layers upon the surface. The four basic types of surface organic matter identified by pedologists are known as peat, mor, moder and mull. Gradational forms can be recognized between these four basic types. Peat is developed in saturated conditions, while the other three types of surface organic matter are only saturated for short periods of time (Fig. 2.8).

The name **peat** is used for organic accumulations composed of fibrous, semi-fibrous or amorphous materials. Unlike the other forms of organic matter, the plant remains are often still recognizable. Different forms of peat may be distinguished by their content of fibrous material. If a peat rich in fibrous material is rubbed, most of the plant fibres can be seen and it is referred to as **fibric**. Material in which the organic matter is almost completely

Fig. 2.7 Flocculated and dispersed soil. The flocculated soil is well-structured and has spaces (pores) through which air and water can move. These spaces are lost when the soil is dispersed.

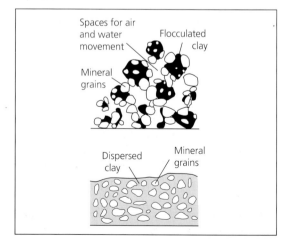

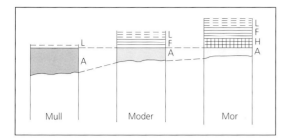

Fig. 2.8 Diagrammatic representation of the thin surface layers of organic matter (L, F and H). These make up the O horizon.

decomposed is called **terric**. (American pedologists use the term **sapric** for completely decomposed material, and that with an intermediate degree of decomposition is described as **hemic**.)

Mor develops beneath a heath or coniferous forest plant community and is associated with strongly acid soils. The plant litter is of low nutritive value and strong acidity severely restricts the range of soil fauna present. Breakdown of the litter is retarded so that three distinct organic horizons can be identified. These are the litter (L), fermentation (F) and humus (H) layers, which are included in the O horizon of the FAO horizon designation system. Much of the organic breakdown in the acid conditions of mor is achieved by fungi, and, as earthworms are usually absent from such soils, there is little incorporation of the humus, which rests abruptly on the mineral soil surface.

Organic matter can also accumulate in the B horizons of Podzols, forming a discrete layer separated from the surface mor and a very thin A horizon by the bleached albic E horizon that is characteristic of these soils. The mechanisms of podzolization will be discussed elsewhere, so a short explanation will suffice here. Organic compounds, often associated chemically with iron and aluminium, are moved down the profile to enrich the B horizon and give its upper part a dark colour, contrasting with the bleached eluvial horizon above and an iron-enriched spodic B horizon below.

Moder is a form of organic matter intermediate between mor and mull. It is often found under woodland conditions in association with Dystric Cambisols, and it is more acid and has a more restricted soil fauna than mull. It comprises decomposing organic matter and faecal pellets of the soil fauna, especially the springtails and mites. Litter (L) and fermentation (F) horizons are identifiable in approximately equal thicknesses. In the case of forms transitional to mull, an increased amount of humus incorporation into the mineral soil occurs as well.

Mull forms in freely drained, base-rich soils with good aeration. Such conditions are good for plant life as well and so there is a plentiful supply of plant litter, and associated with it a rich soil fauna including earthworms. The organic debris is completely broken down by the soil fauna and the humified remains are incorporated into the soil each year, so that none remains from one year to the next. Earthworms, in particular, are responsible for ingesting a mixture of plant and soil material and mixing it together intimately in their casts. In the mull form, the humus has a colloidal character and is intimately associated with the clay minerals, with which it forms the **clay–humus complex**.

The chemical composition of soil organic matter is extremely complex and is thought to be composed of high-molecular-mass substances which show no ordered structure when examined by X-ray diffraction. When analysed by conventional chemical methods, humus has fractions which are soluble in alkalis and in acids. A wide range of compounds and substances results from the activities of micro-organisms which break down the original plant material. These substances often have a phenolic structure with carboxyl groups (COOH) which dissociate to give a negative charge; the magnitude of this charge is dependent upon the pH and gives humus similar but larger cation exchange properties than clays, 200 $cmol_c \, kg^{-1}$. Some of these organic substances are capable of linking with metal ions as chelates, making them more soluble and easy to move in solution.

The clay–humus complex

The chemistry of the soil is largely concerned with the chemical and physical activity of the minute particles of the clay–humus complex. As long ago as 1850, Thomas Way found that soils had the power to retain cations and that natural clays reacted in a similar manner to artificial silicates of lime and aluminium. Subsequent investigations have shown this piece of research to be correct, but the mechanism involved was not understood at the time. Acids, alkalis and their salts dissociate in solution to a certain degree – that is, they form ions with positive and negative charges. Pure water has the same property to a lesser degree, dissociating into hydrogen (H^+) and hydroxide ions (OH^-):

$$NaNO_3 = Na^+ + NO_3^-$$

$$H_2O = H^+ + OH^-$$

As a result of broken edges of the silicate clay crystals and ionic substitution within their structures, the clay mineral particles have a net negative charge. Similarly, the organic particles have a net negative charge derived from broken bonds of organic molecules. Thus the clay–humus particle effectively acts as a highly charged anion, which in colloidal chemistry is known as a **micelle** (Fig. 2.9). In the soil solution surrounding the micelle, attracted to it by the negative charge which they compensate, are numerous cations in a diffuse cloud, forming the Gouy layer. A molecular-thin layer of cations and anions at specific binding sites, known as the Stern layer, occurs at the clay–humus interface. Together, these two layers form the **electrical double layer** upon which models of the exchange system are built. The cations are said to be 'adsorbed' as they are capable of being displaced and exchanged for other cations.

Fig. 2.9 Diagrammatic representation of a clay–humus micelle with adsorbed ions of hydrogen (H^+), calcium (Ca^{2+}) and potassium (K^+) (after Eyre, 1969).

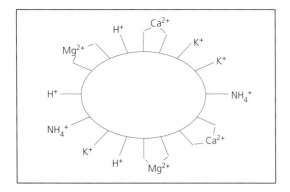

The total amount of exchangeable cations held by the clay–humus complex is the cation exchange capacity (CEC) of the soil, and the **base saturation** is the amount of base cations (Ca^{2+}, Mg^{2+}, K^+ and Na^+) present, expressed as a percentage of the total which includes hydrogen ions (H^+).

The exchange capacity of soils in the humid temperate regions tends to be dominated by the ions of hydrogen and calcium, together with lesser amounts of magnesium, sodium and potassium. In the humid tropics, strongly leached soils are dominated by hydrogen ions and the strong acidity allows aluminium ions (Al^{3+}) to come into solution, as also occurs in base-poor soils of humid temperate regions, exacerbated by the problems of acid rain.

With increasing dryness of climate, there is less leaching, and calcium and magnesium ions dominate the exchange positions of the clay–humus complex in central continental areas. In arid climates, where leaching is minimal and where the ground-water may be rich in soluble salts, sodium ions can come to dominate the exchange positions, resulting in soils of poor structure, in which virtually no commercial or subsistence crops can be grown. A clay–humus complex saturated by calcium and hydrogen ions has a flocculated state, forming stable soil crumbs. When sodium is the dominant cation, the clay and humus particles become dispersed and the soil is difficult to cultivate. Physiologically, plant growth is limited by the presence of salt in the soil because plants cannot draw moisture from the soil into their roots.

Soil structure

Soil structure is an important physical characteristic of any soil. In a soil, structure is produced by the individual particles of sand, silt and clay aggregating into larger units with specific shapes, known as **peds**. Most soils are **pedal**, that is they have structure. Those soils without structure, termed **apedal** soils, may be either **massive** or, in the case of coarse sandy soils, composed of unaggregated individual grains of sand, in which case the structure is referred to as **single grain**. Soil structure is encouraged by the presence of organic matter, and the gums and mucilages formed by bacterial breakdown of organic matter help to bind the peds together. The peds have been described as the 'architecture' of the soil, and the spaces around and through them act as channels to conduct water through the soil. These spaces between the peds, known as **pores**, are also important as they provide a habitat for the soil fauna.

It is not readily apparent from the surface that the total volume of air spaces in an organic-rich, medium-textured topsoil can be as high as 60 per cent, but is usually around 50 per cent. Cultivation reduces the number of larger pore spaces, which are important for the movement of air and water through the soil. An average figure of 45 per cent is quoted for nineteen cultivated Georgia (USA) soils, with 57 per cent pore space in neighbouring uncultivated soils.

Soil is readily classified into six structural types: structureless, platy, crumb, blocky, prismatic and columnar. Structure is described according to the type and size of structure and how well-formed the structure is in the soil. The different types are described in Table 2.2 and illustrated in Fig. 2.10.

Maintenance of soil structure is important for agriculturalists the world over, for unless a soil is well-structured, crop yields are depressed, and structureless soils are more liable to erosion. Soil structure can be weakened by over-cropping or over-grazing, both of which reduce the organic matter content to a level where collapse of structure occurs. The action of heavy farm machinery repeatedly passing over the soil can cause compaction and plough-pans in the subsoil. In the topsoil, structures may be crushed and the wheelings form channels which erosion rapidly exploits.

Soil colour

One of the features a pedologist first looks at when describing the profile of a soil are the horizons present, mainly distinguished by changes in colour. The use of colour as a distinguishing feature for a soil horizon is a simple approach, but colour is indicative of many other, more complex soil properties. In many cases, soil colour is attributable either to the presence of organic matter or to the state of oxidation or hydration of the iron minerals present. Black and very dark brown colours are

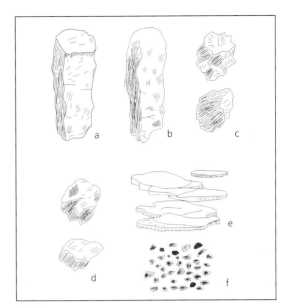

Fig. 2.10 Soil structures are formed by the aggregation of sand, silt and clay particles: (a) prismatic, (b) columnar, (c) angular blocky, (d) subangular blocky, (e) platy, (f) granular or crumb (after USDA, 1951).

indicative of organic matter accumulation, and usually these colours are confined to the surface horizons. Grey colours are associated with removal or segregation of iron, especially in poorly drained conditions where they are accompanied by yellowish or reddish mottles. Reddish-brown colours are usually found in well-drained soils, and whitish colours are normally associated with accumulations of various salts in the soils of arid regions. Where there is strong summer drying of soil, as in areas of Mediterranean climate, soils develop bright red colours of iron in the hematite state. Colours of soils are described using the colour charts of the Munsell colour system which describe soil colours in terms of hue (the basic spectrum colour, e.g. red {R} or yellow {Y}), value (darkness or lightness from white to black) and chroma (the strength of the colour).

Soil air

The atmosphere penetrates into the soil along the pores and fissures. After rain, when excess moisture has drained from the soil, the volume of the remaining air-filled pores is referred to as the **air capacity**.

	Plate-like with one dimension (the vertical) limited and greatly less than other two; arranged around a horizontal plane; faces mostly horizontal	Prism-like with two dimensions (the horizontal) limited and considerably less than the vertical; arranged around a vertical line; vertical faces well defined; vertical angular.		Block-like; polyhedron-like, or spheroidal, with three dimensions of the same order of magnitude, arranged around a point.			
				Block-like; blocks or polyhedrons having plane or curved surfaces that are casts of the moulds formed by the surrounding peds		Spheroids or polyhedrons having plane or curved surfaces which have slight or no accommodation to the faces of surrounding peds	
		Without rounded caps	With rounded caps	Faces flattened; most vertices sharply angular	Mixed rounded and flattened faces with many rounded vertices	Relatively non-porous peds	Porous peds
Class	Platy	Prismatic	Columnar	(Angular) blocky[1]	Subangular blocky[2]	Granular	Crumb
Very fine or very thin	Very thin platy; <1 mm	Very fine prismatic; <10mm	Very fine columnar; <10mm	Very fine angular blocky; <5mm	Very fine subangular blocky; <5mm	Very fine granular; <1mm	Very fine crumb; <1mm
Fine or thin	Thin platy; 1 to 2mm	Fine prismatic; 10 to 20mm	Fine columnar; 10 to 20mm	Fine angular blocky; 5 to 10mm	Fine subangular blocky; 5 to 10mm	Fine granular; 1 to 2mm	Fine crumb; 1 to 2mm
Medium	Medium platy; 2 to 5mm	Medium prismatic; 20 to 50mm	Medium columnar; 20 to 50mm	Medium angular blocky; 10 to 20mm	Medium subangular blocky; 10 to 20mm	Medium granular; 2 to 5mm	Medium crumb; 2 to 5mm
Coarse or thick	Thick platy; 5 to 10mm	Coarse prismatic; 50 to 100mm	Coarse columnar; 50 to 100mm	Coarse angular blocky; 20 to 50mm	Coarse subangular blocky; 20 to 50mm	Coarse granular; 5 to 10mm	
Very coarse or very thick	Very thick platy; >10mm	Very coarse prismatic; >100mm	Very coarse columnar; >100mm	Very coarse angular blocky; >50mm	Very coarse subangular blocky; >50mm	Very coarse granular; >10mm	

1 Sometimes called nut. The word 'angular' in the name can ordinarily be omitted.
2 Sometimes called nuciform, nut, or subangular nut. Since the size connotation of these terms is a source of great confusion to many, they are not recommended.

Table 2.2 Types and classes of soil structures (after USDA, 1951)

Air within the soil is a natural continuation of the atmosphere above the soil, but although it is similar in some respects, it differs in others. Compared with atmospheric air, soil air is usually saturated with water vapour and it has a greater concentration of carbon dioxide.

The figures given in Table 2.3 indicate that the soil air has slightly less oxygen and more carbon dioxide (eight times) than atmospheric air, but the amounts of both gases vary considerably according to the activity of the micro-organisms living in the soil. Addition of leaf litter or organic manure greatly stimulates the soil fauna, which may result in the depletion of oxygen and an increase in carbon dioxide. The exchange of these gases with the atmosphere above the soil is hindered if the soil pores and fissures are small or limited in number. When the pores are filled with water, fresh oxygen cannot easily diffuse in, and such oxygen that may be present in the soil is soon consumed so that anaerobic conditions develop. It is in these conditions that the growth of most plants is inhibited and conditions favouring chemical reduction occur in soils.

Considerable energy is currently being exerted by the scientific community in ascertaining the amounts and rates of change of the so-called 'greenhouse gases' in the atmosphere. As the soil holds large reserves of carbon (about twice the amount held in the vegetation), investigations are taking place to find the potential amounts of carbon dioxide and methane which might be released from soils with changing land-use and climatic conditions. From these investigations it has emerged that soils are an important factor influencing the amount of these trace gases. Specifically, the actions of deforestation and cultivation interrupt the natural cycling of carbon, causing the release of carbon dioxide. Cultivation of rice results in the release of

methane from the flooded, anaerobic soils of paddy fields, mainly through the stems of the rice plants. Denitrifying bacteria release nitrogen into the atmosphere, and nitrogenous fertilizers added to arable soils increase emissions of nitrous oxide from soils to the atmosphere.

The movement of gases into and out of the soil takes place by diffusion, a process which depends upon the differences in concentration of gases between the soil atmosphere and the free atmosphere above the soil. Even in freely drained soils with wide pores, some water is trapped by constrictions, so the process is not straightforward. Changes in atmospheric pressure can cause the soil to 'breathe' and the gustiness of the wind may assist gaseous movement. The passage of water through the soil may also displace air from below the wetting front as it moves downwards.

Oxygen diffuses into the soil, where it is taken up by roots and used in microbial activity. During the summer, the demand for oxygen is between 7 and $35\,g\,m^2\,d^{-1}$ and unless there is a saturated layer, the process of diffusion is sufficiently rapid to meet the demand. Conversely, as a result of biological respiration, carbon dioxide diffuses from the soil pores out into the atmosphere at a rate of between 1.5 and $6.7\,g\,m^2\,d^{-1}$ (but some also dissolves in water), and it has been predicted that, other than in anaerobic pockets, the concentration of carbon dioxide in soil air should not normally exceed 1 per cent.

Soil water

The presence of air and water in the soil is almost complementary, for if the soil is saturated with water the air is driven out. In a poorly drained, saturated soil, almost all the pore space between the peds is occupied by water. If the soil is allowed to drain so that the water contained in the larger pores and cavities is removed, the water which is lost is known as **gravitational water**. About two days after heavy rain or irrigation, a freely drained soil has lost all its gravitational water and is said to be at **field capacity**. In this state, considerable amounts of water remain in the finer pores, held by capillary attraction in pores and attached to the surface of soil mineral particles.

Table 2.3 Average composition of soil air (per cent by volume)

	Oxygen	Carbon dioxide	Nitrogen
Soil air	20.65	0.25	79.20
Atmospheric air	20.97	0.03	79.00

If the soil continues to lose moisture from the reserves of capillary water, the point is eventually reached at which plants wilt because they cannot obtain sufficient moisture to maintain turgor. This **wilting point** is not fixed, for plants vary greatly in their capacity to extract water from the soil. The amount of water held between the field capacity and the wilting point of a soil is referred to as the **available water capacity** (Fig. 2.11). This amount will vary according to the texture, organic matter content and structure of the soil, and it is vitally important when considering the ability of a soil to supply a growing crop with its moisture requirements.

Further amounts of moisture can be extracted from the soil in the laboratory. It is possible to bring the soil to air-dry conditions, but as this is rather a variable state depending upon the humidity of the atmosphere, an oven-dry basis, 105°C, is used for most laboratory determinations. Water held at temperatures above oven-dry is referred to as hygroscopic water and is largely unavailable for plants. This water is virtually part of the mineral structure of the soil and may occur as a coating on mineral grains with a thickness of only a few molecules.

The moisture regime of many soils that have ground-water can be simply demonstrated by drilling 10 cm diameter auger holes to different depths, lining the holes with porous tiles and allowing the water level to come to equilibrium. Observations made at suitable intervals throughout the year will reveal the variation of the water level. Infiltration (the rapidity with which water can enter into the soil) can be measured using a ring infiltrometer in which the time taken for a known volume of water to infiltrate is recorded. Soil permeability can also be measured in an auger hole by the rapidity with which the water level returns to normal following removal of water. In the laboratory, soil permeability may be measured by an instrument called a permeameter, in which the passage of water through a soil sample is measured in either unsaturated or saturated conditions.

In order to bring some uniformity to the measurement of soil moisture contents, a system was developed that measures the suction required to pull the water out of the soil. Originally expressed in terms of the tension exerted by the length of a column of water, the range of the numbers necessitated using a logarithmic scale (pF). At saturation, the length of the column is nil and so the suction pressure (in bars) exerted is 0.0 and the pF is 0.0. At field capacity, the suction pressure (−0.33 bar) is represented by a water column 333 cm long or pF 2.5, and at wilting point the suction pressure (−15 bars) is theoretically a water column of 15,000 cm or pF 4.2. However, in recent years the forces which facilitate the movement of water in soils have been collectively referred to by their potential to cause movement, and their measurement is in kilopascals (kPa). The potential of soil water (Φ) is a measure of the amount by which the free energy of water in the soil is reduced by gravitational, osmotic (plant) and matrix (capillary) potentials, which together make the total potential force available for water movement.

Simply stated, water may move through soils in three ways: it may flow freely through the wider fissures and pores, but it also responds to capillary forces and the osmotic pull exerted by plants. Water may also move in the vapour phase under the influence of a temperature gradient, a phenomenon which can be observed in soils of arid areas.

The soil solution

Any soluble constituents present in the soil will dissolve in the water contained in the soil pores and contribute to the **soil solution**. This is the medium through which plants are supplied with the

Fig. 2.11 The width of a film of moisture around a soil particle determines the tension at which it is held. At the outer limit water flows with gravity, but as drying narrows the water film it is more and more tightly held. Water is available for plants between field capacity and the wilting coefficient.

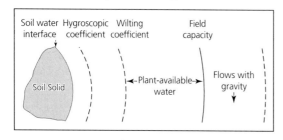

nutrients they require. As has already been observed, inorganic salts dissociate in solution into ions. Many of these ions are attracted to and adsorbed by the clay–humus micelles, but an equilibrium is reached between the ions occupying the exchange positions and those in the soil solution.

In the case of hydrogen ions, their concentration in solution is indicated by the pH scale, in which neutrality is at pH 7. Values below pH 7 are acid and those above pH 7 are alkaline. The general pH range of soils is from pH 3 to pH 10. In humid regions the normal range is from pH 5 to pH 7 and in arid regions from pH 7 to pH 9. Extremely acid conditions, pH 2, may be found in some acid sulphate soils (Thionic Fluvisols), whereas at the other end of the scale, some strongly alkaline soils (Solonetz) may reach a value of pH 10. Soil pH represents an easily determined soil characteristic, which also has a general usefulness. Plant nutrients become less available at the extremes of pH and other elements become available in toxic amounts, so the pH value is often a good guide in the diagnosis of fertility problems.

A significant role of the soil solution is to transport soil constituents from one horizon to another. Movement may be either in solution or suspension; soil constituents will be taken into true solution if they are soluble, or small particles of silt, clay or organic matter may be washed down the profile in suspension. Movement of chemical constituents is also facilitated by chemical linkage (chelation) such as with iron and organic matter, when the iron is mobilized by its association with organic molecules.

In humid climates on level ground, the movement of the soil solution is vertically downwards from the upper eluvial horizons to the lower illuvial horizons of the profile. On sloping sites, soil moisture also moves downslope (laterally through the soil profile), and over a long period of time can produce the sequence of different soils on slopes known as a **catena**. In arid climates, especially where the ground-water table is at shallow depth, movement of soil moisture can be upwards as evaporation draws moisture to the soil surface. Any soluble salts will then be precipitated in the upper soil horizons, where they cause problems for most agricultural crops.

Further reading

Brady, N.C., 1984. *The Nature and Properties of Soils.* 9th edition, Macmillan, London.

Burrough, P.A., 1993. Soil variability: a late 20th century view. *Soils and Fertilizers* **56**:529–62.

Duchaufour, P., 1971. *Précis de pédologie.* 2nd edition, Masson et Cie, Paris.

Eyre, S.R., 1969. *Vegetation and Soils.* Edward Arnold, London.

Foth, H.D., 1978. *Fundamentals of Soil Science.* John Wiley, New York.

Fridland, V.M., 1974. Structure of the soil mantle. *Geoderma* **12**:35–41.

Hole, F.D. and Campbell, J.B., 1985. *Soil Landscape Analysis.* Routledge and Kegan Paul, London.

McBratney, A.B., 1992. On variation, uncertainty and informatics in environmental soil management. *Australian Journal of Soil Research* **30**:913–35.

Mausbach, M.J. and Wilding, L.P. (eds.), 1991. *Spatial Variabilities of Soils and Landforms.* Soil Science Society of America, Madison.

Schroeder, D., 1984. *Soils, Facts and Concepts* (trans. P.A. Gething). Potash Institute, Bern.

USDA, 1951. *Soil Survey Manual.*

White, R.E., 1988. *Introduction to the Principles and Practice of Soil Science.* 2nd edition, Blackwell, Oxford.

Wild, A. (ed.), 1988. *Russell's Soil Conditions and Plant Growth.* 11th edition, Longman, Harlow.

3 Factors of soil formation

The question of how a soil forms inevitably leads first to a consideration of the environmental factors which control the processes of soil formation. Just over 100 years ago, the famous Russian soil scientist Dokuchaev suggested five 'soil formers' which act together to set the limits of soil formation at any one place. These were: parent material, climate, age of the land, plant and animal organisms, and topography. Simply expressed, the concept stated that in the process of soil formation, the parent material is acted upon by the climate and the organisms, over a period of time signified by the age of the land. Topography was also considered, as it has much to do with soil–water relationships and the manner in which gravity can affect soil formation.

Fifty-five years ago, an American soil scientist, Hans Jenny, considered a number of similar 'soil-forming factors', and went on to show how they were functionally related in the form of an equation:

$$s = f'(cl, o, r, p, t,...)$$

in which s, a soil property, is dependent upon (or is a function of) the soil-forming factors of climate (cl), organisms (o), relief (r), parent material (p), and time (t). The three dots imply any other significant soil-forming factors, such as the influence of human beings on soil formation.

The usefulness of this approach is that it is possible to take each soil-forming factor in turn and consider its variation or effects against the others. Whilst the approach is only semi-quantitative, it has the advantage of indicating the relationships of the soil-forming factors, bringing them together for the purposes of discussion. In view of the importance of the factors of soil formation in a consideration of the geography of soils, a brief discussion of their individual roles will be considered.

Climate

Climate is a composite concept which includes the temperature, rainfall, humidity, evapotranspiration, duration of sunshine and many other atmospheric variables. The temperature experienced at any one place sets the speed of any chemical reaction in the soil, and the rainfall percolating through the soil provides a medium in which chemical reactions can take place, as well as providing a mechanism for the movement of soil constituents.

There is a considerable range for both temperature and rainfall throughout the world: rainfall, for example, varies from less than 100 mm in deserts to more than 12,500 mm in the wettest areas, and temperatures that have an annual range of only 0.5 or 1.0°C contrast with those having a range of 43°C. The annual rainfall figures themselves are not always a good indication of the type of soil which will be formed. The total amount of precipitation is significant, but it is as important to assess the effect of seasonal rainfall, and whether it accompanies the cool or the warm season. The intensity of the rainfall is also important, as the effect of short, intense downpours can be very different to long periods of gentle drizzle. These features, as well as the local micro-climate, are important considerations, but unfortunately they are not often recorded.

The rainfall which eventually penetrates into the soil is less than the recorded rainfall, as moisture is diverted through runoff and evaporation from the soil and vegetation surfaces. Plant roots take up water from the soil and, after passing through the plants, it is returned to the atmosphere by the process of evapotranspiration (Fig. 3.1). Water that is not intercepted by plant roots percolates to greater depths and either emerges again in seepages further downslope or joins the ground-water.

Temperature may not seem to have such an

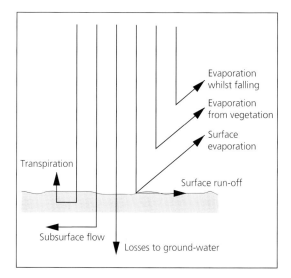

Fig. 3.1 Water entering the soil is not the same as the rainfall; the diagram shows losses incurred before the water reaches the soil. Some water may also be received by downslope movement through the soil.

important role to play in soil formation, but following an idea of Ramann (1928), it is possible to show how it can be significant over a long period of time. In Table 3.1 the relative dissociation of water (into hydrogen and hydroxyl ions) is taken as an index of the rate of chemical activity, and this, multiplied by the length of the weathering period, gives a **weathering factor**. It can be seen that in tropical regions the effectiveness of weathering is almost ten times that in arctic regions and three times that in temperate regions. Weathering has also been in operation for much longer in tropical regions, where it has not been interrupted by a change in climate as during the glacial periods of higher latitudes. Deeper weathering is therefore a characteristic feature of many soils in tropical

regions. Up to 50 m of weathered mantle (regolith) may occur, though the depth is very variable. In temperate regions, the depth to unaltered geological materials may be only one metre or less.

A number of attempts have been made to reduce the effects of climate to a single figure or climatic index. Each has its merits, but most attempts lack a worldwide significance. For example, Thornthwaite's precipitation:effectiveness index works well in North America, but is less accurate in its assessment of the climate of Europe. It is possible to show correlations with rainfall for a number of different soil characteristics. One obvious example is the leaching of calcium carbonate from the soil: the greater the rainfall, the deeper the horizon of calcium carbonate appears in the soil, until it is completely leached out (Fig. 3.2). The formation of clay mineral type and content is also weakly related to the amount of rainfall. Correlations show an increase of clay content accompanying an increase in temperature, and the effect of a higher temperature is also seen in the more rapid decomposition of organic matter in soils of tropical areas.

Unlike the older, climatically based systems of classification, the pedological classification of soils used in this book does not completely mirror the pattern of climate on the Earth's surface. Accordingly, eight climatic zones have been distinguished on the basis of length of growing period, the length of frost-free season and the incidence of rainfall. These 'agro-ecological zones' are now commonly used by scientists involved with soils and agriculture at an international level in the Food and Agriculture Organization of the United Nations (FAO), the Consultative Group of International Agricultural Research (CGIAR), the International Board for Soil Research Management (IBSRAM) and the International Soil Reference and Information Centre (ISRIC).

The length of growing period is estimated from

Table 3.1 Ramann's weathering factor (after Jenny, 1941)

	Average soil temperature	Relative dissociation of water	Days weathering	Weathering factor	
				Absolute	Relative
Arctic	10	1.7	100	170	1
Temperate	18	2.4	200	480	2.8
Tropical	34	4.5	360	1620	9.5

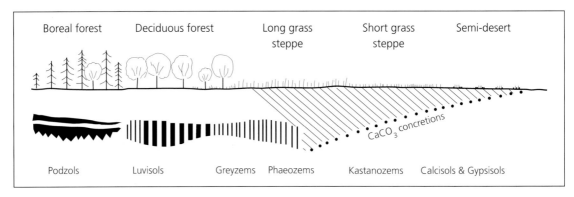

Boreal forest	Deciduous forest	Long grass steppe	Short grass steppe	Semi-desert

CaCO₃ concretions

Podzols	Luvisols	Greyzems	Phaeozems	Kastanozems	Calcisols & Gypsisols

Fig. 3.2 The amount of rainfall can broadly be correlated with the depth to which CaCO, is leached. Thus it is completely removed from Podzol but can appear at the surface of a Calcisol.

the number of days in the year when precipitation exceeds half the evapotranspiration plus a period of time sufficient to remove 100 mm of water from excess water stored in the soil and minus the number of days when the daily mean temperature is less than 6.5°C. The period of time remaining reflects the time when both water and temperature are favourable for crop growth. A period of less than 75 days is used to define an arid climate, between 75 and 270 a seasonally dry climate, and more than 270 days a humid climate.

The frost-free period is defined as the number of days during the year when the average of the extreme minimum temperatures is above 2°C. Using these definitions, the boreal and polar zones have a frost-free period of less than 75 days, the cold zone has a frost-free period of between 75 and 135 days, and the temperate climate has more than 135 days with the average of the six warmest months below 25°C. Within the tropical regions, the seasonally dry sub-tropics are distinguished from the humid tropics by a dry season which extends from 90 to 285 days, whereas the humid tropics have favourable growing conditions all year round.

Organisms

The role of plant and animal organisms in soil formation is of critical importance, for without life there can be no true soil. It has become customary to subdivide the soil organisms into two groups based on size, micro-organisms and macro-fauna, each of which has a particular part to play in soil formation. The green plants synthesize carbohydrates, starches, proteins and other compounds from simple inorganic substances derived from the soil and air by the process of photosynthesis, using energy provided by the sun. When the plants die and the leaves fall to the ground, a rich source of food and energy is provided for the organisms which live in the soil and which are responsible for converting plant debris into the amorphous substance called humus.

Micro-organisms

The numbers of soil-living micro-organisms can be very great indeed (Table 3.2). However, numbers are not necessarily a good guide to their activity, as many organisms may be in a dormant state when sampling occurs; their activity is best measured indirectly by the amount of carbon dioxide evolved. Soil micro-organisms are members of both plant and animal kingdoms and include viruses, bacteria, actinomycetes, protozoa, fungi and algae.

The biomass of bacteria in the soil can amount to a live weight of 3360 kg per hectare (3000 lb per acre). Bacteria live in the thin water films surrounding soil particles and usually have organs of locomotion (cilia or flagella), which enable them to move through the water. Both aerobic and anaerobic bacteria are present in soils, but some normally aerobic bacteria (faculative anaerobes) can also live without oxygen. Aerobic bacteria can rapidly deplete a saturated soil of oxygen, causing chemical reducing conditions. Most soil bacteria

	Broadbalk Field		
	Manured	**Unmanured**	**Grassland**
Insects			
Springtails	40.6	28.3	54.0
Beetle larvae	5.9	0.9	2.3
Fly larvae	19.4	3.8	11.1
All others	3.4	0.5	11.0
Myriapods	4.5	1.8	1.8
Arachnids			
Mites	6.5	1.9	2.9
Spiders	0.17	0.07	1.2
Woodlice	0.04	0.05	–
Gastropods	0.04	–	0.05
Oligochaetes	2.6	0.6	8.4
Nematodes	1.5	0.2	7.6
Totals	84.6	33.2	100.5

Table 3.2 Numbers of small animals found in soil at Rothamsted (1936–1937). Numbers represent millions per acre in top 22 cm (9 inches) (after Russell, 1950)

obtain their energy from organic matter, and in the process produce the substance called humus. Chemotrophic bacteria can make use of inorganic substances; some of these are capable of breaking down sulphur or cyanide compounds as well as complex herbicides and pesticides to obtain their energy requirements. Soil bacteria are preyed upon by protozoans, the most numerous of which belong to the amoebae and the flagellate classes. Both free-living (*Azotobacter*) and symbiotic nodular bacteria (*Rhizobium*) are vitally important for extracting nitrogen from the air, providing a natural source of this essential plant nutrient. Certain algae of the class Chlorophyceae can also fix nitrogen. Less desirable are the denitrifying bacteria (*Pseudomonas*) which reduce nitrate to nitrogen or nitrous oxide, particularly in poorly drained soils.

Of equal importance to the bacteria are the soil-living fungi which can amount to up to 0.2 per cent of the soil volume. Mushrooms and toadstools are the obvious above-soil evidence of the mass of fungal hyphae which ramifies through any decomposable substance within the soil. In some circumstances, such as very strong acidity, fungi are more important than bacteria in the breakdown of organic debris. Organisms with superficial similarities to fungi which occur in neutral or alkaline conditions are the actinomycetes, from which the Nobel-prize-winning soil microbiologist, Waksman, first extracted the antibiotic streptomycin.

Macro-fauna

Many different animals live in the soil; small ones live in the spaces between the soil structures, the larger ones can create their own burrows. In this category, animals belonging to the Arthropoda are the greatest in number, mostly living within the top few centimetres of the soil. In the temperate regions, the springtails (Collembolae) and the mites (Arachnidae) are the most populous (Fig. 3.3). The springtails are responsible for breaking organic matter down into small fragments; many of the mites are carnivorous, feeding upon the springtails.

The earthworms (Oligochaeta), the subject of studies by Darwin and the famous English naturalist Gilbert White, play an important role in the mixing of organic matter with mineral matter. *Lumbricus terrestris*, for example, can be seen to

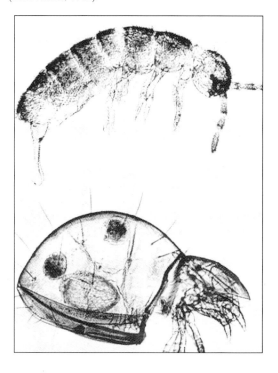

Fig. 3.3 Soil fauna: examples of a collembola (top) and a mite (from Russell, 1961).

actively draw fallen leaves into its burrow. As it feeds, the earthworm ingests a mixture of soil and organic matter which is intimately mixed in the worm's digestive system; the resulting wormcast is a close mixture of humus and soil, slightly alkaline and richer in plant nutrients than the surrounding soil which has not passed through the earthworm. Casting on the soil surface by earthworms eventually leads to the development of a deep, organic-rich topsoil at the A horizon which is gradually thickened. The activities of earthworms – burying organic matter, burrowing, casting and soil mixing – are responsible for the production of the humus form known as 'mull'. Only *Allolobophora longa* and *Allolobophora nocturna* cast on the surface; the other species cast in cavities below the soil surface. Cultivation, which kills about 25 per cent of earthworms, and the lower amount of plant litter associated with arable land have the effect of reducing the earthworm population.

In addition to his evolutionary studies, Charles Darwin (1809–1882) was interested in the activities of earthworms. He measured the weight of worm-casts and calculated that they amounted to 10 tons per acre per year, and that in 50 years the whole volume of soil down to 9 inches (23 cm) would have been brought to the surface by the worms. To measure the effect, Darwin spread chalk and ashes on the surface of the soil in 1842 and by 1871 observed that these were buried by a layer of 7 inches (17.5 cm) of soil. When a later investigator checked the same experimental plot in 1942, the position of the layers of chalk and ashes had not changed.

Whilst the role of the earthworms is beneficial, the same cannot be claimed for the nematodes. This group of creatures is parasitic on plants and animals, and those that live in the soil are no exception. Many nematodes attack plants and reduce yields, as well as transmitting viruses of plant diseases. During drought or in the absence of a host, nematodes are capable of forming a cyst in which the eggs are protected until conditions improve. The species *Heterodera rostochiensis*, the potato root eelworm, is stimulated by exudates from growing potato roots to break out of its cyst and to infect the new plants of the following crop.

Many arthropods spend all or some part of their life cycle in the soil. Centipedes (Chilopoda) are active predators on other soil fauna, but the food of millipedes (Diplopoda) is decaying plant litter, a diet which they share with the woodlice (Isopoda). Both reduce the plant litter to very small particles which are then attacked more readily by micro-organisms. Crop pests such as leather jackets (Diptera) and wireworms (Coleoptera) are larval forms which live in the soil and feed on plant roots. Some insects lay their eggs in the soil and, when hatched, the larvae enter the plants, returning to the soil to pupate before emerging as the adult form.

The colonial insects, ants (Hymenoptera) and termites (Isoptera), are both important inhabitants of the soil. The termites are restricted to tropical areas but ants occur widely in the soils of temperate areas. Both species create their own sheltered environments within the soil, the termites constructing mounds several metres high, with galleries penetrating deep into the subsoil. Ants are predacious, but termites bring plant material into their nests which they 'cultivate' in their underground fungus gardens. It has been estimated that termites are capable of transferring over 1 tonne per hectare per annum ($t\,ha^{-1}\,a^{-1}$) of subsoil to the surface of the soil.

Slugs and snails (Gastropoda) feed mainly on organic debris, which they break down and make more readily available for bacterial colonization. In moist, clayey soils, slugs living just below the soil surface can be a pest, eating new shoots of seeds before they emerge from the soil.

Small mammals, including moles, shrews, rabbits and gophers, and some larger animals, such as foxes and badgers, make their homes in the soil. Their role is restricted to loosening and mixing the soil through their activities. Some birds, too, may influence the nature of the soil. Certain species nest below ground, and small stones from crow's crops have been observed to accumulate below popular roosts in Wisconsin USA.

Larger mammals may be responsible for some soil disturbance such as at salt-licks or mud-wallows, and grazing herbivores provide quantities of dung which contribute to the soil organic matter content. The activities of human beings, however, have the most profound effects on soils and these are considered in Chapter 8.

Plants

Although vegetation is ultimately dependent upon the climate, it can also function as an independent variable. A good example occurs where an oak-wood is replaced by a coniferous plantation: the demands made on the soil are changed and the type of litter supplied to the soil is different, leading to increased podzolization. Where oakwood has colonized Chernozem soils, leaching is encouraged and the soils become degraded.

The regular fall of litter to the soil surface from the vegetation, together with decaying roots, supplies the soil with its organic matter and many of the soil fauna with their nutrient supply. Inputs of litter from forests range from about 2 t ha^{-1} a^{-1} in temperate regions to 10 t ha^{-1} a^{-1} in the tropical rain forest. In an old grassland the annual input of carbon (as roots) was between 2.0 and 2.5 t ha^{-1}. The supply of organic matter to cultivated land from roots is in the order of 0.3 to 1 t ha^{-1} of carbon for small grains, but amounts are dependent upon the quantity of fertilizer applied.

In seasonal environments, the soil microbial population responds rapidly to the availability of food, increasing in number until frost or other adverse conditions inhibit their activity. The activity of the soil flora and fauna converts the plant debris into humus, producing the forms of soil organic matter known as mull, moder or mor, described in Chapter 2.

A most significant zone of interaction between plants and the soil is in the surroundings of roots, sometimes referred to as the **rhizosphere**. The presence of roots provides conditions that encourage the growth of the microbial population. Debris sloughed off plant roots provides food for free-living forms of micro-organisms, and exudates from the roots add to the nutrient supply. Mycorrhizae, symbiotic associations between fungi and plant roots, enable many plants to gain easier access to nutrients. The rhizosphere organisms include nitrogen fixers; their contribution to the nitrogen budget of the soil is described as 'uncertain but significant' and may amount to up to 39 kg ha^{-1} a^{-1}.

Relief

The well-known effects of relief on climate include depression of temperature and increase in rainfall. As an important soil-forming factor, increasing elevation combines with climate to give a succession of different soil-forming conditions, leading to changes in the soil type produced. The succession of soil zones on the slopes of high tropical mountains exhibits this soil pattern very well. A sequence from Ferrallitic Soils on the shore of Lake Malawi to soils at the snowline is given in Fig. 3.4.

Also associated with upland areas is a greater incidence of cloudiness and hence less solar warming; evapotranspiration is also reduced, leading to colder, wetter soil conditions which slow plant decomposition and favour the development of thicker organic horizons. Such conditions are particularly prevalent, for example, in the northern and western uplands of the British Isles.

The compass direction in which a slope faces is described as its **aspect**; the aspect of a slope can greatly affect the amount of solar warming received, especially in the temperate climate zones. Differences in soils will develop in response to the different conditions on sun-facing compared with shaded slopes (Fig. 3.5).

Slope also influences the movement of water on the land and through soils. Sites on the crests of hills and steep slopes actively shed water into low-lying areas which receive proportionately more water for

Fig. 3.4 Altitudinal sequence of soils from Lake Malawi to the snowline.

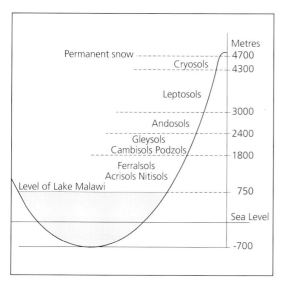

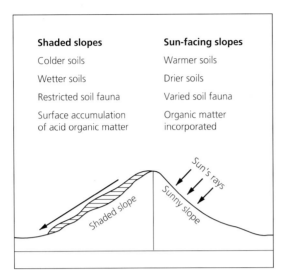

Shaded slopes	Sun-facing slopes
Colder soils	Warmer soils
Wetter soils	Drier soils
Restricted soil fauna	Varied soil fauna
Surface accumulation of acid organic matter	Organic matter incorporated

Fig. 3.5 The effect of aspect and relief on soils situated on shady and sunny slopes.

percolation through the soil profile. Consequently, lower slopes remain wetter for longer periods as water drains from soils higher upslope. Level sites are described as 'normal', although most sites have some slope, even if it is extremely slight (Fig. 3.6).

Gravity acts upon slopes with a vector which exerts its influence in the direction of the slope. There is a tendency for soil material always to be drawn in a downslope direction, whether it is in solution or in the solid state. The action of water, with the mobilization, transport and redeposition of soil materials by overland flow, throughflow and seepage, always works in a downslope direction.

Fig. 3.6 The effect of slope on water availability for soil formation.

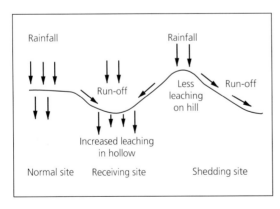

Each wetting–drying cycle and freeze–thaw cycle also imperceptibly moves material downslope in the process known as creep. The long-term effects are shown in the nature of slopes and the inter-linked soils formed upon them. This relationship of a linked sequence of soils with position on the slope is known as a **catena**.

The word 'catena' relates to the way links of a chain, suspended at each end but left to hang freely, form a loop. The soils on a hillside are like the links forming the loop, arranged in sequence from inter-fluve crest to valley floor. The soil relationships of the catena were first identified by Milne in the 1930s in East Africa, and the concept has since proved very useful in the interpretation of soil–landscape relationships in virtually all environments. The catena was the basis for the development of a nine-unit landsurface model, which is helpful in understanding the linkage between processes which operate on slopes and the nature of the soils which develop. The nine landsurface units and their diagnostic properties are summarized in Fig. 3.7. The processes include the effects of gravity and water on the mobilization, transport and redeposition of soil materials by overland flow, throughflow, streamflow and mass movements. This pedogeomorphological approach brings together many aspects of Earth surface processes relevant to pedologists, and is sometimes referred to as a soil–water–gravity model.

The shape of the landscape also influences the movement of weathered debris. Around a concave valley head, creep will tend to concentrate potential soil parent material and soils will be deeper, whereas around the convex nose of a spur of higher land it will tend to be dispersed outwards over a wider area of lower land. As a general rule, soils will be deeper on footslopes where downslope creep has resulted in the accumulation of weathered material and eroded soil. These footslope accumulations are referred to as **colluvium**.

Certain American authors have found that successful prediction of soil attributes can be made using digital terrain models, enabling a link to be made between topography and quantifiable soil characteristics. A strong correlation has been observed between measured soil attributes, slope gradient and a 'wetness index'.

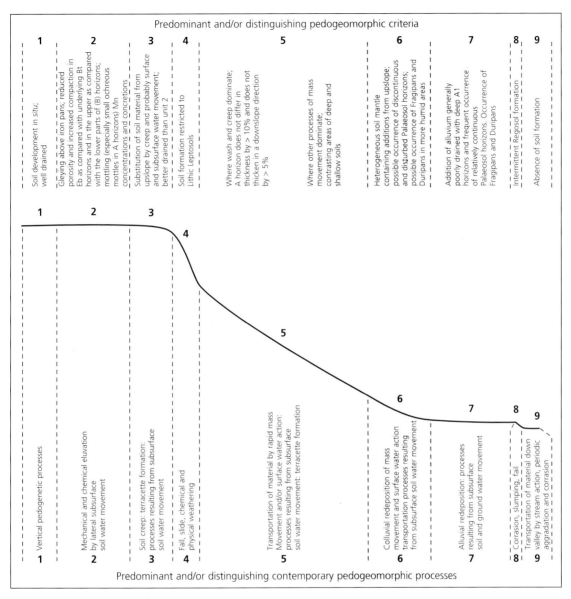

Predominant and/or distinguishing pedogeomorphic criteria

1 Soil development in situ; well drained

2 Gleying above iron pans, reduced porosity and increased compaction in Eb as compared with underlying Bt horizons and in the upper as compared with the lower parts of (B) horizons; mottling (especially small ochreous mottles in A horizons) Mn concentrations and concretions

3 Substitution of soil material from upslope by creep and probably surface and subsurface water movement; better drained than unit 2

4 Soil formation restricted to Lithic Leptosols

5 Where wash and creep dominate; A horizon does not differ in thickness by > 10% and does not thicken in a downslope direction by > 5%

6 Heterogeneous soil mantle containing additions from upslope; possible occurrence of discontinuous and disturbed Palaeosol horizons; possible occurrence of Fragipans and Duripans in more humid areas

7 Addition of alluvium generally poorly drained with deep A1 horizons and frequent occurrence of relatively continuous Palaeosol horizons. Occurrence of Fragipans and Duripans

8 Intermittent Regosol formation

9 Absence of soil formation

1 Vertical pedogenetic processes

2 Mechanical and chemical eluviation by lateral subsurface soil water movement

3 Soil creep: terracette formation: processes resulting from subsurface soil water movement

4 Fall, slide, chemical and physical weathering

5 Transportation of material by rapid mass movement and/or surface water action: processes resulting from subsurface soil water movement: terracette formation

6 Colluvial redeposition of mass movement and surface water action transportation processes resulting from subsurface soil water movement

7 Alluvial redeposition: processes resulting from subsurface soil and ground water movement

8 Corrasion, slumping, fall

9 Transportation of material down valley by stream action, periodic aggradation and corrasion

Predominant and/or distinguishing contemporary pedogeomorphic processes

Fig. 3.7 The nine-unit landsurface model (after Conacher and Dalrymple, 1977).

Parent material

The parent material was described by Jenny (1941) as 'the initial state of the soil system', but it is more generally described as the consolidated or unconsolidated material, little affected by the present weathering cycle, from which the soil has developed. The more simple definition, that it is the material which lies beneath the true soil horizons, could be misleading, as many soils have developed from composite parent materials of differing origins and not simply from the rock which happens to lie at some depth beneath. For example, a soil can develop in a thick glacial till or loess layer overlying an almost unweathered rock; it is possible that there may be thin layers of both glacial drift and loess present in which the soil has developed, or the soil may be developed in both the superficial layers and the bedrock beneath.

It is useful at this point to distinguish between weathering and soil formation; the former is a geological process producing the **regolith**, and the latter is a pedological process, often working on and changing further the results of weathering into soils. Briefly, weathering involves the physical disintegration of the rocks, and the geochemical processes of solution, hydrolysis, carbonization, oxidation and reduction, as well as the rearrangement of the structure of some clay minerals and the formation of others. The soil-forming processes are considered in more detail in Chapter 4.

Weathering and soil formation can proceed either separately or together. In old, deep soils, such as occur in many inter-tropical areas, weathering will occur at depth, well below the genetic soil horizons which have formed near the surface. In younger soils, which are usually much shallower, the two processes may operate almost simultaneously within the same few centimetres of soil.

In most environments, the balance of soil-forming factors is such that different rocks, when weathered, will produce a regolith which in turn will give rise to different soil types, depending on the inherent mineral composition. This has been demonstrated in Scotland, where Cambisols form on basic igneous rocks and Podzols on acid igneous rocks under identical climatic conditions. The differences between calcareous and non-calcareous parent materials are of sufficient importance to be reflected in many soil classifications. The presence of large reserves of bases, in particular calcium and magnesium, maintains the iron, aluminium and humic constituents in a flocculated state, thus inhibiting movement and so retarding the development of horizons within the soil profile. In Wales, outcrops of the Carboniferous Limestone on Black Mountain, Dyfed, give rise to Cambisols at an elevation and under a rainfall which ensure Humic Gleysols on adjacent non-calcareous parent materials. Similarly, in the Peak District of Derbyshire, England, the limestones have a cover of Cambisols whereas the surrounding sandstones and shales only support moorland with Humic Gleysols and Gleyic Podzols.

Extremely porous, quartzose, sandy parent materials rapidly achieve a mature soil profile because they contain few soluble materials, and any constituents in solution or suspension can move easily through the profile and out of the soil. Thus many coarse, sandy parent materials throughout the geological succession develop Podzols upon their weathered mantles. Some of the most striking Podzols are found on the coarse-textured glacio-fluvial sands and gravels of former glaciated areas as well as on the sandstones of the Tertiary formations. Cambic Podzols, and Dystric and Chromic Cambisols are commonly found on steeply sloping sites, for example in Wales and Scotland, where they are developed from weathered debris of Lower Carboniferous strata.

In contrast, clay soils are usually slow-draining and slower to develop a fully mature profile than freely drained soils. Wide expanses of till plains in the lowlands of England have fine-textured Eutric Gleysols or Gleyic Luvisols (Surface-water Gley Soils); similar parent materials in the uplands develop peatyness and typical soils are Dystric Gleysols (Peaty Gleys).

Frequently, alluvial materials are sorted into layers with different particle sizes by fluvial action. They are often silty and possess organic matter in variable amounts and to greater depths than other soils. A combination of alluvial materials together with a covering of neutral or calcareous peat can provide highly fertile Terric Histosols (Earthy Peat Soils) when drained. Unfortunately, the action of draining and cultivation causes oxidation of the peat and most of the former peats of the Fens of eastern England have now disappeared, leaving humose silty mineral soils.

In the sub-humid and semi-arid lands, conditions are suitable for the development of soils rich in the clay mineral montmorillonite (smectite). Leaching of soil constituents from the upland areas to the lowlands provides the raw materials for recombination of elements into new minerals. Along the valley floors of the savanna lands, black, montmorillonite-rich clays have formed. These dark-coloured, deeply cracking clayey soils are discussed under the heading of Vertisols in Chapter 6.

Where blown sand, loess or volcanic ash accumulates, or where land is completely disrupted by opencast mining, new parent materials are made available for the processes of soil formation to work upon. The changes which take place in these materials demonstrate how the early stages of soil formation take place. The direction or rate of soil formation may be changed gradually or abruptly when the other factors of soil formation change, for example climate, or where the natural processes are interrupted by the actions of human beings.

Time

Soils, like organisms, change with the passage of time and gradually develop new features as they proceed from youth, through maturity, to old age. Young soils retain many of the features of the parent material from which they developed, but as they become more mature, the pedological features increase at the expense of the characteristics of the parent material. This progression starts with the addition of the first fragment of organic matter to a new parent material and continues with the development, and increasing clarity, of the genetic horizons. By the time a soil is in equilibrium with its environment, it can be considered to be a mature soil. Most of the early forms of soil classification are based on the characters of the mature soil profile.

There are several examples of soil formation that has taken place over a known period of time. Often, these examples are related to catastrophic events, such as the eruption of Krakatoa in 1883, which was well-documented, or to the development of soils on lavaflows, landslide debris and earthflows. The retreat of glacier fronts has left behind an expanse of new parent material upon which soil formation has begun. Records of the earlier position of glaciers provide an opportunity to date accurately the beginning of soil formation.

Examples are also available where the draining of a lake has exposed its floor to the processes of soil formation; one of the best-documented examples is the draining of the polders from the bed of the IJsselmeer in The Netherlands. The initial changes in the new parent material have been described as a process of **ripening**, during which profound physical, chemical and biological changes take place as the soil develops.

The development of a sequence of dunes parallel to the coast has occurred in several parts of the world, providing information on the rate of soil formation. Similar sequences of successive mining spoil heaps show changes taking place as soil development occurs, including accumulation of organic matter and acidification, which can be related to the time which has elapsed since the mining spoil heaps were dumped.

In many inter-tropical regions, it is possible to establish a sequence of soil development correlated with the morphology of the landscape, thus linking together two branches of geographical study. The position of a soil on the landscape gives its age relationships (Fig. 3.8). In the example, the time-scale of geomorphology and that of soil formation are working in parallel, although for most soils the time-scale of soil formation is shorter than that concerned with the formation of geomorphological features.

In the British Isles, it is generally accepted that soil formation dates from the end of the Pleistocene, about 10,000 years BP. Most of the soils formed during the interglacial periods were eroded by subsequent glaciation, but a few relict soils remain to give some indication of the earlier soil cover. Pockets of soil material, often eroded

Fig. 3.8 Age and position of soils on the landscape. Different geomorphic surfaces give rise to soils of different maturity.

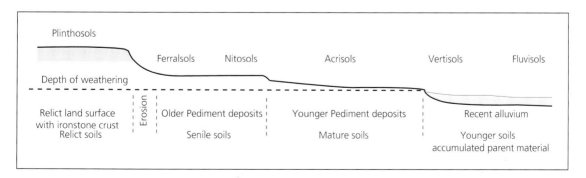

29

and redeposited, that remain in Scotland and South Wales indicate warmer conditions during the last interglacial period. Evidence of soils formed in colder conditions is preserved within the sequence of glacial deposits in East Anglia.

Changes of climate are known to have occurred during post-glacial times and the effects of this have been preserved in soils. Following the Iron Age period of British pre-history, increased podzolization occurred in southern Britain. Many soil profiles have features which suggest that the present soil-forming factors are different from those of the past, reflecting climatic change. The evidence is to be seen in the lower soil horizons that have yet to be brought into equilibrium with the present environmental conditions.

Modelling soils

The modeller's approach, which aims to build in the mind's eye a simple but comprehensible picture of a complex reality in the real world, has five main components. The first of these concerns the **external variables** or factors such as temperature, precipitation and, in more recent times, the influence of pollutants on soils. Secondly, there are the **state variables**, the parameters of the soil system as shown by the amount of various constituents and concentrations of nutrients. Such chemical, physical and biological relationships may be linear or non-linear and can be demonstrated by mathematical equations. It is necessary to choose parameters carefully for specific soils. These parameters must be calibrated realistically by comparison with known observations. Associated with these parameters is the idea of **sensitivity**; for example the impact of some parameters may change dramatically with the seasons. It is necessary to **conceptualize** the processes in diagrammatic or mathematical form, demonstrating the interaction of the various elements of the model. Finally, the model has to be **verified** for its internal logic and the accuracy of its output. In recent years, models have been used extensively to obtain a better understanding of crop growth, nitrogen cycling, nutrient uptake, carbon content, organic matter turnover and soil–plant moisture relationships.

The functional relationship of the soil-forming factors shown by Jenny is but one extremely useful approach to the study of soils using a conceptual model. However, there are some real difficulties in applying this particular approach in every case. The significant problems of giving climate, organisms or parent material a value which can be substituted in the equation can only be resolved by the use of subjective decisions. Furthermore, it is almost impossible to isolate completely the variables: relief and climate are often closely related and with them the nature of the associated plant and animal ecosystems. Later, after attempting more complex soil–ecological equations, Jenny simplified his model to three state factors:

$$s = f'(Lo, Px, t)$$

where Lo = the initial state of the system, Px = the external flux potentials and t = the age of the system. Following this lead, Runge has proposed a factorial model which lays more stress on energy relationships:

$$s = f'(o, w, t)$$

in which o = organic matter production, w = water for leaching and t = time. Other modellers have attempted to use changes in chemical or mineralogical composition in models which try to balance the inputs and outputs of the soil system.

Since Jenny's *Factors of Soil Formation* was published in 1941, there have been many developments in the use of models. Two main types of model are used in soil studies: concrete models and conceptual models. The former implies experimental soil columns in the laboratory through which solutions can be percolated, as well as lysimeters in the field containing undisturbed soil profiles which can be weighed and the inputs and outputs measured. Conceptual models include mental, verbal, structural and mathematical forms.

An important step forward has been the recognition of the soil as an open system, stemming from the proposals of Simonson. The biogeochemical cycling of elements, as suggested in Chapter 1, can form a useful outline model for soil genesis, as well as illustrating the path of plant nutrients or pollutants through the soil and its associated plant and animal ecosystems (Fig. 3.9). Weathering of the rocks is an input which becomes the mineral part of

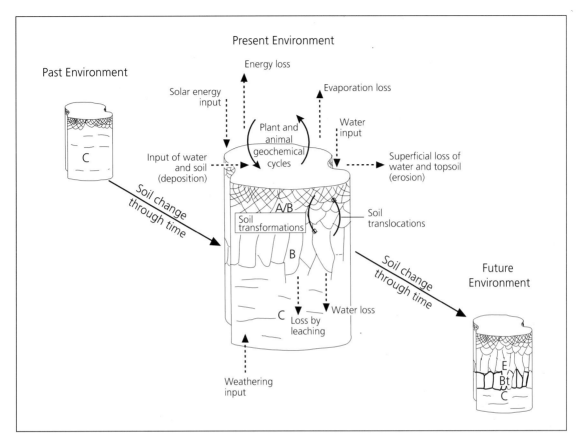

Fig. 3.9 The soil as an open system. A soil area, or pedon, is shown as part of a system evolving through time. Profile characteristics result from additions (inputs) and losses (outputs), as well as through translocations and transformations within the profile.

the soil; some of the elements released by weathering will be plant nutrients and these become an output of the soil system and an input of the associated biological cycle. Recycling will occur when the plant dies and its component elements are returned in the plant litter, decomposed and taken up again by a later generation of plants. Losses from the system occur when dissolved minerals are carried away by the drainage water, or crops are harvested.

An advantage of the systems approach lies in the idea of 'feedback' loops, which help to regulate and maintain the soil system. Any model of soils has to be a dynamic model because soils change over time. It may be a rapid change, as with changes of

land-use, or it may be a slower change in response to the factors controlling their development. Some of the oldest tropical soils may well approach the steady-state or dynamic equilibrium advocated by systems theorists, but even these soils are subject to change if one of the factors of soil formation changes.

Modelling forms an important aspect of pedology when, with limited amounts of basic information, it becomes necessary to extrapolate from one set of data to another. A new area of study, which is evolving rapidly, involves **pedotransfer functions** to derive surrogate data for use when observations were not made at the time a soil was sampled. To date this has applied particularly to soil physical data: insufficient data were gathered in the earlier days of soil surveys, and are now expensive, time-consuming and labour-intensive to obtain. Most progress has been made with pedotransfer functions that estimate water contents at certain matric potentials, or estimate the soil-water retention or other physical parameters. The soil attributes used most commonly by modellers include particle size, organic carbon content and bulk density, and predicted values of soil-water retention, saturated and unsaturated soil conductivity have been used. These attributes of soils are necessary for modelling the movement of water, plant nutrients and pollutants through soils (transport models). They are incorporated in models of the uptake of nutrients by crops and are also used in models predicting soil erosion. With restricted funding for soil studies, the use of these pedotransfer functions becomes increasingly attractive, and they have the added advantage that they can be handled by computer and interfaced with geographical information systems to give a spatial dimension to the studies.

Further reading

Anlauf, R., Kersebaum, K.Ch., Liu Ya Ping, Nuske-Schüler, A., Richter, J., Springob, G., Syring, K.M. and Utermann, J., 1990. *Models for Processes in the Soil: Programs and Exercises*. Catena Verlag, Hannover.

Birkeland, P.W., 1984. *Soils and Geomorphology*. Oxford University Press, Oxford and New York.

Bouma, J. and Van Lanen, H.A.J., 1987. Transfer functions and threshold values: from soil characteristics to land qualities. In: Beek, K.J., Burrough, P.A. and McCormack, D.E. (eds.) *Quantified Land Evaluation Procedures*. ITC Publication No. 6, Enschede.

Conacher, A.J. and Dalrymple, J.B., 1977. The nine-unit landsurface model: an approach to pedogeomorphic research. *Geoderma* **18**:1–154.

Dalrymple, J.B., Blong, R.J. and Conacher, A.J., 1968. An hypothetical nine unit landsurface model. *Zeitschrift für Geomorphologie* **12**:60–76.

Daniels, R.B. and Hammer, R.D., 1992. *Soil Geomorphology*. Wiley, New York.

Darwin, C.R., 1881. *The Formation of Vegetable Mould through the Action of Worms with Observations on their Habits*. Murray, London.

Gerrard, A.J., 1981. *Soils and Landforms*. George Allen and Unwin, London.

Jenkinson, D.S., 1990. The turnover of organic carbon and nitrogen in soil. *Philosophical Transactions of the Royal Society London* **B 329**:361–9.

Jenny, H., 1961. Derivation of state factor equations of soils and ecosystems. *Soil Science Society of America Proceedings* **25**:385–8.

Jenny, H., 1994. *Factors of Soil Formation. A System of Quantitative Pedology*. Dover Publications, New York.

Milne, G., 1935. Some suggested units of classification and mapping, particularly for East African soils. *Soil Research* **4**:183–98.

Mitchell, C.W., 1991. *Terrain Evaluation*. Longman Scientific and Technical, Harlow.

Moore, I.D., Gessler, P.E., Nielsen, G.A. and Petersen, G.A., 1993. Soil attribute prediction using terrain analysis. *Soil Science Society of America Journal* **57**:443–52.

Ramann, E., 1928. *The Evolution and Classification of Soils* (trans. C.L. Whittles). Heffer, Cambridge.

Richter, J., 1987. *The Soil as a Reactor: Modelling Processes in the Soil*. Catena Verlag, Hannover.

Runge, E.C.A., 1973. Soil development sequences and energy models. *Soil Science* **115**:183–93.

Russell, E.J., 1950. *Soil Conditions and Plant Growth*. 8th edition, Longmans Green and Co., London.

Russell, E.J., 1961. *The World of the Soil*. Collins Fontana Library.

Simonson, R.W., 1959. Outline of a generalized theory of soil genesis. *Soil Science Society of America Proceedings* **23**:152–6.

Simonson, R.W., 1995. Airborne dust and its significance to soils. *Geoderma* **65**:1–43.

Smeck, N.E., Runge, E.C.A. and Mackintosh, E.E., 1983. Dynamics and general modelling of soil systems. In: Wilding, L.P., Smeck, N.E. and Hall, G.F. (eds.) *Pedogenesis and Soil Taxonomy. 1. Concepts and Interactions*. Developments in Soil Science 11A, Elsevier, Amsterdam.

Wood, M., 1989. *Soil Biology*. Blackie, Glasgow.

4 Processes of soil formation

The processes of soil formation modify the regolith and give it the acquired characteristics which distinguish soil from parent material. These processes include weathering, clay formation, leaching, eluviation, podzolization, calcification, ferrallitization, salinization, alkalization, solodization, rubefaction, gleying, accumulation of organic matter, and pedoturbation. These processes are not mutually exclusive: podzolization and gleying can be seen to take place simultaneously in cool, humid regions of the world; gleying and salinization are frequently seen in low-lying areas of semi-arid parts of the world. The results of the soil-forming processes are to produce the characteristic features of soils. These are used in the identification and classification of soils.

Weathering

Originally, rock minerals were formed deep in the Earth's crust at temperatures and pressures very different from those at the surface. When eventually revealed at the Earth's surface by geological action, these rock minerals are unstable in their new environment and are susceptible to weathering by the processes of hydrolysis or acid decomposition, oxidation, reduction, hydration and carbonation.

Weathering is an important precursor of soil development but it also occurs alongside specific soil-forming processes, especially in shallow or young soils. It can be considered under the headings of either physical or chemical weathering. Physical weathering is most obvious in arctic and desert regions where free water is limited, but elsewhere chemical weathering is dominant in the production of soil parent materials. Water is critically important in the process of chemical weathering. Charged with dissolved carbon dioxide and the breakdown products of organic matter, rain-water forms an acid solution which attacks unweathered rocks and their constituent minerals. At the same time, the movement of water through the soil and regolith removes the soluble products from the site of weathering and so prevents equilibrium concentrations being reached in the soil solution. This ensures that rock decomposition continues.

Studies of the soil solution, the liquid component of the soil, have shown that weathering of the common feldspar minerals takes place in two stages: mineral breakdown followed by organic complexation. An example is the hydrolysis of orthoclase feldspar to kaolinite, releasing potassium ions and silicic acid into the soil solution. Feldspar minerals have a complex composition, reflected in their surface form, which is porous; this allows the acidic soil solution to penetrate and exploit any weaknesses present. Hydrolysis of clay minerals occurs because the dipole form of the water molecules orients them with their positively charged side towards the mineral. Their opposite, negatively charged side attracts hydrogen ions (i.e. protons, H^+) which, after satisfying the overall negative charge, enables other hydrogen ions to enter the lattice structure of the clay particle and exchange with potassium, sodium or calcium ions within the mineral, thus disrupting its structure. The process is encouraged further by the formation of organo-metal complexes (chelates), which enables the breakdown products to pass into solution and percolate down the soil profile.

Other weathering processes which take place in the regolith include oxidation and reduction. Iron and manganese minerals are particularly involved, and often their state of oxidation gives typical colours to soil horizons. Iron oxides and hydroxides are present as very small particles, coating other, larger mineral grains such as quartz. When the iron oxides are removed, the uncoated quartz grains give the typical grey colour of the albic E horizon. The chemical process of reduction also takes place and is very important in waterlogged conditions; reduction makes iron and manganese more soluble and oxidation–reduction processes produce the typical grey and yellowish-red colours of the mottling of gley soils. Dissolution removes many minerals, and carbonation affects calcareous material such as calcium carbonate, which is attacked by carbonic acid producing soluble calcium bicarbonate.

Weathering results in loss of the features of rock structure and leads to development of the regolith. In the temperate regions, depth of weathering is normally one or two metres only, but in the humid tropics much greater depths of weathered material can be seen. Extremely deep weathering profiles occur, in which the present-day soil is formed only in the immediate surface. Below the soil, in the parent rock, a series of different layers may be identified, separated by 'weathering fronts'. These layers include the ironstone, pallid and mottled zones of laterites, and a plasmic zone in which the fabric of the primary rock is destroyed and replaced by new soil parent material. At the base of the weathered profile lies the saprolite, where the rock is completely rotten but retains its rock structures, and the saprock, which still contains weatherable minerals. Some or all of these layers may be present, depending upon the erosional history of the site.

Clay formation

Soils developed from recent alluvial sediments may contain the minerals illite, vermiculite and chlorite, which have been formed elsewhere and transported to their present site. However, in many soils, as a result of the chemical elements liberated during the weathering process, the ingredients are present for new clay minerals to be formed within the soil. Some clay minerals are formed simply by alteration, but clay formation, together with the production of different colours by oxidation, and structural changes caused by wetting and drying cycles, is an important contributor to the development of a **cambic B horizon** (Plate A7).

In semi-arid or sub-humid regions, active weathering on the interfluve areas releases silica and magnesium which become concentrated in alluvial lowlands, where recombination may occur to produce smectite clays. Where the soil solution becomes over-saturated with aluminium hydroxides and silica, allophane together with the minerals imogolite and halloysite contribute to the resultant clay fraction. This occurs particularly in regions where volcanic ejecta are weathering to form soil parent materials.

In the humid tropical regions, kaolinite, the iron oxides ferrihydrite and goethite, and the aluminium oxide gibbsite form a group of **low activity clays**. These clays, with a very low cation exchange capacity (CEC) and a low base saturation, are produced throughout the inter-tropical region, where the silica content of the soil solution is very low and the concentration of other elements is also very dilute.

Leaching

This is the term given to the process by which soluble constituents are removed from the soil. In any part of the world where rainfall exceeds evaporation, readily soluble salts are dissolved by water percolating downwards. Consequently, soluble salts are removed in the drainage water and do not persist in the soil profile. Calcium carbonate and even sparingly soluble minerals are dissolved and carried away over a long period of time (Fig. 4.1).

In most humid climates, however, not all of the calcium, magnesium, potassium and sodium is present as free salts in the soil; some is held as cations by the clay–humus complex. A process of proton exchange takes place in which hydrogen ions are exchanged for the cations, gradually acidifying the soil. After prolonged attack by acid weathering and leaching, as has occurred in some soils of the humid tropical regions, only quartz, kaolinite, gibbsite and a few other very stable minerals remain in the soil, in part protected by a coating of iron oxides composed of goethite, with a yellowish-brown colour, or hematite with a bright red colour. In association with clay formation, leaching is responsible for the development of the cambic B horizon.

The leaching process is checked when soils are limed for agricultural purposes. Plants also tend to reduce the effect of leaching, as they bring elements in solution from the subsoil through their roots to the stems and leaves. These elements are then released by the death and decomposition of the

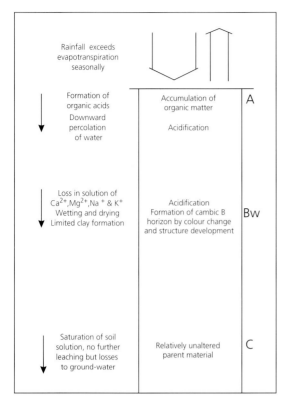

Fig. 4.1 The process of leaching.

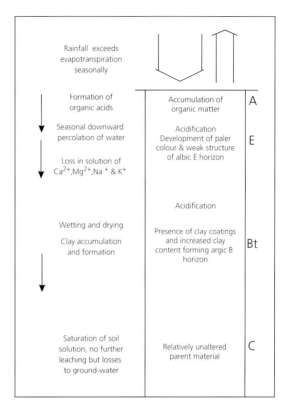

Fig. 4.2 The process of clay eluviation.

plant on the soil surface. Burrowing animals, too, tend to bring material to the surface by their activities, and this is also in opposition to the leaching process.

Clay eluviation

In the past, the term 'eluviation' simply implied the removal of substances from the A horizon of a soil. Recently, it has become customary to distinguish between loss by solution (leaching) and eluviation, which refers specifically to the loss in suspension of material from a soil horizon. Finely dispersed humus and clay particles, as well as other weathering products, can move as colloidal suspensions from upper, **eluvial** horizons to **illuvial** horizons lower in the profile, where they are redeposited (Fig. 4.2). This process appears to be encouraged by a climate in which a period of desiccation results in the soil shrinking and cracking. As the soil dries, the suspended material is deposited from the soil solution on the sides of the peds and along pores.

Pedologically, one of the most important results of eluviation is the development of a B horizon enriched in clay, which is referred to as an **argic B horizon** (also called an argillic horizon, a Bt horizon or a 'textural' B horizon) (Plate A8). In some soils the clay content is appreciably raised by this phenomenon of eluviation. The results of eluviation can be seen as clay coatings on subsurface soil structures, which are also observable by microscopic examination in thin sections of soil samples.

The argic horizon often has a prismatic or subangular blocky structure. In order to qualify as argic, a horizon must have an increased clay content: if the overlying horizon has less than 15 per cent clay, the argic horizon must have over 3 per cent more; if the overlying horizon has between 15 and 40 per cent clay, the argic horizon must have 20 per cent more; and if the overlying soil has a clay content of more than 40 per cent then an argic horizon must have 8 per cent more.

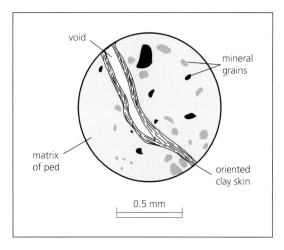

Fig. 4.3 A thin section of soil as seen through a microscope, showing oriented clay lining the walls of a pore.

Eluviation is regarded as a purely mechanical washing of fine particles suspended in the soil solution from the upper into the lower horizons. For this reason the process is also referred to by the French name of *lessivage* and the group of related soils in France are called *Sols Lessivés*. In well-developed examples, clay skins can be seen with a hand lens or even with the naked eye (Fig. 4.3). It is also possible to observe the downward movement of silt particles from the eluvial horizon of grey wooded soils in Canada and the Derno-podzolic Soils of Russia. This results in a characteristic white tonguing of the E horizon into the B horizon, a feature which is referred to by the term 'glossic'.

Podzolization

The process of podzolization is prevalent in soils of the cool humid parts of the world, but it is also responsible for the development of extremely deep soils on quartzitic sands in tropical regions. The results of podzolization are readily distinguishable because the processes that operate are more severe and the profile formed is more distinctive, both in appearance and in its physical and chemical properties, than in the case of soils formed only by leaching or eluviation (Fig. 4.4).

Podzolization involves the development of an extremely acid humus form known as mor, which

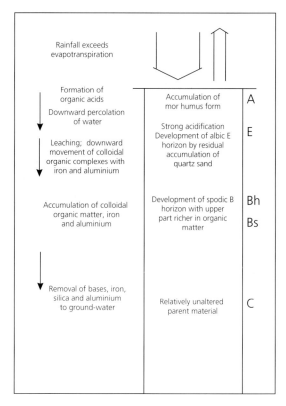

Fig. 4.4 The process of podzolization.

forms because the rate of decomposition of debris from plants such as heath or coniferous trees is slow, allowing extremely acid litter, fermentation and humus horizons to accumulate (Fig. 2.8). Rain-water falling on the vegetation acquires soluble organic breakdown substances from the plants; as it percolates through the surface organic horizons, further organic breakdown substances are added to it before it enters the mineral soil. This acidified soil solution is capable of disrupting the structure of the clay minerals, releasing the constituent elements. Silica and aluminium from the clays, iron from iron minerals and coatings on mineral grains, complexed with organic matter, are mobilized and removed from the surface horizons as the solution percolates downwards through the soil profile.

As even the most sparingly soluble elements are eventually removed by this process, there is a tendency for the almost insoluble quartz grains of sand to form a relative accumulation in the immediate subsurface as the other soil components are removed. In this way, the strongly bleached, grey **albic E horizon**, typical of Podzols, gradually forms (Plate A6). The A horizon, with its accumulation of organic matter, remains thin in the absence of earthworms to mix the organic and mineral materials.

The iron and aluminium oxides, which were mobilized, together with the organic matter, from the eluvial horizons and moved down the soil profile in the soil solution, are eventually deposited in an illuvial B horizon which has been given the name **spodic B horizon** (Plate A10). This is defined as occurring below an A horizon or an E horizon and at a depth greater than 12.5 cm. A spodic B horizon must have one or more of the following: a sub-horizon more than 2.5 cm thick, continuously cemented by a combination of organic matter with iron or aluminium or with both; a sandy or coarse-loamy texture with distinct dark pellets of coarse silt size or with sand grains covered with cracked coatings of organic matter and aluminium with or without iron; and one or more sub-horizons must have the following features:

(a) if there is 0.1 per cent or more extractable iron, the ratio of iron plus aluminium extracted by pyrophosphate at pH 10 to the percentage of clay is 0.2 or more, or if there is less than 0.1 per cent extractable iron, the ratio of aluminium plus organic carbon to clay is 0.2 or more; and

(b) the sum of pyrophosphate-extractable iron plus aluminium is half or more of the sum of dithionite-citrate extractable iron plus aluminium; and

(c) the thickness is such that the index of accumulation of amorphous material in the sub-horizons that meet the preceding requirements is 65 or more. This index is calculated by subtracting half the clay percentage from the CEC (expressed in $cmol_c\,kg^{-1}$ clay) at pH 8.2 and multiplying the remainder by the thickness of the sub-horizon (in centimetres); the results of all the sub-horizons are then added.

Strongly acid conditions developed in all Podzol soils limit the range of soil fauna present as well as the range of plants that can be successfully grown.

Earthworms are noticeably absent and the soil undergoes little faunal pedoturbation, so the pronounced horizons of the Podzol profile are allowed to develop.

Calcification

The process of calcification is characteristic of soils in low-rainfall semi-arid and arid areas and continental interior situations. Leaching is slight, and although downward movement does take place, the soluble constituents are not removed from the soil profile. After seasonal rains or snowmelt, these soils are wetted only to a depth of 1 to 1.5 m, where the impetus of the downward-percolating moisture is lost and it begins to be drawn back to the surface to re-evaporate (Fig. 4.5). Successive wetting and drying cycles in the soil lead to the deposition of calcium carbonate in a **calcic horizon** (Plate A12), usually in the lower B or upper C horizons of the soil profile. To qualify as a calcic

Fig. 4.5 The process of calcification/gypsification.

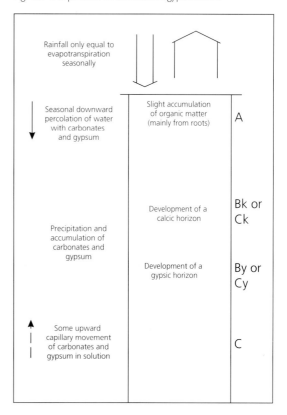

horizon there must be a zone of at least 20 cm where calcium carbonate is accumulating and the amount must be in excess of 15 per cent of the fine earth and 5 per cent more than in a lower horizon.

Calcium carbonate accumulation may be in the form of fine particles diffused throughout the soil matrix (Plate A31), as concretions of soft, powdery lime (Plate A26), or as discrete nodules. However, in some cases it is in the form of continuous, strongly cemented layers which may occur at depth or at the surface where erosion has exposed them. The name **petrocalcic horizons** has been given to these layers (Plate A13).

In arid areas, processes similar to those which lead to the accumulation of carbonates in the soil profile can result in the accumulation of gypsum in a **gypsic horizon** (Plate A14). The gypsum can occur as scattered crystals through the matrix of the soil (Plate A32), as crystallaria ('desert roses') or as a massive **petrogypsic horizon** (Plate A15). Where both calcic and gypsic horizons occur in the same profile, the gypsic usually lies below the calcic horizon.

Ferrallitization

The process of ferrallitization is characteristic of soil formation in the humid tropical regions of the world. In the past, this process has been referred to as laterization, latosolization, kaolinization or desilicification; these terms have become confused in their definition and use, so the term ferrallitization is preferred. In simple terms, this process involves the net loss of silica, the formation of kaolinite and the relative accumulation of the sesquioxides of iron and aluminium (Fig. 4.6). The accumulation of Fe and Al gave this process of soil formation its name. On basic parent rocks the process is fairly rapid, leading to the formation and accumulation of the iron minerals goethite and hematite, but gibbsite may be formed instead of kaolinite. On acid rocks the process is much slower and clay formation is restricted to the kaolinite group of clay minerals. In both cases, the clay minerals frequently are coated and cemented with iron oxides. The resulting soil material is usually porous and therefore freely drained, and is yellowish-brown or red in colour, depending upon the

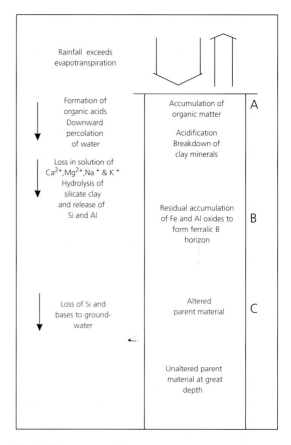

Fig. 4.6 The process of ferrallitization.

degree of hydration of the iron oxides. Because of the cohesion given by the iron oxide coatings the clay does not easily disperse in water and so the soil is relatively resistant to erosion.

The process of ferrallitization is accompanied by strong leaching of the soil, so pH values are low. The rapid decay and recycling of the elements contained in leaf-fall from the forest trees keep the limited amounts of plant nutrients and bases in circulation between plant and soil. Geomorphological stability and a prolonged exposure to the humid tropical environment allow time for the production of a highly weathered, low base-status **ferralic B horizon** (Plate A11), alternatively known as the oxic horizon.

To qualify as a ferralic B horizon ferrallitization must have proceeded to such a degree that the soil material is more than 30 cm thick, has a particle size of sandy loam or finer, contains less than 10 per cent weatherable minerals, possesses less than 5 per cent rock structure, and any clay increase must be gradual. The ferralic B horizon is also characterized by a CEC equal to or less than 16 $cmol_c\,kg^{-1}$ clay as measured by the ammonium acetate method at pH 7.0. In extreme cases the amount of exchangeable bases (Ca, Mg, K, Na) may be reduced to less than 1.5 $cmol_c\,kg^{-1}$, with the presence of unbuffered 1 M KCl-extractable Al or a delta pH (pH KCl - pH H_2O) of +0.1 or more. In these cases the soil is said to possess **geric properties**.

Salinization

In arid climates the rainfall is irregular and is insufficient to remove soluble salts from the soil. With occasional rain they are moved down the profile, but when dry conditions resume they may be drawn upwards again. In semi-arid areas salts may be washed from soils of the upland areas, and there is a redistribution of salts into the soils on the lower parts of the landscape. In most cases, the occurrence of soils affected by salinization is associated with those areas in arid and semi-arid regions where there is a high ground-water level and imperfect or poor natural drainage. Frequently, these areas are the alluvial plains and other areas which in moister climates would produce considerably greater yields of crops.

Regrettably, many soils are suffering salinization as a result of excessive use of irrigation water without adequate drainage, which has raised the ground-water to a level where capillary rise brings salts into the soil. The water is evaporated, leaving the salt in the soil. These soils often develop a surface encrustation of salt and are known as Solonchak soils (Fig. 4.7). Such soils are described as having **salic properties** (Plate A16). This term refers to an electrical conductivity of the saturation extract of more than $15\,dSm^{-1}$ at 25°C within 30 cm of the surface, or of more than $4\,dSm^{-1}$ if the pH exceeds 8.5. The salt may originate from a salt-rich geological substratum, or it may be derived from salt sea-spray, blown inland by onshore winds, which gradually accumulates in the unleached soils of arid and semi-arid areas.

Soils in which the presence of salt in the profile results from natural processes are called primary

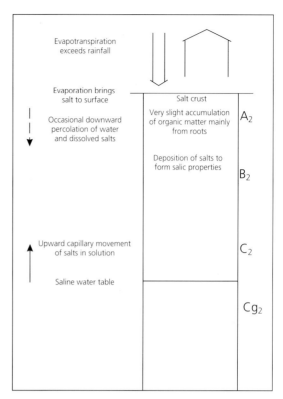

Fig. 4.7 The process of salinization.

saline soils. In hot, dry countries the use of irrigation water containing even small quantities of soluble salts can result in the salinization of soils as the water is evaporated. The resulting soils are described as secondary saline soils as they only occur through human interference in the natural environment. In both primary and secondary saline soils, the depth to the water table is of critical importance.

Alkalization

The process of alkalization occurs when sodium ions come to dominate the exchange positions of the clay–humus complex of a soil. This is achieved when slight leaching removes the soluble neutral salts. The solubility of calcium and magnesium is lower than that of sodium, which therefore remains in the soil solution after the divalent ions have been precipitated. Drying can also concentrate sodium ions remaining in solution so that they monopolize the exchange positions on the clay–humus complex, giving the soil a **natric B horizon** (Plate A9). A natric B horizon is defined as one which has the properties of an argic horizon, but with a columnar structure and with more than 15 per cent of the exchange capacity occupied by sodium ions within the upper 40 cm of the horizon. The soils become strongly alkaline (pH >8.5) and sodium carbonate is formed within the soil. The process results in Solonetz soils; these are extremely difficult to manage as the organic-rich topsoil becomes completely dispersed when wet, and the natric horizon itself is either very plastic when wet or as solid as concrete when dry.

Solodization

The process of solodization, or removal of sodium ions from the clay–humus complex, results in a range of soils from the Solodized Solonetz to the Solod. In these soils, the metal cations, mainly sodium, are gradually leached out and once the neutral salts have been removed the exchangeable sodium hydrolyses, increasing the hydroxyl ion concentration in the soil solution. This results in dispersion of the organic and mineral colloids. As the metal cations of the salts are gradually replaced by hydrogen ions, a strongly acid soil eventually results, called a Solod. The process of change from a salty soil to a Solod can be initiated by a change in climate, such that increased rainfall affects soils, by water from snowmelt accumulating in low-lying areas to give increased leaching, or by irrigation.

Rubefaction

Certain soils, formed under cool wet winters and hot dry summers, have a marked red colour caused by an even distribution of iron oxides throughout the profile. The term was introduced to describe the reddening observed in many soils of the Mediterranean countries of Europe. An irreversible loss of water from iron oxide gels leads to the production of a hematite coating on soil particles, which gives the bright red colour.

The reddening process increases with the age of the soil and so there is some correlation between colour and soil history: many brightly coloured Red Earths in Australia clearly have had a long pedogenetic history. Outside the present-day areas of Mediterranean climate, bright red palaeosol remnants along the coast of south Wales in the UK have been used as evidence for a warmer climate during the last major interglacial period of the Pleistocene.

Gleying

The presence of water in the soil for long periods brings about anaerobic conditions, as explained in Chapter 2. This can happen in all climatic zones, and the process of gleying produces features which enable the pedologist to recognize the hydromorphic character of the soils and to consider these soils together as a group of Gley or Hydromorphic Soils. Poorly drained soils frequently occur on plateau sites or on the lower parts of the landscape, and are often developed from parent materials related to those of adjacent freely drained soils.

The process of gleying involves the reduction of iron compounds and either their complete removal from the profile or their segregation into mottles or concretions. Usually the gleying process is accomplished with saturated conditions in the presence of organic matter. The metabolic activity of the bacteria is responsible for the oxygen deficit, and the reducing conditions develop best where the soil solution is stagnant. A strongly gleyed soil or gleyed horizon is frequently an unrelieved grey or bluish colour, but where some oxygenation takes place there will be mottles of rust-coloured ferric oxide.

For soils developed in a strongly seasonal climate, a number of these reactions are combined into a process of soil formation referred to as **ferrolysis**. Cycles of oxidation–reduction in the soil environment allow the leaching of displaced cations in the reduced phase and the acid weathering of clay minerals in the oxidized phase at the beginning of each cycle. The process is driven by energy derived from bacterial decomposition of soil organic matter. In the reduced state, iron is changed to the ferrous form and replaces adsorbed basic cations, which are partly leached out of the soil. As the soil is oxidized again in the dry season, the exchangeable iron is changed from the ferrous to the ferric state with the production of protons (H^+), which contribute to the next cycle of disruption of clay minerals.

Two basic types of Gley Soil are widely recognized by pedologists. Where water is held upon a slowly permeable or an impervious horizon within 50 cm of the soil surface, producing mottling, a Surface-water Gley or Pseudogley Soil results, with **stagnic properties** (Plate A18); where water rises up through the soil from an impermeable layer at depth beneath the soil, to give mottling within 100 cm of the soil surface, a Ground-water Gley or True Gley is produced, with **gleyic properties** (Plate A17). It is usual to find Ground-water Gley Soils in areas which receive an inflow of surface- and ground-water. In this case, the soil must be permeable if the water is to be able to move between the soil structures and saturate the lower soil horizons of the profile.

With anaerobic conditions in the soil, the decomposition of plant residues on the surface is slow and their incorporation into the soil is minimal. Therefore peat often develops on soils with a high level of ground-water. The colour of the soil in these profiles is usually an unrelieved grey, reflecting the presence of ferrous iron compounds. If the soil dries occasionally there may be a few mottles of rust-coloured ferric oxide.

Surface-water Gley Soils can occur almost anywhere on the landscape where a slowly permeable horizon, such as a Bt horizon or an iron pan, prevents the free downward passage of water through the soil profile. Localized gleying results, particularly on the surfaces of pores and peds, which become grey. In contrast, the ped interiors retain the brighter colours of ferric iron, giving an overall impression of mottling when revealed in a soil pit or exposure. Soils with such mottles scattered throughout their profiles closely resemble the Pseudogley Soils described by German authors.

Accumulation of organic matter

Plant leaves and other debris that fall onto the soil surface, if undisturbed, may accumulate to form an organic horizon that is not saturated with water for more than a few days in the year. This horizon is composed of three layers. In the litter layer (L), the process of decomposition (already begun on the plants) turns the easily recognizable leaves a dark brown colour, but the type of leaf is still recognizable. In the fermentation layer (F), plant litter loses its distinguishing characteristics, and eventually in the lowest layer (H) becomes a black amorphous substance referred to as **humus**. Humus is a complex polyphenolic organic substance with many active chemical functional groups. These unincorporated organic layers, lying on the surface of the mineral soil, are not normally saturated, and are collectively referred to as the O horizon. They are not, however, a diagnostic horizon for classification purposes.

Decomposition is a complex process during which a succession of soil fauna break the material down into smaller pieces, with fungi and bacteria eventually causing the complete disintegration of the plant tissue into chemical elements and compounds which can be recycled by the plants through their roots. The dark-coloured, more resistant humus remains to darken the soil surface horizon. Although an average figure for the turnover of all organic matter is given in the literature (20–22 years), some organic matter fractions are fairly rapidly recycled, with a turnover time of between two and three years. Use of radioactive carbon dating enables estimation of the mean residence time of the stabilized and more resistant material. The turnover time of these more stable forms of soil carbon, measured at Rothamsted, England, ranges from 1450 years in the topsoil to 12,100 years at 2 m below the surface. Analysis of the average of ^{14}C age in some representative topsoil samples of soil organic matter from North America ranges from $210–440 \pm 120$ years in surface soils in Iowa and North Dakota, to 25,300 years $\pm$ 9 per cent for a frozen peat soil in Alaska.

The process of darkening of soil material by organic substances is known as **melanization**. The presence of organic substances in the soil confers stability to the soil structures. Organic substances also act as a source of energy for the soil fauna, and the gradual release of elements from the humus is a source of plant nutrients.

Accumulation of incorporated organic material in soils takes place in four distinctive diagnostic surface horizons. These are the ochric, mollic and umbric A horizons, and the histic H horizon.

Most of the soil organic matter comes from above-ground leaves and stems of plants. Where the accumulation of humus is relatively slow, because of the nature of the organic debris available or the prevailing climatic conditions, incorporation is slight and an **ochric A horizon** is formed (Plate A4). An ochric A horizon is a thin A horizon which has too light a colour, too high a chroma and too little organic carbon to be mollic or umbric (see below). An ochric A horizon can be hard and massive when dry, and may be of the moder type in humid areas or mull in drier climates.

The type of humus associated with calcareous soils is mull, produced by the natural vegetation of grasses and the action of earthworms. Grasses have well-developed root systems which, when alive, ramify through the soil, and when dead supply large amounts of organic matter to the soil. The aerial parts of the grasses also return to the soil as organic matter when they die back after the growing season, or are burnt. The lack of leaching in semi-arid climates and a combination of summer drought and winter frost in continental areas, typically the steppes or prairies, limit the rate of organic decomposition so that over many years a very rich and deep **mollic A horizon** (Plate A2) accumulates.

Essential features of the mollic horizon include the following: even after ploughing to a depth of 18 cm, the surface horizon should have a strong structure which is not massive or hard when dry; it should have colours with a chroma of less than 3.5 when moist and a value darker than 3.5 when moist and 5.5 when dry, and a colour value that is at least one unit darker than the C horizon; the base saturation should be 50 per cent or more; the organic carbon content should be at least 0.6 per cent, although if there is much finely divided lime in the horizon the colour criteria may be waived and then the organic carbon content should be more than 2.5 per cent; thickness must be more than 10 cm if resting directly upon hard rock or a petrocalcic, petrogypsic horizon or a duripan; where the solum is less than 75 cm a mollic horizon must be more than 18 cm, but where soil depth is more than 75 cm it must be 25 cm (this includes transitional horizons in which A horizon characteristics are dominant); finally, there should be less than $250 \, mg \, kg^{-1}$ citric-soluble phosphate present. Similar dark-coloured, strongly structured horizons that have all the preceding characteristics except that the base saturation is below 50 per cent are termed **umbric A horizons** (Plate A3).

In conditions of very poor drainage, peat formation is encouraged in association with the gley soils present. Basically, there are two types of peat: the moor peat which is strongly acid, and the fen peat which is neutral or mildly alkaline. Further subdivision can be made based on botanical composition, structure and degree of decomposition of the organic remains. The characteristics of these two peat forms result from the way in which they have developed. The acid moor peat develops on upland areas where high rainfall results in the leaching of all the bases so that acidity dominates and there is very slow decomposition of plant debris, forming a **histic H horizon** (Plate A1). As a consequence, the organic matter accumulates above the level of the mineral soil and can eventually develop into a raised bog if the rainfall is sufficient. A raised bog is one in which the plants are sustained from the nutrients brought in by the rain.

Fen peats are developed where organic matter accumulates in waters liberally supplied with bases and which have a neutral or mildly alkaline pH. These conditions occur mainly in lowland alluvial situations. When adequately drained, the soils developed upon such parent materials are usually very fertile with high land values, as in the Fens of eastern England.

Pedoturbation

All clays swell and contract to some degree when they pass through cycles of wetting and drying, and this results in the development of structure and cambic horizons. Pedoturbation occurs where the movement of soil material is more obvious. Where the supply of bases is plentiful, as in the seasonally dry tropics, low-lying areas of the landscape frequently develop soils rich in montmorillonite. This clay mineral has a great capacity to expand as it takes up and releases moisture; as it does so, the individual peds expand, and press and move against each other causing polished faces to be formed, called slickensides. The surface expression of this pedoturbation is frequently a mound-and-hollow micro-relief, often referred to as 'gilgai' after an

Australian aboriginal word. Many soils throughout the world have these features, referred to as **vertic properties** (Plates A22 and A23).

In sub-arctic regions, freeze–thaw cycles can also result in the mixing of different layers of soil material in the subsoil, forming features described as 'festoons'. In many soils, mixing by soil fauna is an important feature of their development. The lack of well-developed soil horizons in Brown Earths is partly caused by the continual mixing of the soil by earthworms in the process of faunal pedoturbation.

Conclusion

The processes of soil formation may be described as 'bundles' of processes which operate within a soil. These processes, which may vary in intensity, can be seen more simply as one or more of the categories (additions, losses, transfers or trans-formations) from the generalized theory of soil genesis proposed in 1959 by Simonson. These four categories include the following.

Further reading

Brinkman, R., 1979. *Ferrolysis: a Soil-forming Process in Hydromorphic Conditions*. Pudoc, Wageningen.

Buol, S.W., Hole, F.D. and McCracken, R.J., 1988. *Soil Genesis and Classification*. Iowa State University Press, Ames.

Jackson, R.M. and Raw, F., 1970. *Life in the Soil*. Arnold, London.

Ross, S.M., 1989. *Soil Processes*. Routledge, London.

Simonson, R.W., 1959. Outline of a generalized theory of soil genesis. *Soil Science Society of America Proceedings* **23**:152–6.

Wild, A. (ed.), 1988. *Russell's Soil Conditions and Plant Growth*. 11th edition, Longman, Harlow.

Additions

- water, from rainfall, irrigation, seepage or capillary rise from ground-water
- radiant energy from the sun
- fresh and decayed organic matter added to the surface (O horizon) or incorporated in the surface horizon (Ah horizon)
- organic matter added to the Bh horizon of Podzols
- iron compounds added to the Bs horizon of Podzols and the Bg horizon of Gley Soils
- silicate clay added to the Bt horizon as clay coatings or void infillings
- calcium and magnesium carbonates added to A, B or C horizons
- silica or other cements added to indurated horizons

Losses

- moisture through evaporation, transpiration or drainage
- heat
- organic matter from the A horizon
- silicate clay from the A and E horizons
- carbonates from the A, B or C horizons
- silica by weathering of primary minerals
- iron through leaching and gleying
- aluminium through leaching

Transfers

- movement of mineral grains from open to tighter packing arrangements (pedocompaction)
- mixing of organic and mineral soil components by wetting and drying, freezing and thawing and animal activity (pedoturbation)
- movement of iron compounds into nodules and concretions as a result of gleying

Transformations

- decay of plant remains into humus
- weathering of primary minerals to form silicate clays, oxides and hydroxides of iron and aluminium
- transformation of soil components into new forms (e.g. clay into clay coatings).

5 Soil classification

Classification is only a contrivance to order a subject, perhaps to understand and remember its content more easily, and it should certainly show how any one part of the subject is related to the whole. A classification also serves to create a 'language' or nomenclature for exchanging knowledge, and is indispensable for conceiving mapping units on a soil map. As far as soils are concerned, classification is still in the process of development, and throughout the last century, numerous attempts were made to group soils into natural, homogeneous classes with common properties. A final valuable role of classification is that it serves as a basis from which further enquiry can proceed.

Soils are not discrete individuals, like animals or plants, but gradually change laterally from one to another – they are said to form a **continuum** upon the Earth's surface. Because soils are not readily separated from one another, classification has proved to be a considerable challenge, and the history of soil science is marked by the various attempts to bring order into the subject.

Although earlier forms of soil classification are now mainly of historical interest, they remain relevant to present-day pedology because they show how concepts developed, and many of the names introduced in earlier classifications remain in the literature and may still be used, even though the system of classification itself has fallen into disuse.

Soil classification is fundamental to a study of the soils of the world, and so it is an important consideration in a book devoted to world soils. Equally, classification is essential for making a soil map. However, classification requires a wide knowledge of the subject before it can be fully understood. Students new to pedology may find it helpful to read further and gain some insight into the broad major types of soil formation before returning again to this chapter. For the time being, you are recommended to proceed with the approach adopted at the end of this chapter in which the soils of the world can be traced using the key in Fig. 5.1.

Origins

The earliest attempts to classify soils may be traced to China 4000 years ago when nine classes were recognized, but the evidence suggests that this was more a classification of land than of soil. In Europe, the earliest documented assessment of soils dates from Greco-Roman times, when soils were placed in categories ranging from best to worst for the growth of crops.

Throughout much of historical time, soils were grouped by their texture: clayey soils, loamy soils, sandy soils and organic soils. Although simple to use and with very practical significance for the agriculturalist, this simple means of classifying soils includes such a wide range of different soil types that, outside a purely local setting, texture alone cannot be used meaningfully in a classification system unless combined with other criteria.

In Chapter 1 it was stated that soil studies in modern times developed from two branches of learning: geology and agro-chemistry. No early forms of classification emerged as a result of the agro-chemical approach, but in the 19th century the growth of geological knowledge led to a recognition of the importance of the underlying rocks as parent materials for soils. Somewhat inevitably, this linkage was transferred to soil classification, so names such as 'limestone soils', 'sandstone soils' and 'alluvial soils' came into common usage amongst those who cultivated the land. These terms can still be heard in use, even though perfectly good pedological names are available.

The modern period

It is generally accepted that present-day soil science

began in the 1880s with the ideas of Dokuchaev in Russia. He recognized that soil was an **independent natural body** which could be studied on the basis of the interpretation of the morphology of the soil as revealed in its profile, supported by laboratory investigations. It was observed by Dokuchaev and his colleagues that many soil types had a definite geographical distribution associated with particular climate regions and vegetation types. This led to the development of the names **zonal**, **intrazonal** and **azonal soils**, which are often used to describe soils which strongly reflect the climatic zone in which they occur, the overriding effect of soil-forming processes such as gleying, or the nature of the parent material, respectively. Dokuchaev is credited with producing the first natural soil classification based on observable features in the soil profile.

Russian soil scientists have persisted with this broad zonal approach, based on 'genetic principles of Dokuchaev's school of soil science', for the classification of the soils of their country. More recently, these soil types have been accommodated into four defined bioclimatic zones: polar, boreal, subboreal and sub-tropical. For example, the boreal zone includes classes of cryogenic, podzolized and non-podzolized soils, further subdivided by length of growing season, frost-free period and weathering type.

In the USA, also during the late 19th century, Hilgard noted that soils in the state of Mississippi were associated closely with surface geology, but in California he recognized that climate was also important for its influence on the accumulations of carbonates and more soluble salts in the soils of drier regions. However, the ideas of Dokuchaev only became assimilated into the soil science of the USA in the 1930s, after Marbut had translated a German version of Glinka's *The Great Soil Groups of the World and their Development* into English.

The concepts of soil series and soil type as mapping units in the USA were introduced in 1903, and this was followed by a linkage to ten physiographic soil provinces in 1906. From 1921 onwards, recognition of the difference between the darker-coloured soils of the Great Plains, where the climate is drier, and the lighter-coloured soils further east led to their classification in 1927 into Pedocals and Pedalfers, respectively. Classification, involving concepts of maturity and drainage, in Great Soil Groups came in 1935, and was elaborated by Baldwin, Kellogg and Thorp in 1938. The Great Soil Groups continued to be used in US classifications until 1964. In 1951, the Soil Survey Staff began work on a new classification with a series of 'approximations'; this led to the publication of the *Seventh Approximation* in 1960 which became *Soil Taxonomy* in 1975.

In Britain, an essentially geological approach was used to describe soils in reports commissioned by the British Board of Agriculture on the state of agriculture in many counties at the end of the 18th century. The concept of 'residual (or sedentary) soils', developed over the solid geological strata, and 'transported soils', formed in glacial drifts, windblown materials, colluvium and alluvium, can be traced back to the middle of the 19th century. This geological approach to soil classification continued to be used by Hall and Russell in their report on the agriculture and soils of Kent, Surrey and Sussex in the first decade of the 20th century. During the period from 1900 to 1914, attempts were made to map soils using the 'drift' maps of the Geological Survey. Fortunately, it was appreciated that the correlation was not perfect and, although an important factor, the parent material was only one of a number of influences determining the type of soil developed at any one place. In the years following the end of the First World War in 1918, visits by American soil surveyors and the appointment of soil survey assistants to the regional agricultural chemists led to the adoption of a system based on American experience, in which soils were mapped as soil series determined by the characteristics of the soil profile. Much of the early work in soil survey in Britain was done under the supervision of G.W. Robinson in the University of Wales at Bangor, who produced a classification of world soils (Table 5.1). Unfortunately he did not make a classification of British soils, although he reviewed the current state of knowledge of British soils in *Soils, their Origin, Constitution and Classification*.

Robinson's classification of world soils reflected the approach of soil scientists and the limited knowledge of soils and their distribution before and immediately after the Second World War.

Soils with free drainage	Completely leached (pedalfers)	Presence of raw humus	1. Humus Podzols
			2. Iron Podzols
		Absence of raw humus	3. Brown Earths
			4. Degraded Chernozems
			5. Prairie Soils
			6. Yellow Podzolic Soils
			7. Red Podzolic Soils
			8. Tropical Red Loams
			9. Ferrallites
	Incompletely leached (pedocals)		10. Chernozems
			11. Chestnut Soils
			12. Brown Desert Soils
			13. Grey Desert Soils
Soils with impeded drainage	Absence of soluble salts	Sub-arctic	14. Tundra
		Temperate	15. Gley Soils
			16. Gley Podzols
			17. Peat Podzols
			18. Peat Soils
		Sub-tropical and tropical	19. Vlei Soils
	Presence of soluble salts		20. Saline Soils
			21. Alkaline Soils
			22. Soloti Soils

Table 5.1 Classification of world soils (after Robinson, 1947)

Although it was based on mature profiles and included drainage, degree of leaching and type of humus as criteria for separating soils into meaningful groupings, in many respects climate was used as a surrogate for actual soil knowledge. For the soil criteria which he used, he drew upon the experience of Marbut's 1927 system and subsequent modifications for classification of soils in the USA. In his system, Robinson also foreshadowed ideas later expressed by Kubiena (1953), whose system of classification was outlined in his book *The Soils of Europe*.

Kubiena grouped profiles by their horizon sequence as indicated by the horizon designations, A, B, C, etc., and the type of humus played an important role in the second stage of his classification. With five basic groups of soils, this classification had the great merit of simplicity and illustrated the use of profile morphology in soil classification: A(C) Raw Soils, AC Rankers and Rendzinas, A(B)C Brown Soils, ABC Podzols and B/ABC Salt-crust Soils. Kubiena's ideas had considerable influence upon the subsequent development of soil classification in Europe. Grouping soils by the degree of development of the soil profile can be seen in French, Belgian, German and British systems of classification. The study of humus form and the micro-morphological structure of the soil are other aspects introduced by Kubiena which have since found much favour worldwide.

The Soil Survey of England and Wales adopted a classification based on diagnostic horizons in 1973 (Table 5.2). In a similar manner to the USDA *Soil Taxonomy* and the FAO–Unesco *Soil Map of the World*, the system has a limited number of diagnostic horizons, which include a podzolic B horizon (containing enrichment with organic matter, iron and aluminium), an argillic B horizon (with an

Major Group	Group
1 Terrestrial Raw Soils	1.1 Raw Sands
	1.2 Raw Alluvial Soils
	1.3 Raw Skeletal Soils
	1.4 Raw Earths
	1.5 Man-made Raw Soils
2 Hydric Raw Soils	2.1 Raw Sandy Gley Soils
	2.2 Unripened Gley Soils
3 Lithomorphic Soils	3.1 Rankers
	3.2 Sand-rankers
	3.3 Ranker-like Alluvial Soils
	3.4 Rendzinas
	3.5 Pararendzinas
	3.6 Sand Pararendzinas
	3.7 Rendzina-like Alluvial Soil
4 Pelosols	4.1 Calcareous Pelosols
	4.2 Non-calcareous Pelosols
	4.3 Argillic Pelosols
5 Brown Soils	5.1 Brown Calcareous Earths
	5.2 Brown Calcareous Sands
	5.3 Brown Calcareous Alluvial Soils
	5.4 Brown Earths
	5.5 Brown Sands
	5.6 Brown Alluvial Soils
	5.7 Argillic Brown Earths
	5.8 Paleo-argillic Brown Earths
6 Podzolic Soils	6.1 Brown Podzolic Soils
	6.2 Humic Cryptopodzols
	6.3 Podzols
	6.4 Gley Podzols
	6.5 Stagnopodzols
7 Surface-water Gley (Stagnogley) Soils	7.1 Stagnogley Soils
	7.2 Stagnohumic Gley Soils
8 Ground-water Gley Soils	8.1 Alluvial Gley Soils
	8.2 Sandy Gley Soils
	8.3 Cambic Gley Soils
	8.4 Argillic Gley Soils
	8.5 Humic Alluvial Gley Soils
	8.6 Humic Sandy Gley Soils
	8.7 Humic Gley Soils
9 Man-made Soils	9.1 Man-made Humus Soils
	9.2 Disturbed Soils
10 Peat (organic) Soils	10.1 Raw Peat Soils
	10.2 Earthy Peat Soils

Table 5.2 Classification of soils in England and Wales (after Avery, 1973)

increased content of clay), a cambic B horizon (with pedological reorganization but not enrichment) and gleyed B horizon (showing reduction and segregation and/or loss of iron), as well as different forms of surface horizon. This classification has evolved from previous work and retains many of the names currently familiar to users of soil maps.

Of the ten major groups in this British classification, some are recognizable immediately whilst others are new or reorganized. Major departures from the earlier British system of classification include the Lithomorphic Soils, which bring together shallow AC soils such as Lithosols, Rendzinas and Rankers. Pelosols are a small group of clayey soils typically found on calcareous argillaceous materials, some of which possess vertic properties, i.e. they expand and contract as they wet and dry and have slickensides on the peds. The Brown Soils and the Podzols have undergone stricter definition, with the controversial Brown Podzolic Soils, having podzolic B horizons and without an albic E horizon, being allocated to the Podzols. Stricter definition is apparent in the two major groups of poorly drained soils, now brought into line with the European concepts of Pseudogley and Gley Soils. These soils differ in water held in the profile through a perched water table, stagnic conditions, and true gley resulting from ground-water saturating the profile. This classification gives a more satisfactory grouping of British soils than the previous classification, and also maintains a working relationship with systems developed in France and Germany as well as with the legend of the FAO–Unesco *Soil Map of the World*.

The classification that evolved for France, and for those countries with which France has close historical ties, has as its essential criteria the degree of development of the soil profile, types of clay mineral present, presence of sesquioxides and the degree of modification from the parent material, the type of organic matter and the effects of gleying (CPCS, 1967). There are twelve classes (Table 5.3). Many of the criteria can be traced back to those suggested by Kubiena (1953) in his simple system of classification, although considerable elaboration has been introduced to take into account later knowledge. Within each of the twelve classes, subclasses are distinguished by

I   *Raw Mineral Soils*
    (A)C profile without organic horizons

    1.1   Non-climatic Raw Mineral Soils
    1.2   Arctic Desert Soils
    1.3   Hot Desert Soils

II *Weakly Developed Soils*
    AC profile lacking in calcium

    2.1   with Permafrost
    2.2   Rankers
    2.3   Grey Sub-desert Soils
    2.4   Non-climatic Weakly Developed Soils

III *Vertisols*
    AC or A(B)C profile with expanding clays

    3.1   with reducing conditions and
          no external drainage
    3.2   with external drainage

IV *Andosols*
    A(B)C profile with high exchange capacity derived
    from volcanic ash

    4.1   of cold climates
    4.2   of tropical climates

V   *Calcareous Soils*
    AC or A(B)C profile derived from calcareous
    or gypsiferous parent materials

    5.1   Rendzinas
    5.2   Brown Calcareous Soils
    5.3   Gypsiferous Soils

VI *Isohumic Soils*
    AC or A(B)C profile rich in well-humified
    organic matter

    6.1   of humid regions
    6.2   of cold regions
    6.3   of regions with rain in the cool season
    6.4   of regions with rain in the hot season

VII *Brown Soils*
     A(B)C or ABC profile with mull humus

    7.1   of humid temperate climates
    7.2   of continental temperate climates
    7.3   of boreal climates
    7.4   of tropical climates

VIII *Podzols*
     ABC profile with mor humus

    8.1   of temperate climates
    8.2   of cold climates
    8.3   with gleying

IX   *Sesquioxide-rich Soils*
     ABC profile with separation of iron oxides
     and medium to high exchange capacity

    9.1   Ferruginous Tropical Soils
    9.2   Red Mediterranean Soils

X   *Ferrallitic Soils*
     ABC profile with loss of silica and separation
     of the oxides of iron and aluminium

    10.1 weakly leached
    10.2 moderately leached
    10.3 strongly leached

XI   *Hydromorphic Soils*
     Profile with gleying and organic matter accumulation

    11.1 Organic Soils
    11.2 Peaty Mineral Soils
    11.3 Non-humic Gley Soils

XII *Halomorphic Soils*
     Profile with soluble salts

    12.1 Salic Soils with stable structure
    12.2 Sodic Soils with unstable structure

Table 5.3 Classes and subclasses of the classification used in France (after CPCS, 1967)

different pedo–climatic conditions or other significant characteristics such as base status in the Isohumic Soils and the presence of clay illuviation in the *Sols Lessivés* of the Brown Soils. Currently, a complete re-evaluation of French soil classification is under way; preliminary documents for a new system have been published using a morphogenetic approach in which soils are grouped by combinations of reference horizons and diagnostic solums (AFES, 1992).

A great difficulty associated with most of the older zonal classifications of soils is that they were produced for central concepts of virgin soils under natural or at least semi-natural vegetation, whereas much of the landscape has been affected greatly by the work of mankind. Certainly, it is possible to have different phases of the same soil series under natural conditions and agriculture, but in many cases the alteration from the natural condition has been profound. Also, the zonal soils were described only in quantitative terms and so many problems arose with marginal cases between the different zonal soil groups.

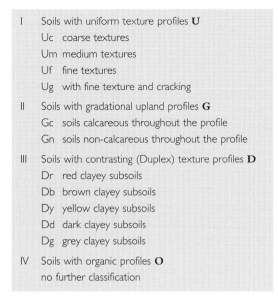

I   Soils with uniform texture profiles **U**
    Uc   coarse textures
    Um medium textures
    Uf   fine textures
    Ug with fine texture and cracking

II   Soils with gradational upland profiles **G**
    Gc soils calcareous throughout the profile
    Gn soils non-calcareous throughout the profile

III Soils with contrasting (Duplex) texture profiles **D**
    Dr   red clayey subsoils
    Db brown clayey subsoils
    Dy yellow clayey subsoils
    Dd dark clayey subsoils
    Dg grey clayey subsoils

IV Soils with organic profiles **O**
    no further classification

Table 5.4 Classification of Australian soils (after Northcote, 1960)

It is unfortunate that many of the older classifications of soils were based on the presence or absence of certain types of humus, for this can so easily be changed by forest clearance or cultivation. Transient features are not the best criteria to adopt for classification. Consequently, FAO and USDA have used the presence of specific mineral surface and subsoil horizons as diagnostic criteria to classify and map soils. Soil properties that do not change materially with land-use and agricultural practice are most suitable, and, of these, texture is the most readily observed feature. Thus a classification can be built quite objectively upon soils with uniform texture (U), soils with texture which gradually changes with depth (G) and soils with an abrupt change in texture somewhere in the profile (D). This idea was followed through in a key for classification of Australian soils (Table 5.4). A new classification system, recently proposed and tested, is based on diagnostic horizons compatible with international systems of soil classification (Table 5.5).

Other persistent soil features are the nature and proportions of clay minerals present, the cation exchange capacity, the amount and type of exchangeable cations, and the degree of leaching. These criteria were incorporated into a scheme of classification which seemed to have much to offer pedologists in a physicochemical approach to world soils (Table 5.6). Subsequent appreciation of the effects of acid rain upon soils indicates the potential value contained in this approach, which could be used to highlight the vulnerability of certain soils to excessive leaching.

Other soil classifications have been developed for specific purposes. For example, in semi-arid areas where there is pressure to increase the area of

Table 5.5 Classification system for Australian soils (after Isbell, 1993)

Name	Characteristics	Approximate equivalent FAO units
Anthroposols	Man-made soil	Anthrosols
Calcarosols	Calcareous throughout	Calcisols
Chromosols	Strong texture contrast, often bright coloured	Luvisols
Dermosols	Well-structured but lacking texture contrast	Cambisols, Phaeozems
Ferrosols	Structured B horizon with high iron content	Ferralsols
Hydrosols	Seasonally or permanently wet soils	Gleysols, Solonchaks
Kandosols	1:1 clay minerals	Cambisols, Acrisols, Nitisols?
Kurosols	Abrupt clay increase in B horizon	Planosols
Organosols	Dominantly organic material	Histosols
Podzols	Accumulation of organic matter, aluminium or iron	Podzols
Rudosols	Rudimentary development of profile	Regosols, Leptosols, Fluvisols
Sodosols	Abrupt clay increase in B horizon, sodic	Solonetz
Tenosols	Weak profile development except for A horizon	Cambisols, Chernozems
Vertosols	Swell–shrink cracking clays with slickensides	Vertisols

Class	Example
0 Soils showing no or only rudimentary differentiation	Regosols, Fluvisols
1 Soils effectively unleached containing soluble salts, mainly sodium chloride	Solonchaks
2 Slightly leached soils (second stage of leaching) dominated by sodium ions, often containing gypsum	Solonetz, Gypsisols
3 Moderately leached soils (third stage of leaching) dominated by Ca^{2+} and Mg^{2+} ions and containing secondary carbonate	Chemozems, Kastanozems
4 Leached soils (fourth stage of leaching) dominated by Ca^{2+} and H^+ ions, without secondary carbonate	Cambisols, Luvisols
5 Strongly leached soils (fifth stage of leaching) dominated by H^+ and Al^{3+} ions	Podzols, Ferrallsols

Table 5.6 Classification of soils by extent of leaching (after Hallsworth, 1965)

irrigated lands, the presence and nature of salts in the soil are two important criteria in deciding which soils can be brought into cultivation. These, and other relevant features, must be taken into account in classifying soils for irrigation development plans.

Numerical methods in classification

Traditionally, classification techniques in soil science, as in biological sciences, drew upon the Linnaean principles allied to the evolutionary theory of Darwin. Classification in science was pursued with great enthusiasm by natural scientists of the 19th century, which led one well-known British scientist to comment 'if only scientists had measured rather than classified!' It is evident that there are differences when soils are compared with plants and animals, which are distinct individuals, each with its own genetically controlled characteristics.

An alternative to the descriptive approach is to make as many measurements and observations as possible about the attributes of soils and then to use these in the compilation of 'natural groups'. These soil groupings, based upon as many features as possible, would contain the greatest content of information, each feature being given equal weight, and the overall similarity of the soils included would be a function of the number of features held in common. What appealed to many soil scientists was that this approach was also objective in that it was not prejudiced by any nebulous, unquantifiable ideas of genesis. This approach was first proposed by Adanson some 200 years ago, but at that time only limited use could be made of it. However, since the 1960s the means to make such all-embracing comparisons has become available, and at the present time, using computers, any natural feature which forms an array of natural groups, such as soils, can be dealt with using forms of numerical taxonomy.

The first attempts to use numerical methods, using available soil descriptions and analyses, indicated the possibilities as well as the pitfalls of numerical methods. It was soon established that multivariate methods of analysis were appropriate to soil studies because soils had many properties which typically are interrelated. From simple inspection of the raw data it is not always easy to see the relationships present. With numerical classification the aim is to produce groupings which are as alike as possible but which do not overlap with other groups. The first step is to lay down the rules and then uniformly apply them. Decisions have to be made about the use of similarity coefficients or distance measurements between individuals and variables, and about the strategy to be used (e.g. nearest-neighbour relationship). The output of this method can be presented in the form of taxonomic dendrograms. Unfortunately, the results obtained were of little more value than those obtained using conventional classification methods.

Other statistical methods can be applied, such as ordination and the calculation of the principal components. An examination by Rayner (1966) of 23 profiles from Glamorganshire, Wales, used similarity matrices in a form of ordination which can be more widely used than principal components analysis. Multivariate analysis of variance can be used to test whether groups are significantly different. Similarly, multiple discriminant analysis can be used to describe the scatter in space of the measured attributes. Canonical correlation may be used to study the interrelationships between two sets of measurements made on the same individuals (e.g. field and laboratory properties). Alternatively, it is possible to start with a number of groups and then allocate a new individual to one of those groups. Measurements of the new individual are compared and allocation is made to the group for which probability of membership is highest.

After an initial burst of enthusiasm, numerical methods of soil classification tended to languish. Currently, the scene is in the process of changing again; the need for soil data as inputs for environmental assessments is pressurizing soil science to adopt statistical sampling methods and to make greater use of existing data. These data are needed to provide more information about soils through extrapolation of observations to local, regional or world values by **pedotransfer functions**. These functions are used to relate soil characteristics to more complex characteristics needed for simulation modelling.

In the final analysis, the value of numerical classification of soils rests upon how far the classes can be delineated geographically and at an acceptable cost. The legibility of the map and degree of homogeneity of the map units are important features, and soil surveyors in conventional mapping have to use their professional expertise to achieve them.

International systems

As more knowledge has become available about the soils of the world in the second half of the 20th century, it has been appreciated that because soils form a continuously variable cover on the Earth's surface, usually without abrupt changes, any classification system must have clear criteria for separation of soil classes, and yet must retain sufficient flexibility to encompass the inherent natural variability. The impetus given earlier by Dokuchaev and his followers for classification of the soils of the world was lost as the original concept of zonal, intrazonal and azonal soils was found to be an inadequate basis for further work. Central concepts were developed but the limits between soils were poorly defined, which led to overlap and confu-

sion. Considerable problems were also encountered in the relationship between soils that were being mapped by soil surveyors in the field, and the rather theoretical pattern of world soils revealed by the earlier forms of world soil classification.

As mentioned previously, it was to overcome some of these difficulties that the American Soil Survey Staff produced a new and comprehensive system of soil classification, eventually published in 1975 as *Soil Taxonomy*, but still referred to by some people as the 'Seventh Approximation' as it was the culmination of a long period of development involving six earlier versions. A series of working groups, including scientists from outside the USA, have continued the development of the system with further amendments right up to the present day. This system avoids the use of all the old folk and colour names for soils and instead uses a new, specially created vocabulary for the description of soils. At first, the system was subject to considerable criticism, mainly because of its terminology, but it has now become one of the international systems of reference for soils and so has to be considered in any book on the soils of the world.

The second international system of classification which is widely used began as a legend for the FAO–Unesco *Soil Map of the World*, not specifically as a soil classification. It has two levels only at the present time, Major Soil Groupings and Soil Units. Discussions are in progress to develop a third level of classification for this system.

Soil Taxonomy

As described in Chapter 1, soils are formed of a number of horizons, which result from the action of the processes of soil formation. *Soil Taxonomy* recognizes horizons as components of soils, but for classification purposes the smallest unit which can be called a soil is known as a **pedon**. Development of the concept of the pedon, defined in Chapter 1, is important for the geography of soils because it formally defines soil with three dimensions, producing mappable areas when one or more pedons are grouped together in a mapping unit or **polypedon**, which in turn can be related to morphological facets of the landscape.

To identify and classify soils in *Soil Taxonomy*, a limited number of horizons were recognized as reflecting widespread, common results of the processes of soil formation. These were designated **diagnostic horizons** and strictly defined in terms of morphology and chemical characteristics. In order to qualify for a particular soil grouping, a soil had to possess the measured criteria laid down in these definitions. Two types of diagnostic horizons are specified according to position in the soil profile: seven **epipedons** are identified at the surface, and a further nineteen **subsurface horizons** are identified at depth below the soil surface. Brief descriptions of these horizons are shown below.

Other horizons which are recognized include the indurated horizons of certain soils. A **duripan** is

Epipedons

Mollic epipedon: a dark-coloured, thick surface horizon, typical of steppe soils, with over 50 per cent of the exchange capacity dominated by base cations.

Umbric epipedon: a dark-coloured surface horizon, with less than 50 per cent of the exchange capacity dominated by base cations.

Ochric epipedon: epipedons which are too light in colour, too low in organic carbon, or too thin to belong to mollic or umbric epipedons. The most common form of surface horizon.

Mellanic epipedon: a black, thick surface horizon occurring in soils developed in volcanic ash. Organic matter is usually associated with allophane or aluminium–humus complexes, resulting in low bulk density.

Histic epipedon: a peaty surface horizon, saturated with water for part of the year, and having a large amount of organic carbon.

Anthropic epipedon: similar to a mollic epipedon, but man-made with a large amount of phosphate accumulated by long-continued farming.

Plaggen epipedon: a man-made surface horizon more than 50 cm thick raised above the original soil surface with characteristics that depend upon the original soil from which it was derived.

Subsurface horizons

Albic horizon: a bleached, light-coloured horizon from which clay and free iron oxides have been removed.

Agric horizon: a compact horizon formed immediately below the plough layer by cultivation, which has been enriched by clay and humus.

Argillic horizon: an illuvial horizon enriched with clay to a significant extent.

Natric horizon: a clay-enriched illuvial horizon, the cation exchange complex of which has a high sodium content.

Cambic horizon: a horizon in which the parent material has been changed into soil by formation of soil structure, liberation of iron oxides, clay formation and obliteration of the original rock structure.

Calcic horizon: a horizon enriched with calcium carbonate in the form of powdery lime or secondary concretions, more than 15 cm thick.

Gypsic horizon: a horizon enriched with calcium sulphate, more than 15 cm thick.

Salic horizon: a horizon enriched with salts more soluble than gypsum, more than 15 cm thick.

Spodic horizon: an illuvial horizon enriched with organic matter, iron and aluminium. Alternatively called the podzol B horizon.

Oxic horizon: a horizon with a very low content of weatherable minerals, in which clay is composed largely of kaolinite and sesquioxides, having a low exchange capacity and being poorly dispersable in water.

Kandic horizon: a clayey subsurface horizon with similar characteristics to the oxic horizon but with more clay than the overlying surface horizon and an abrupt change of texture between the surface and lower horizons.

Glossic horizon: a horizon more than 5 cm thick in which an upper albic E horizon penetrates (tongues) down into a lower argillic, natric or kandic horizon.

Placic horizon: a thin, black or reddish-brown, brittle pan, cemented with iron, iron and manganese or an iron–organic complex. It forms a barrier to roots.

Sombric horizon: a freely drained, dark subsurface horizon containing illuvial humus with a low CEC and low base saturation which may be mistaken for a buried A horizon. It is not associated with aluminium or dispersed by sodium.

Sulphuric horizon: a mineral or organic horizon more than 15 cm thick which has a pH of 3.5 or less and contains the mineral jarosite or more than 0.05 per cent water-soluble sulphate.

a horizon cemented by silica or aluminium silicate; a **fragipan** is a compact, slowly permeable loamy subsurface horizon with a high bulk density, brittle when moist and hard when dry. A **petrocalcic horizon** is a cemented calcic horizon; similarly, a **petrogypsic horizon** is a cemented gypsic horizon.

In addition, several other diagnostic soil characteristics are used to classify a soil in *Soil Taxonomy*. These include: **andic properties**, which are present in soils composed of volcanic glass, with a low bulk density and high retention of phosphates; **aquic conditions**, which result from continuous or periodic saturation; **sulphidic materials**, which are subsoil materials containing oxidizable sulphur compounds; **plinthite**, which is a material found in the subsoils of tropical regions, rich in sesquioxides and kaolinite, strongly weathered and poor in humus, which irreversibly hardens into iron crusts and irregular aggregates when dried.

To place a soil in this USDA classification it is necessary to use a key which can be found in the original monograph and its successive supplements. A simplified flow chart may be used in a semi-quantitative manner to allocate soils to one of the orders (Table 5.7), but for accurate work it is essential to refer to the most recent version of the published *Keys to the Soil Orders*.

Soil mapping series, identified in the field, are related through **families** which stress common conditions for plant growth, **subgroups** which define central concepts, and **great groups** in which soils are grouped together on the kind and degree of expression of horizons, soil moisture regime and base status. There are over 200 of these great groups, in which the presence or absence of diagnostic horizons becomes an important criterion. The great groups are arranged in 57 **suborders**, characterized by similar genetic processes; subdivision is by the presence or absence of wetness, soil moisture regime, climatic regime and, in Histosols, the state of organic fibre decomposition. Finally, the suborders are arranged in eleven **orders** in which the soil-forming processes are indicated by the presence or absence of the major diagnostic horizons described previously. The names of orders and suborders of the classification are given in Table 5.8.

It can be seen from Table 5.8 that the names of

If a soil has:	Order
– more than 30% organic matter to a depth of 30 cm	Histosols
– more than 35 cm of andic soil properties and no albic horizon	Andisols
– a spodic horizon	Spodosols
– an oxic horizon within 1.5 m, or more than 40% clay and a kandic horizon	Oxisols
– more than 30% clay in all horizons; cracks to 50 cm	Vertisols
– dry conditions more than 50% of the year; no mollic horizon	Aridisols
– an argillic or kandic horizon with a low base saturation	Ultisols
– a mollic epipedon	Mollisols
– an argillic or kandic horizon with a high base saturation	Alfisols
– other soils with an umbric, mollic or plaggen epipedon or a cambic horizon	Inceptisols
– other soils	Entisols

Table 5.7 Simplified key to orders in *Soil Taxonomy* system (after Buol *et al.*, 1989)

the soil orders are compounded from certain 'formative elements' plus the ending –isols or –osols. Weakly or recently formed soils (Entisols) take as their formative element the **ent** from the word recent; soils of the desert areas (Aridisols) take as their formative element the **id** from arid. Other formative elements include **ept** from *inceptum*, or beginning, for the Inceptisols, soils with moderately formed horizons; **ult** from the word *ultimus* for soils with very strongly leached horizons; and **ist** from *histos* (tissue) for organic soils. Suborder names are then built by adding other formative elements to those of the orders, such as **aqu** for wetness, **fluv** for soils on alluvial materials, **ud** for characters associated with soils of humid climates, **ust** for soils associated with dry climates, etc. Combining these elements gives names such as Aquents, Fluvents, Ochrepts, Udults or Ustox. A further list of formative elements is used to provide a third syllable for the great group name, for example **cry** (from cryo-, cold) added to Aquent gives Cryaquents, or **dystr** (from dys-, ill and troph-, food) added to

1	Alfisols. Soils with an argillic horizon and moderate to high base content	
	– with features of gleying	Aqualfs
	– in cold climates	Boralfs
	– in humid climates	Udalfs
	– in seasonally dry climates	Ustalfs
	– others in semi-arid climates	Xeralfs
2	Andisols. Soils on volcanic materials	
	– with features of gleying	Aquands
	– in very cold climates	Cryands
	– usually dry in most years	Torrands
	– in humid climates	Udands
	– in seasonally dry climates	Ustands
	– on glassy materials	Vitrands
	– others in semi-arid climates	Xerands
3	Aridisols. Soils of desert and semi-desert areas	
	– in very cold climates	Cryids
	– with a salic horizon	Salids
	– with a duripan	Durids
	– with a gypsic or petrogypsic horizon	Gypsids
	– with an argillic or natric horizon	Argids
	– with a calcic or petrocalcic horizon	Calcids
	– other Aridisols	Cambids
4	Entisols. Weakly developed soils	
	– with features of gleying	Aquents
	– with strong artificial disturbance	Arents
	– on fresh alluvial deposits	Fluvents
	– with sand or loamy sand texture	Psamments
	– other Entisols	Orthents
5	Histosols. Soils developed in organic materials	
	– occasionally saturated; >75% fibric material	Folists
	– saturated for >6 months; >75% fibric material	Fibrists
	– saturated for >6 months; partly altered material	Hemists
	– saturated for > 6 months; highly altered material	Saprists

6	Inceptisols. Moderately developed soils	
	– with features of gleying	Aquepts
	– with plaggen epipedon	Plaggepts
	– in tropical climates	Tropepts
	– with an umbric epipedon	Umbrepts
	– other Inceptisols	Ochrepts
7	Mollisols. Soils with a dark A horizon and high base status	
	– with albic and argillic horizons	Albolls
	– with gleying	Aquolls
	– in cold climates	Borolls
	– on calcareous parent materials	Rendolls
	– in humid climates	Udolls
	– in seasonally dry climates	Ustolls
	– in semi-arid climates	Xerolls
8	Oxisols. Soils with an oxic horizon or plinthite	
	– with features of gleying	Aquox
	– in very wet (perhumid) climates	Perox
	– usually dry in most years	Torrox
	– in humid climates	Udox
	– in seasonally dry climates	Ustox
9	Spodosols. Soils with a spodic horizon	
	– with features of gleying	Aquods
	– in very cold climates	Cryods
	– with little iron in the spodic horizon	Humods
	– other Spodosols	Orthods
10	Ultisols. Soils with an argillic horizon and low base content	
	– with features of gleying	Aquults
	– with a humose A horizon	Humults
	– in a humid climate	Udults
	– in seasonally dry climates	Ustults
	– in semi-arid climates	Xerults
11	Vertisols. Cracking clay soils	
	– with features of gleying	Aquerts
	– in very cold climates	Cryerts
	– in humid climates	Uderts
	– in seasonally dry climates	Usterts
	– in semi-arid climates	Xererts
	– usually dry in most years	Torrerts

Table 5.8 Names of orders and suborders of *Soil Taxonomy* system (after Soil Survey Staff, 1994)

Ochrept gives Dystrochrepts, which are acid, infertile soils often found on glacial outwash plains.

The complete classification of an individual soil in this system would be as follows. At the family level, the particle-size class is given as well as the clay mineralogy and the temperature regime within which the soil occurs. A Podzol soil (Spodosol) with poor drainage and a fragipan is used as an example:

Order	Spodosols
Suborder	Aquods
Great Group	Fragiaquods
Subgroup	Typic Fragiaquods
Family	Typic Fragiaquod, coarse loamy, mixed, frigid.

When first introduced, the American system stimulated much discussion. Now that the controversy has died down, many references are made to it by pedologists and soil survey organizations throughout the world. It has not been adopted by many European countries as they already had their own sophisticated systems of classification. However, it has been adopted by many developing countries and it is being used increasingly as an international standard of comparison for soils throughout the world.

The FAO–Unesco Soil Map of the World legend

There is really only one truly international contender for the title of World Soil Classification and that is the legend created for the FAO–Unesco 1:5,000,000 *Soil Map of the World*, compiled by FAO beginning in 1961. This map, in seventeen sheets covering the whole world, is a unique document as it has been compiled from over 800 soil surveys; it is the only available map of the soils of the world compiled on a uniform basis at this scale. There has been a revision of the legend, published in 1990, and a start has been made on revision of those parts of the world where new data have become available, such as in South America, or where the original data were inadequate, as in China. At present there is no prospect of a new publication of the map, but the FAO–Unesco *Soil Map of the World* has been digitized and is now available for use on computers using geographical information systems. The legend, specifically *not* called a classification originally, has increasingly functioned as a world classification for soils since its inception, even for detailed soil maps. Since 1990, a working group of the International Society of Soil Science has been working on the *Soil Map of the World* legend to convert it into a World Reference Base for soil classification. The documentation on this project was presented to members of the society at the World Congress of Soil Science held in Mexico in 1994.

On the FAO–Unesco *Soil Map of the World*, soil units have been distinguished on the basis of the state of knowledge at the time of publication of their genesis, morphology and distribution, as well as their significance as a natural resource for food production. Where possible, traditional names for soils

have been retained, but where doubt or confusion surrounded the use of an older term, a new name was selected. The following brief descriptions of the soil units, termed **Major Soil Groupings**, are not definitions, but are given to introduce the reader to the terminology of the mapping units on this unique soil map (the order is as they occur in the key).

Histosols (from Greek *histos*, tissue): soils with more than a defined amount of organic soil material, organic soils.

Anthrosols (from Greek *anthropos*, man): soils in which the influence of human activities dominates soil formation.

Leptosols (from Greek *leptos*, thin): weakly developed shallow soils.

Vertisols (from Latin *vertere*, to turn): clayey soils which crack widely when dry and swell when moist.

Fluvisols (from Latin *fluvius*, river): soils developed on river deposits showing alluvial stratification.

Solonchaks (from Russian *sol*, salt and *chak*, salty area): soils in which salt accumulation is a dominant process.

Gleysols (from Russian *gley*, wet soil): waterlogged soils dominated by the effects of poor drainage and anaerobic conditions.

Andosols (from Japanese *an*, dark and *do*, soil): soils composed of volcanic materials, often with a dark-coloured surface horizon.

Arenosols (from Latin *harena*, sand): soils with a texture of sand or loamy sand.

Regosols (from Greek *rhegos*, blanket): weakly developed soils with a texture finer than sandy loam.

Podzols (from Russian *pod*, under and *zola*, ash): soils with a bleached, ashy-coloured horizon immediately beneath the surface and a spodic B horizon.

Plinthosols (from Greek *plinthos*, brick): soils of mottled appearance which harden on exposure to the atmosphere.

Ferralsols (from Latin *ferrum*, iron and *alumen*, aluminium): soils composed of kaolinite, quartz and relatively enriched with oxides of iron and aluminium.

Planosols (from Latin *planus*, flat): soils on flat relief with seasonal saturation caused by restricted permeability in lower horizons.

Solonetz (from Russian *sol*, salt and *etz*, strongly expressed): soils dominated by the presence of sodium salts.

Greyzems (from the colour grey and Russian *zemlja*, earth): soils with uncoated sand grains present in an organic-rich surface horizon, associated with the forest steppe region.

Chernozems (from Russian *chern*, black and *zemlja*, earth): dark-coloured, deep soils rich in organic matter, and calcareous lower in the profile, associated with the grass steppe/prairie.

Kastanozems (from Latin *castanea*, chestnut and Russian *zemlja*, earth): calcareous soils rich in organic matter with a brown (chestnut) colour, associated with semi-arid grass steppes.

Phaeozems (from Greek *phaios*, dusky and Russian *zemlja*, earth): dark-coloured soils rich in organic matter with deep leaching of carbonates, associated with the forest steppe.

Podzoluvisols (from podzol and luvisol): soils with a clay-enriched lower horizon into which an upper albic horizon is deeply tongued.

Gypsisols (from gypsum): soils dominated by the presence of gypsum in the form of crystals or concretionary layers of calcium sulphate.

Calcisols (from calcium): soils dominated by the presence of calcium carbonate as either powdery lime or concretionary layers.

Nitisols (from Latin *nitidus*, shiny): soils with deep clay-enriched lower horizons with shiny ped surfaces.

Alisols (from Latin *alumen*, aluminium): acid soils with a clay-enriched lower horizon, high exchange capacity and low saturation by bases.

Acrisols (from Latin *acetum*, strongly acid): acid soils with clay-enriched lower horizons, low exchange capacity and low saturation by bases.

Luvisols (from Latin *luere*, to wash): soils with clay-enriched lower horizons, high exchange capacity and high saturation by bases.

Lixisols (from Latin *lixia*, washing): soils with clay-enriched lower horizons, low exchange capacity and high saturation by bases.

Cambisols (from Latin *cambiare*, to change): moderately developed soils with lower horizons having colour or structure changes from the parent material which permit the identification of a cambic B horizon.

Allocation of soils to these 28 Major Soil Groupings is determined by the presence or absence of a limited number of diagnostic horizons, diagnostic properties or materials. Many of the basic concepts and differentiating criteria of *Soil Taxonomy* have been adopted in the FAO–Unesco system, some in a slightly simplified form and others slightly expanded. However, soils are classed in a more traditional way, using both established and newly devised names. The mollic, umbric and ochric A horizons are closely modelled on the epipedons of the same names in *Soil Taxonomy*, but to these has been added the **fimic** A horizon; the subsurface argillic horizon has been redefined as the **argic** B horizon; and the oxic horizon is redefined as the **ferrallic** B horizon. A simplified flow chart for the FAO–Unesco key is given in Fig. 5.1. To place a soil in the FAO–Unesco system the key should be worked through in strict order from the beginning until the appropriate place for a soil is found. The terminology of the various diagnostic horizons and properties has been explained in Chapters 3 and 4. Classification is only approximate with this simplified key.

Within each of these Major Soil Groupings, between three and nine different varieties of **Soil Units** are distinguished at a second level of classification by the addition of an adjectival word before the soil name (e.g. Humic Cambisol, Calcic Luvisol). The most common of these are descriptive of the topsoil character (e.g. humic, umbric) or of the fertility (e.g. eutric, dystric), or some characteristic of the B horizon (e.g. calcic, gypsic, gleyic, luvic). Proposals have been made for a third level of subdivision for the system, **Soil Subunits**, but as yet only suggestions have been put forward and the matter is under active discussion by a working group of the International Society of Soil Science.

Framework for discussion of world soils

From this chapter it is evident that there are many different ways of classifying soils, and that each system has its merits. As the Australian soil scientist, Leeper, expressed it: 'when scientists discuss methods of analyzing a solution for traces of phosphate, they are practical, reasonable and unemotional. When the same men discuss the classification of

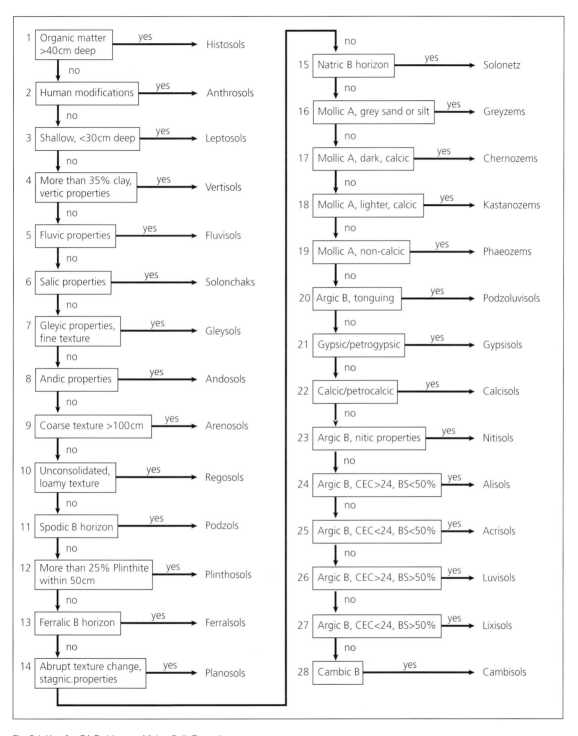

Fig. 5.1 Key for FAO–Unesco Major Soil Groupings.

soils these virtues are liable to evaporate!' The problems of soil classification are often bound up with local requirements and national prestige, and decisions taken at a local level sometimes cannot be accommodated at a national or international level.

Geographically, soils are the product of all the regional and local environmental factors, both physical and cultural, and thus soils provide a regional or zonal indication of environmental uniformity. As stated at the beginning of this chapter, classification helps us to remember relationships between the different soils, to predict their behaviour and to remember their properties. Equally important is that soil classification enables us to communicate with each other about soils using a common language, in which the terminology is clearly and accurately defined.

The next seven chapters of this book present a review of the main soil types of the world, and their profiles are illustrated in the pages of colour illustrations. For each of the 28 Major Soil Groupings of the FAO–Unesco *Soil Map of the World*, a brief account will be given of their distribution and extent, mode of formation and classification. The 28 Major Soil Groupings, following FAO (1990) and Driessen and Dudal (1991), have been arranged in nine sets according to their composition, organic or mineral, a dominant soil-forming factor such as parent material, topography or age, or specific combinations of climate or vegetation. A similar approach is adopted here, but the number of groups has been reduced to seven.

1. The first set of soils, those conditioned by their parent materials, is dealt with in Chapter 6. These include: **Histosols**, soils formed from organic materials; **Andosols**, soils developed in volcanic materials; **Arenosols**, soils developed in deep sandy materials; **Regosols**, soils developed in loamy materials; and **Vertisols**, soils formed in materials rich in clays which expand and contract strongly as they wet and dry.
2. Soils which are weakly developed, as a result of their topographic position or youthfulness, constitute the second group and are discussed in Chapter 7. The set includes three major soil groupings of mineral soils. These are the **Fluvisols** and **Gleysols**, which are usually developed on level topography. Elsewhere, soils which do not have strongly developed horizons are placed in the **Cambisols**.
3. The third grouping is of soils overwhelmingly changed by human activities: these are now sufficiently important to warrant consideration as a separate group, **Anthrosols**, in Chapter 8.

The remaining Major Soil Groupings reflect the nature of the climate and vegetation, which is determined by their geographical position in broad latitudinal belts around the globe. These soils are presented in Chapters 9 to 12.

4. Mineral soils characteristic of mid-latitude, cool, humid climates (but which also occur in other regions) are described in Chapter 9. Leaching and podzolization are dominant processes and the soils include **Luvisols**, **Podzoluvisols**, **Planosols** and **Podzols**.
5. Central continental areas, the steppes and prairie lands, are characterized by mineral soils of the **Chernozems**, **Kastanozems**, **Phaeozems** and **Greyzems**. These soils, with dark colours in their surface horizons and accumulation of carbonates, are discussed in Chapter 10.
6. Arid and semi-arid soils, described in Chapter 11, include **Solonchaks**, **Solonetz**, **Gypsisols** and **Calcisols**. These soils contain soluble or sparingly soluble salts not present in the mineral soils of more humid regions.
7. The **Plinthosols**, **Ferralsols**, **Nitisols**, **Acrisols**, **Alisols** and **Lixisols** are soils characteristic of tropical and sub-tropical regions. They develop under a regular rainfall and strong leaching, with the ferrallitization process dominant. These soils are presented in Chapter 12.

A consideration of soils at a world scale has the disadvantage that many generalizations have to be made which do not recognize the complexity of the soil pattern at a local level. Despite this, it is important to realize that many relationships can still be seen between the different factors of the environment which together produce the soil cover and also influence the use of soils as a natural resource.

Plate A1. Histic H horizon: saturated organic material, 20–40 cm thick. (ISRIC)

Plate A2. Mollic A horizon: dark-coloured, deep, base-rich A horizon. (ISRIC)

Plate A3. Umbric A horizon: dark-coloured, deep, base-poor A horizon. (ISRIC)

Plate A4. Ochric A horizon: light-coloured, thin A horizon. (ISRIC)

Plate A5. Fimic A horizon: man-made surface horizon, 50 cm or more thick.

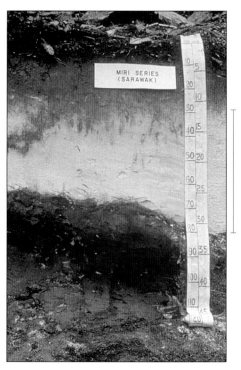

Plate A6. Albic E horizon: whitish-grey, bleached horizon, free of clay and iron oxides. (ISRIC)

Plate A7. Cambic B horizon: colour and structure are different from the parent material.

Plate A8. Argic B horizon: increased clay content. (ISRIC)

Plate A9. Natric B horizon: increased clay content and saturated with sodium salts. (ISRIC)

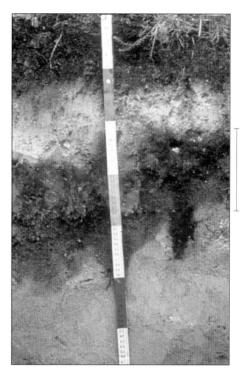

Plate A10. Spodic B horizon: enriched with aluminium, organic matter and iron. (ISRIC)

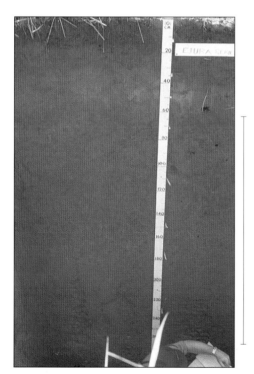

Plate A11. Ferralic B horizon: deep, clayey horizon with low CEC, with few weatherable minerals and little dispersible clay.

Plate A12. Calcic horizon: 15 cm or more thick, enriched with calcium carbonate. (ISRIC)

Plate A13. Petrocalcic horizon: massive, cemented horizon, indurated with calcium carbonate. (ISRIC)

Plate A14. Gypsic horizon: 15 cm or more thick, enriched with calcium sulphate.

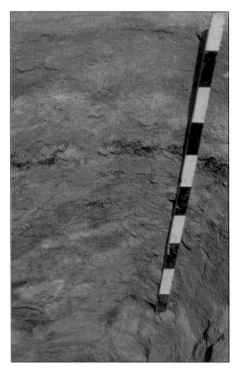

Plate A15. Petrogypsic horizon: massive, cemented horizon, indurated with calcium sulphate.

Plate A16. Salic properties: the presence of salts in the soil gives the saturation extract an electrical conductivity of 15 dS m^{-1}, or 4 dS m^{-1} if pH is >8.5.

Plate A17. Gleyic properties: dull colours result from saturation by ground-water. (ISRIC)

Plate A18. Stagnic properties: dull colours result from saturation by surface-water.

Plate A19. Fluvic properties: stratified fluvial, lacustrine or marine sediments with variable organic carbon content.

Plate A20. Nitic properties: strongly formed, clayey, angular blocky peds with shiny surfaces.

Plate A21. Ferric properties: coarse, bright red mottles associated with Luvisols, Alisols, Lixisols and Acrisols.

Plate A22. Vertic properties a): deep wide cracks in clayey soils.

Plate A23. Vertic properties b): parallelepiped blocky structures with polished 'slickensides' surfaces. (ISRIC)

Plate A24. Plinthite: iron-rich, humus-poor mixture of clay which irreversibly hardens upon drying.

Plate A25. Petroferric phase: hardened plinthite, referred to as ironstone.

Plate A26. Soft powdery lime: soft white coatings or crystals of calcium carbonate.

Plate A27. Placic phase: soils with a thin iron pan.

Plate A28. Permafrost: layer of soil which is permanently at or below 0°C. (ISRIC)

Plate A29. Yermic phase: soils having desert pavement with desert varnish, infilled cracks and surface platy layer with vesicular pores.

Plate A30. Takyric phase: clayey textured soils which crack into polygonal elements when dry.

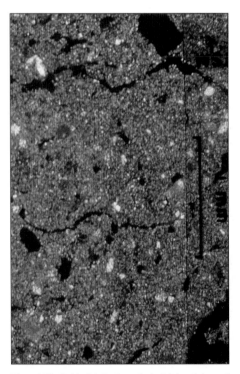

Plate A31. Calcic fabric: the whole fabric of the soil is penetrated with calcium carbonate.

Plate A32. Gypsic fabric: the fabric of the mineral soil is replaced by gypsum crystallaria.

Plate B1. Terric Histosol, Wales, UK. Highly decomposed organic materials with only small amounts of visible plant fibres; very poor drainage.

Plate B2. Urbic Anthrosol, Germany. Industrial wastes covered with a layer of soil material; methanogenesis is occurring. (ISRIC)

Plate B3. Rendzic Leptosol, Romania. A mollic A horizon overlies limestone with calcium carbonate equivalent of more than 40 per cent.

Plate B4. Lithic Leptosol, Switzerland. Continuous hard rock occurs within 10 cm of the soil surface. (ISRIC)

Plates B1 to B32. Examples of soil profiles

Plate B5. Calcic Vertisol, Texas, USA. This is a dark-coloured soil with cracks, having marked parallelepiped structures with slickensides.

Plate B6. Eutric Fluvisol, England, UK. Fluvic properties and weak ochric A horizon are present.

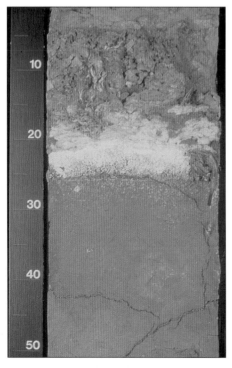

Plate B7. Sodic Solonchak, Turpan, China. This is an imperfectly drained saline soil with thick, dirty white salt pan, high pH and high electrical conductivity. (ISRIC)

Plate B8. Dystric Gleysol, England, UK. The presence of strong mottling and low base saturation places this soil in the Dystric Soil Unit.

Plate B9. Umbric Gleysol, Germany. Soils with gleyic properties belong to the Gleysols; with an umbric A horizon this soil is an Umbric Gleysol. (ISRIC)

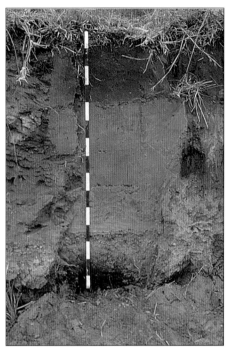

Plate B10. Vitric Andosol, Kenya. This profile is well-drained, has andic properties with a coarse texture and therefore is a Vitric Andosol. (ISRIC)

Plate B11. Luvic Arenosol, South Africa. The texture is coarser than sandy loam to more than 100cm, but thin clay lamellae place it in the Luvic Soil Unit. (ISRIC)

Plate B12. Eutric Regosol, Mali. Lacking any diagnostic horizon other than an ochric or umbric A horizon, this profile is a Regosol; with a high base saturation it belongs to the Eutric Soil Unit. (ISRIC)

Plate B13. Haplic Podzol, England, UK. Beneath a heath vegetation a well-developed E horizon and spodic B horizon can be seen. There is no gleying and no placic horizon.

Plate B14. Carbic Podzol, Indonesia. There is a deep E horizon (can be 10m deep) developed in coarse sands, and a highly organic B horizon. There is little iron present in the B horizon. (ISRIC)

Plate B15. Dystric Plinthosol, Ghana. Hardened nodules are present at a depth of 80cm, comprising more than 25 per cent by volume; low saturation with bases.

Plate B16. Rhodic Ferralsol, Malaysia. The presence of a ferralic B horizon and the bright red colours (redder than 5YR) place it in the Rhodic Soil Unit. (ISRIC)

Plate B17. Umbric Planosol, South Africa. There are stagnic properties overlying a slowly permeable B horizon within 125cm of the soil surface. (ISRIC)

Plate B18. Haplic Solonetz, South Africa. A natric B horizon is present, with characteristic rounded tops to the structures in the B horizon. (ISRIC)

Plate B19. Haplic Greyzem, Russia. A mollic A horizon, which has uncoated sand/silt grains, overlies an argic B horizon.

Plate B20. Haplic Chernozem, Ukraine. A deep (1m) mollic A horizon is present, and krotovinas are visible in the C horizon. (D. Gunary).

Plate B21. Calcic Kastanozem, Ukraine. A shallow, lighter-coloured mollic A horizon with calcium carbonate accumulation places this soil in the Calcic Soil Unit. (ISRIC)

Plate B22. Haplic Phaeozem, Czech Republic. There is a deep, dark mollic A horizon with no gleying, clay or calcium carbonate accumulation. (ISRIC)

Plate B23. Stagnic Podzoluvisol, Germany. There is a deeply tonguing E horizon over an argic B horizon with slow drainage. (ISRIC)

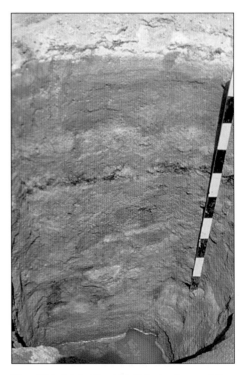

Plate B24. Petric Gypsisol, Bahrain. Accumulation and crystallization of gypsum in this profile has produced a massive petrogypsic horizon.

Plate B25. Petric Calcisol, Australia. Accumulation of calcium carbonate in the lower horizon of this soil has become cemented into a rock-like layer.

Plate B26. Haplic Nitisol, Mexico. The deeply extended argic B horizon of this profile has angular blocky peds with shiny surfaces so the soil qualifies as a Nitisol.

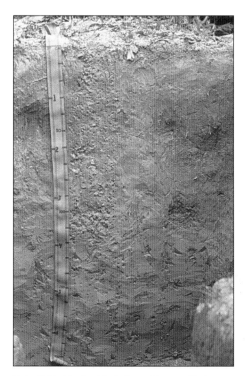

Plate B27. Haplic Alisol, Peru. The profile has an argic B horizon with CEC of >24 $cmol_c\,kg^{-1}$ and saturation with aluminium ions. (ISRIC)

Plate B28. Acrisol, Jinxian Province, China. The profile has an argic B horizon with low CEC, but the B horizon has less than 50 per cent saturation, so it is a Haplic Acrisol. (ISRIC)

Plate B29. Haplic Luvisol, England, UK. There is an increased clay content in the B horizon, but the absence of other diagnostic features places this soil in the Haplic Soil Unit.

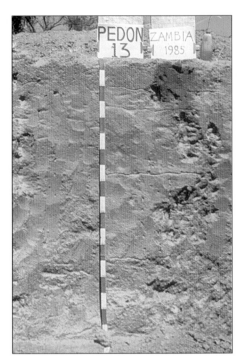

Plate B30. Haplic Lixisol, Zambia. The soil has an argic B horizon with a CEC of more than $24\,cmol_c\,kg^{-1}$, a high silt:clay ratio and a base saturation of >50 per cent. (ISRIC)

Plate B31. Dystric Cambisol, Wales, UK. The presence of a cambic B horizon can be seen by its change in colour and structure.

Plate B32. Cryosol, Canada. This soil hummock from near the Mackenzie delta has an ice core. (ISRIC)

Further reading

AFES, 1992. *Référential pédologique: principaux sols d'Europe*. INRA, Paris.

Avery, B.W., 1973. Soil classification in the Soil Survey of England and Wales. *Journal of Soil Science* **24**: 324–8.

Baldwin, M., Kellogg, C.E. and Thorp, J., 1938. Soil classification. In: *Soils and Men*. Yearbook of Agriculture for 1938, USDA, Washington, pp.979–1001.

Buol, S.W., Hole, F.D. and McCracken, R.J., 1989. *Soil Classification*. Iowa State University Press, Ames.

Butler, B.E., 1980. *Soil Classification for Soil Survey*. Clarendon Press, Oxford.

CPCS, 1967. *Classification des sols*. ENSA, Grignon.

de Gruijter, J.J., 1977. *Numerical Classification of Soils and its Application in Survey*. Pudoc, Wageningen.

Driessen, P.M. and Dudal, R. (eds.), 1991. *The Major Soils of the World*. Agricultural University Wageningen, Katholieke Universiteit, Leuven.

FAO, 1990. *FAO–Unesco Soil Map of the World. Revised Legend*. World Soil Resources Report No. 60, FAO, Rome. Reprint ISRIC, 1994.

FAO, 1993. *World Soil Resources: an Explanatory Note on the FAO World Soil Resources Map at 1:25,000,000 Scale*. World Soil Resources Report No. 66, FAO, Rome.

Hall, A.D. and Russell, E.J., 1911. *Report on the Agriculture and Soils of Kent, Surrey and Sussex*. HMSO, London.

Hallsworth, E.G., 1965. The relationship between experimental pedology and soil classification. In: Hallsworth and Crawford (eds.), *Experimental Pedology*. Butterworths, London, pp. 354–71.

Isbell, R.F., 1993. *A Classification System for Australian Soils (3rd Approximation)*. CSIRO, Townsville.

Kubiena, W.L., 1953. *The Soils of Europe*. Murby, London.

Marbut, C.F., 1928. A scheme for soil classification. *Proc. 1st International Congress of Soil Science*, 1927, Washington. Vol. 4, pp. 1–31.

Northcote, K.H., 1960. *A Factual Key for the Recognition of Australian Soils*. Soils Division, Divisional Report 4/60, CSIRO.

Rayner, J.H., 1966. Classification of soils by numerical methods. *Journal of Soil Science* **17**: 79–92.

Robinson, G.W., 1949. *Soils: their Origin, Constitution and Classification*. 3rd edition, Murby, London.

Rosanov, B.G., 1990. *Soil Classification*. Centre for International Projects, USSR State Committee for Environmental Protection, Moscow.

Simonson, R.W., 1989. *Historical Highlights of Soil Survey and Soil Classification with emphasis on the United States, 1899–1970*. Technical Paper No. 18, International Soil Reference and Information Centre, Wageningen.

Soil Survey Staff, 1975. *Soil Taxonomy*. Agriculture Handbook 436, USDA, Washington.

Soil Survey Staff, 1994. *Keys to Soil Taxonomy*. 6th edition, USDA, Washington.

Spaargaren, O.C., 1995. *World Reference Base for Soil Resources*. ISSS, ISRIC, FAO, Wageningen/Rome.

Strzemski, M., 1975. *Ideas Underlying Soil Systematics*. National Centre for Scientific, Technological and Economic Information, Warsaw.

Webster, R., 1977. *Quantitative and Numerical Methods in Soil Classification and Survey*. Clarendon Press, Oxford.

6 Soils conditioned by their parent materials

One feature of most modern soil classification systems is their recognition that soil formation is a dynamic process, and that not all soils of the world are mature and in a steady state of equilibrium with the prevailing environment. In the discussion of time as a factor in soil formation, it was demonstrated that soils of all ages may occur in landscapes, from those which are young and weakly developed to those which are mature and some which might even be described as senile. This chapter considers soils in which the stage of development is controlled by their parent materials: either the nature of the parent materials outweighs other factors determining soil genesis, or the parent materials are resistant to the processes of soil formation. It has been suggested that their morphology and mineralogical composition reflect the youthfulness of the soil profile because fewer horizons with less complex features occur in these soils than are seen in other soil groupings.

Accumulation of preserved plant debris provides the parent material for **Histosols**, a group of soils, quite distinct from all other soils, which have formed in mineral parent materials. Soils formed in volcanic deposits, **Andosols**, are developed in materials that are rich in weatherable minerals such as feldspars, ferromagnesian minerals and volcanic glass. The **Arenosols** are developed in sandy materials, and **Regosols** in loamy and finer materials. Both these groups are derived from unconsolidated rock debris with only slightly developed surface diagnostic horizons. **Vertisols** develop in very clayey materials which crack widely when dried, and often have evidence of pedoturbation in their subsoils. An additional Major Soil Grouping, at present not in the legend of the FAO–Unesco *Soil Map of the World*, is the **Cryosols**, which are affected by the presence of permafrost.

Histosols

Peat and organic soils, formed from more or less well-preserved plant tissue and hence known as 'Histosols' (from Greek *histos*, tissue), are developed in very poorly drained conditions, often in association with hydromorphic mineral soils (Gleysols). Histosols are a distinctive Major Soil Grouping because, unlike other Major Soil Groupings, they are formed from organic materials, with mineral matter occurring at depth or as a minor constituent, and often not directly influencing the processes of soil formation. The most extensive areas of Histosols occur in the boreal regions of North America, Europe and Asia, where they are estimated to cover 200 million hectares. A further 40 million hectares are in tropical regions, especially in southeast Asia, for example on lowlands beside the Sunda Strait in Sumatra (Plate B1).

An arbitrary division between peats (Histosols) and peaty mineral soils (Histic Soil Units) has been drawn where the depth of organic soil materials lying on the mineral soil surface exceeds 40 cm (60 cm if the material is mainly sphagnum peat with a bulk density of less than $0.1\,\mathrm{Mg\,m^{-3}}$). Histosols develop from organic soil materials more than 40 cm thick which are saturated with water for long periods or are artificially drained, and which have 18 per cent or more organic carbon if the mineral fraction contains more than 60 per cent clay, or 12 per cent organic carbon if there is no clay in the mineral soil.

Accumulation of organic matter is encouraged by saturated anaerobic conditions which inhibit bacterial activity. These conditions result when heavy rainfall, seepage, regular flooding and high levels of ground-water maintain the soil in a saturated condition. In very cold climates too, organic breakdown is restricted by low temperatures, and although biomass production is also low, decomposition is insufficiently rapid to break down all the plant litter produced, so an organic accumulation occurs. Extreme acidity and the presence of organic toxins also cause the slow organic breakdown and accumulation of plant debris. The different types of saturated organic materials in Histosols include: **sapric** material (USDA), which is well-decomposed so that when rubbed between the fingers or on a sieve most of the fibrous material disintegrates; **hemic** material (USDA), which is intermediate in character; and **fibric** material (FAO and USDA), which is relatively undecomposed. A fourth, less common form of organic material, only saturated for short periods, is described as **folic** (FAO).

There are several types of peats which may be identified broadly by their position in the landscape and the nature of the accumulation. A simple division used in Ireland consists of **blanket bog, raised bog** and **fen**. Blanket bogs occur in the uplands and are normally acid, but fen occurs in lowland areas where peats may be acid, neutral or calcareous, depending upon the surrounding geological and pedological conditions.

On the uplands of western Europe, particularly in northern Scotland, Wales, England and Ireland, strongly acidic blanket bog covers large areas over 300 m above sea level. This blanket bog is often only 30 to 40 cm thick, but can attain a depth of 150 cm, and deeper accumulations can be found in declivities. The sapric organic materials from which it is formed are black, strongly acid, and consist of few identifiable plant remains, with very little mineral matter included. It supports a growth of cotton grass (*Eriophorum*) and sphagnum moss, but with partial drainage heather may invade and become dominant.

The upland blanket bogs rely on a plentiful and well-distributed rainfall for their existence, but most lowland bogs develop where there is saturation resulting from seepages or high levels of the ground-water table. Variations of water level in the past are responsible for determining the type of peat that develops in a specific area. In really wet conditions, a reedswamp community of phragmites may form the peat; in drier conditions carr peat may accumulate, in which woody fragments of alder, birch or willow trees are included. Such materials

can accumulate up to the level of the ground-water table. The form of lowland peat most important for agriculture is fen peat, which is developed where base-rich waters are associated with the accumulation of organic matter. Where limestone outcrops occur and calcareous waters drain into the accumulating organic materials, they can provide a source of bases to enrich the peat, which, when drained, can form very fertile soils, as is the case in the Fens of eastern England. Fen or basin peats are usually fairly well decomposed and the material from which they are composed is described by pedologists as sapric or hemic material.

In areas of high rainfall, peat can continue to grow above the water table in what is described as a 'raised bog' (or ombrogenous peat) which holds water like a sponge (Fig. 6.1). Usually composed predominantly of sphagnum moss, the plants which form these peats are totally dependent upon the rainfall for their nutrients, as the saturated mass of organic material isolates them from the basin peats and mineral soils at depth below the peat. The acid conditions, saturation and lack of plant nutrients limit the growth of most plants on raised bogs, but the sphagnum continues to grow as its lower parts become humified. As the name suggests, a raised bog grows into the shape of a low dome and the brown peat is strongly acid in reaction.

In tropical conditions, for example in Sumatra, peats accumulate in low-lying areas of coastal plains. In brackish water situations of coastal locations, incursion of sea-water can induce the formation of sulphides in the accumulating organic and mineral materials, which, if drained and oxidized, can become extremely acid. Any proposed agricultural development of coastal peats should be preceded by an assessment of the sulphidic materials present. If the material contains more than 0.75 per

Fig. 6.1 Basin peat and raised bog formation.

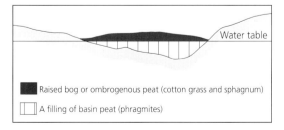

Raised bog or ombrogenous peat (cotton grass and sphagnum)

A filling of basin peat (phragmites)

cent of sulphides and there is little calcium carbonate present, it will become strongly acid when drained. Where drainage has taken place, a sulphuric horizon may develop with a pH value of less than 3.5, containing yellow mottles of the mineral jarosite with a hue of 2.5Y and a chroma of 6 or more. Such soils are classified as Thionic Histosols. They can also occur in temperate regions where the mineral pyrite is oxidized, for example in disturbed materials from opencast coal-mining activities.

Within the Major Soil Grouping of Histosols, Soil Units are identified on the basis of the type of organic material present and the temperature regime (Fig. 6.2). The **Gelic Histosols** occur in arctic regions where the permafrost is within 200 cm of the soil surface. **Thionic Histosols** have either a sulphuric horizon or sulphidic material within 125 cm of the soil surface. Although common in tropical regions, these soils are also seen in temperate parts of the world. The remaining Soil Units are distinguished by the nature of the organic material present. **Folic Histosols** are well-drained and are never saturated with water for more than a few days at a time. **Fibric Histosols** comprise raw or weakly decomposed organic materials in which the content of fibre is dominant to a depth of 35 cm. **Terric Histosols** have highly decomposed organic materials in which fibrous plant remains are of minor importance.

Profile of a Terric Histosol (Saprist*) from Wales UK

Profile SN 50/5584, Soil Survey of England and Wales
(Parent material: peat)
Diagnostic criteria: histic H horizon;
organic material more than 40 cm.

Oh$_1$	0–10 cm	Black (10YR 2/1) very slightly stony humified peat (stones are artifacts) with moderately developed fine granular structure; wet; abundant fibrous roots; clear smooth boundary
Oh$_2$	10–20 cm	Dark brown (7.5YR 3/2) stoneless humified peat, massive; wet; many fibrous roots; clear smooth boundary
Oh$_3$	20–70 cm	Black (10YR 2/1) stoneless humified peat, massive; wet; clear smooth boundary
Oh$_4$	70–100 cm	Very dark greyish brown (10YR 3/2), stoneless humified peat, massive; wet

Selected analyses

Horizon	Oh1	Oh2	Oh3	Oh3	Oh4
Depth (cm)	0–10	10–20	20–45	45–70	70–100
Org. C(%)	–	37	39	39	56
pH H$_2$O (1:2.5)	–	3.9	3.5	3.4	4.1
Rubbed fibre (%)	–	9	2.5	3.0	9.3

Comment: the profile is strongly acid throughout. Organic material is described by the soil surveyor to a depth of more than 40 cm as raw oligo-amorphous humified peat. Fibrous material in profile is from roots and is not dominant, so classification points to a Terric Histosol.

* *Soil Taxonomy* name is given in parentheses

Fig. 6.2 Classification of Histosols.

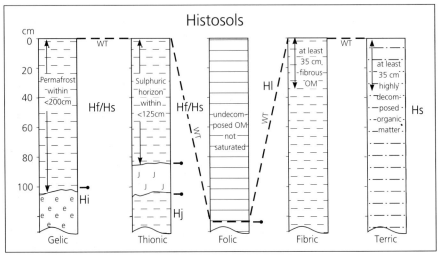

Andosols

Soils with features worthy of special comment are the Andosols, named from soils formed on base-rich volcanic deposits in Japan (from Japanese *an*, dark and *do*, soil). The strong influence of the pyro-clastic parent material determines that these soils occur in all parts of the world where there is active volcanicity, from Alaska in the tundra to Indonesia in the tropics (Fig. 6.3). Andosols are soils with a dark brown to black surface horizon having a thick, fine crumb-structured, friable A horizon overlying a crumb-structured cambic B horizon in which there is no illuvial clay accumulation. Young Andosols may have an AC profile. The Andosols have a low bulk density, and when handled they are not sticky. This rather variable group of soils covers over 110 million hectares throughout the world and includes both very fertile soils and also phosphate-retentive, infertile soils (Plate B10).

The mineralogy of the igneous ejecta from which Andosols are formed can vary considerably

Fig. 6.3 Landscape with volcanic parent materials upon which Andosols are developed.

from place to place, but volcanic glass, feldspars, ferromagnesian minerals and quartz are the most common constituents. In roadside cuts, the soil and its parent material can be seen to be a succession of ash layers. The whole of the developing profile is very porous and the particles forming the soil have a large surface area. Weathering can proceed rapidly, and produces a range of colloidal minerals including allophane, imogolite and ferrihydrite, all of which become closely associated with humic acids. In acid Andosols, the colloidal complex con-sists of iron and aluminium chemically linked (chelated) with humic acids. It is this combination of mineral and organic colloids which gives the Andosols their characteristic dark surface horizon and high (8–30 per cent) organic matter content. A significant chemical characteristic of Andosols is that their cation exchange capacity increases (by between 40 and 80 per cent) as pH values increase. A field test used to diagnose Andosols is to measure the active aluminium by the pH in NaF (molar sodium fluoride): if the pH value is over 9.5 the soil is almost certainly an Andosol.

Andosols are stable, very friable and highly per-meable soils with a high moisture retention capa-city, except in coarse-textured or very young Andosols. In many cases, the minerals allophane or imogolite are present as secondary minerals. In the weathering process, compounds are released which react with organic materials to form stable, organ-ic-rich mollic or umbric A horizons. The presence of volcanic glass can be determined in the field with a hand lens, and allophane by the active aluminium (sodium fluoride) test. Andosols also have the power to strongly fix phosphate so that it is unavailable for plants. An outstanding physical characteristic of many Andosols is their low bulk density. Soils must possess at least one of these **andic properties** in order to belong to the Andosols. However, redistribution of constituents within the profile caused by rapid weathering can result in strongly indurated horizons lower in the profile, referred to in Latin America as 'talpetate' or 'cangahua'.

The first requirement for an Andosol is that it possesses andic properties within 35 cm of the soil surface. To be an Andosol, a soil must have one or more of these properties. They include: a stipulated

---

Profile of a Vitric Andosol (Typic Dystrandept) from La Palazzina, Italy

ISRIC Profile IT 16
(Parent material: volcanic tuff (Holocene))
Diagnostic criteria: umbric A horizon and andic properties.

O$_l$	3–0 cm	Leaves, slightly decomposed; abrupt smooth boundary
Ah$_1$	0–4 cm	Black (10YR 2/1) silty clay loam with weak fine crumb structure; slightly sticky; slightly plastic; very friable; very porous; common fine and very fine roots; non-calcareous; abrupt smooth boundary
Ah$_2$	4–29 cm	Very dark brown (7.5YR 2/2) clay loam with massive structure; slightly sticky; slightly plastic; porous; many fine and few coarse roots; non-calcareous; clear irregular boundary
Bw	29–47 cm	Strong brown (7.5YR 5/6) gravelly sandy loam with weak medium angular blocky structure; non-sticky; non-plastic; very friable; porous; clay and sesquioxide coatings on ped faces; common fine and few medium roots; frequent volcanic ash fragments; non-calcareous; clear smooth boundary
BC	47–117 cm	Strong brown (7.5YR 4/6) gravelly sandy loam with very weak coarse subangular blocky structure; non-sticky; non-plastic; porous; patchy clay and sesquioxide coatings on ped faces; very frequent volcanic ash fragments; non-calcareous

Selected analyses

Horizon	Ah1	Ah2	Bw	BC
Depth (cm)	0–4	4–30	30–50	50–110
Clay (%)	27	15	3	4
Bulk density (Mg m^{-3})	–	0.50	0.58	0.58
pH H$_2$O (1:2.5)	4.6	4.9	5.6	5.9
Org. C (%)	14.5	5.85	1.42	0.53
CEC	66.6	39.2	37.1	32.9
Base sat. (%)	15	2	1	3

Comment: very dark surface horizon qualifies as an umbric A horizon as it has low base saturation. Soil has andic properties. The B horizon qualifies as cambic.

minimum amount of aluminium and iron extractable by ammonium oxalate from the fine earth (if there is <5 per cent glass, i.e. strongly weathered, the $Al_{ox}+1/2Fe_{ox}$ should be >2.0, but if there is >60 per cent glass, i.e. slightly weathered, the $Al_{ox}+1/2Fe_{ox}$ needs to be only 0.4 per cent); bulk density is 0.9 Mg m^{-3} or less; the retention of phosphate is more than 85 per cent; more than 60 per cent of the soil material is composed of volcanic clastic fragments coarser than 2 mm. Other criteria concern the content of volcanic glass in the silt and sand fractions. Some Andosols have thixotropic properties as shown by their smeary consistency.

From a chemical point of view, it is convenient to subdivide the Andosols into two categories. Group 1 contains soils with low bulk density, in which active aluminium is dominant and with a high capacity for phosphate retention. Group 2 contains soils with normal bulk density, low amounts of active aluminium, with halloysite as the main clay mineral, accompanied by poorly crystalline silicates and sometimes smectite.

Having established that the soil belongs to the Major Soil Grouping of Andosols, the successive Soil Units in the key (Fig. 6.4) are: **Gelic Andosols**, which have permafrost within 200 cm of the surface; **Gleyic Andosols**, which have gleyic properties within 100 cm of the surface; **Vitric Andosols**, which are glassy and do not have a smeary consistency or a fine texture; **Mollic** and **Umbric Andosols**, which have a mollic or umbric A horizon, respectively. Any remaining Andosols are placed in the **Haplic Andosols**.

Arenosols

Coarse-grained (sandy) soils are classified in the Major Soil Grouping of Arenosols. These soils have a texture which is coarser than a sandy loam to a depth of at least 1 m, they do not have fluvic or andic properties, and are lacking diagnostic horizons other than an ochric A and albic E horizon. It is estimated that Arenosols cover 900 million hectares or about 7 per cent of the terrestrial area of the world (Plate B11).

The parent materials for Arenosols are unconsolidated sands derived from recent dunes, beach ridges and plains of redistributed sands, for example the Kalahari Sands of southern Africa, or deeply weathered sandstones. Arenosols may be found in virtually all climates, from the arctic to the tropics

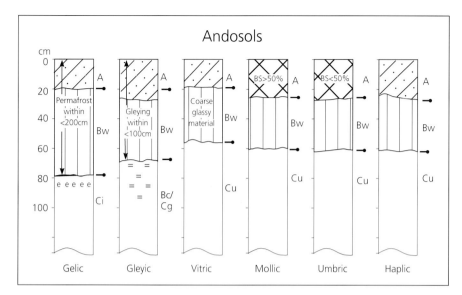

Fig. 6.4 Classification of Andosols.

and from wet and dry regions. They are most extensive in the arid regions of the world, but they are also common in the humid tropics where their extremely permeable nature and the high rainfall ensure deep and thorough leaching. Small areas occur elsewhere in the world on suitable parent materials. The dominant mineral present in the parent material of Arenosols is quartz, but the processes which have resulted in the accumulation of these large sand masses have also concentrated minerals such as ilmenite, rutile and tourmaline,

and in Australia they are mined for these minerals. Calcium- or gypsum-rich sands can occur in the arid regions.

Having decided that a soil qualifies as an Arenosol, there are currently seven possible Soil Units in this Major Soil Grouping (Fig. 6.5): **Gleyic Arenosols** have gleyic properties within 100 cm of the soil surface; **Albic Arenosols** have an albic E horizon, with minimum thickness of

Fig. 6.5 Classification of Arenosols.

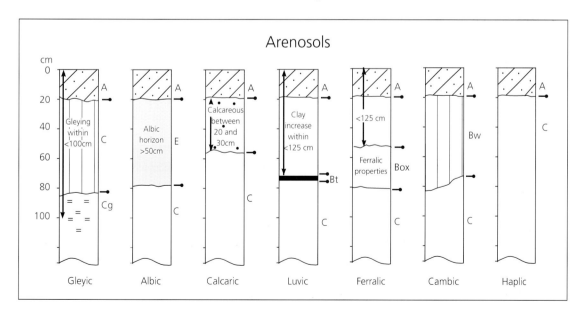

Profile of a Luvic Arenosol (Argic Quartzipsamment) from Cliffdale, Pietermaritzburg, Natal

ISRIC Profile ZA 14
(Parent material: sandstone)
Diagnostic criteria: ochric A horizon.

Ah	0–22 cm	Reddish-brown (5YR 5/3) structureless sand; non-sticky; non-plastic; loose; no mottles; no cutans; many fine roots; non-calcareous; clear wavy boundary
C₁	22–60 cm	Brown (7.5YR 5/2) structureless sand; non-sticky; non-plastic; loose; no mottles; no cutans; no roots; animal burrows; non-calcareous; gradual smooth boundary
C₂	60–140 cm	Pinkish-grey (5YR 6/2) structureless sand; non-sticky; non-plastic; loose; no mottles; thin clay lamellae; no roots; non-calcareous

Selected analyses

Horizon	A	C11	C12	C21/C22
Depth (cm)	0–22	22–35	35–120	120+
Clay (%)	3	2	3	22
pH H$_2$O (1:2.5)	5.9	5.8	5.7	5.6
Org. C (%)	0.43	0.31	0.27	0.16
CEC	3.5	0.9	0.9	0.4
Base sat. (%)	46	78	44	25

Comment: a sand with a weakly developed ochric A horizon and no diagnostic B horizon. The thin clay lamellae in the lower C horizon were not considered to qualify as an argic horizon, but their presence does place this soil in the Luvic Arenosol Soil Unit.

50 cm, within 125 cm of the soil surface; **Calcaric Arenosols** are calcareous at least between 20 and 50 cm from the surface; **Luvic Arenosols** have an increase of 3 per cent clay or more or lamellae of clay accumulation within 125 cm of the surface; **Ferralic Arenosols** have ferralic properties (low CEC); **Cambic Arenosols** show changes in colour or structure typical of a cambic B horizon. Any remaining Arenosols are placed in the **Haplic Arenosols**.

Strongly developed 'tropical Podzols' with a deeply developed albic E horizon are classified as Albic Arenosols (Plate B14). The extreme depth of this horizon normally excluded these soils from the Podzol Major Soil Grouping as it has been defined. Often 4–5 m in depth, in extreme cases the E horizon can be 12 or 13 m deep, as in some of the oldest (Pleistocene) dune formations in the Cooloola National Park on the Queensland coast of Australia. The Australian examples of Arenosols often have interrupted spodic B horizons composed of patches of iron-cemented sand with 'pipes' passing through to further E horizon material beneath, so the local name of 'pipy Podzols' has been given to these soils.

Arenosols of arid regions generally have a much simpler pedological history. They usually occur on accumulations of aeolian sands and have minimal profile development. A shallow ochric A horizon can develop if these sands become fixed by vegetation, but remobilization by wind is always possible. In temperate regions Arenosols are less common, but where they occur they often contain coatings of iron on sand grains, or thin lamellae of clay, which are too insignificant to qualify as a diagnostic B horizon of any sort. Therefore, by default they fall into the category of Arenosols.

Regosols

Unconsolidated, partly weathered materials, which showed little evidence that they had been affected by soil formation, were difficult to place in the older climate-based classifications. A group of soils called Regosols was first described by Thorp and Smith (1949) as 'an azonal group of soils consisting of deep unconsolidated rock (soft mineral deposits) in which few or no clearly expressed soil characteristics have developed; they are largely confined to recent sand dunes and to loess or glacial drift of steeply sloping ground'. Since then, the major group of Regosols has been more closely defined as soils developed on fine-grained, unconsolidated materials which do not have fluvic, gleyic, andic or vertic properties, and no diagnostic horizons other than an ochric or umbric A horizon, or contain sufficient soluble salts to meet the requirement for salic properties. Their profile is simple, being limited to an ochric A horizon overlying the parent material (Plate B12). However, where the parent material is gravelly, the sand may be blown away to leave a residual surface layer of stones, referred to as

Profile of a Eutric Regosol (Aquic Ustorthent) from Oyo State, Nigeria

ISRIC Profile NG 02

Diagnostic criteria: ochric A horizon.

Ah	0–13 cm	Brown (7.5YR 4/4) loamy coarse sand with moderate fine crumb structure; loose; porous; many fine and medium roots; gradual smooth boundary
BC₁	13–32 cm	Dark brown (10YR 4/3) loamy sand with weak fine crumb structure; loose; porous; many fine and common coarse roots; few ferruginous and manganiferous concretions; diffuse boundary
BC₂	32–62 cm	Brown (7.5YR 4/4) slightly gravelly loamy sand with very weak fine blocky structure; loose; porous; common fine and medium roots; ferruginous and manganiferous concretions; clear wavy boundary
C	62–82 cm	Brown (7.5YR 4/4) gravelly loamy sand with weak fine subangular blocky structure; friable; porous; common fine and few medium roots; ferruginous and manganiferous concretions; clear wavy boundary
2Btb	82–132 cm	Brown (5YR 4/4) very gravelly sandy clay loam with moderate fine subangular blocky structure; hard; porous; many fine distinct mottles; plinthite fragments; clear wavy boundary
3C	132–155 cm	Very gravelly sandy loam; old concretionary colluvium

Selected analyses

Horizon	Ah	BC	C	2Btb
Depth (cm)	0–13	13–62	62–82	82–132
Clay (%)	6	7	10	31
pH H₂O (1:2.5)	6.1	6.0	6.2	6.1
Org C (%)	1.2	0.4	0.2	0.3
CEC	4.3	1.3	0.7	0.9
Base sat. (%)	57	77	83	61

Comment: rather too coarse in the upper part of the profile for a Regosol, but finer-textured material lower down does meet the textural criteria. A soil with only an ochric horizon which at 82 cm passes into a (possible) buried soil with many ironstone concretions.

a 'desert pavement'. Examples of such profiles occur in Israel, where the desert pavement is underlain by a thin sandy/silty horizon in which there are vesicles, thought to be formed by air bubbles when the soil is (occasionally) wetted. These soils are locally known as 'reg' soils.

Regosols are found throughout the world in all climate zones and at all elevations. Altogether, these soils cover an area of 580 million hectares, mainly in the sub-arctic regions, but also in mountainous and desert regions, where the processes of soil formation are retarded by drought or frost. As a result, the content of weatherable minerals may be high and profile development is minimal.

Subdivision of the Regosols into Soil Units includes: **Gelic Regosols**, with permafrost within 200 cm of the soil surface; **Umbric Regosols**, with a dark-coloured umbric A horizon; **Gypsic Regosols**, which are gypsiferous between 20 and 50 cm below the soil surface; **Calcaric Regosols**, which are calcareous between 20 and 50 cm below the soil surface; **Dystric Regosols**, which have a base saturation of less than 50 per cent, at least between 20 and 50 cm below the soil surface. Any remaining Regosols are placed in the **Eutric Regosols** (Fig. 6.6).

Vertisols

Dark brown or black clay-rich soils developed upon parent materials rich in bases form a special group of soils called Vertisols. They are extensively developed in areas subject to a strongly alternating climatic regime of wet and dry seasons. These soils are low in organic matter and are subject to strong pedoturbation, which is said to continually overturn the upper part of the soil profile. The **vert** from invert has been used to make the name of these interesting soils. The FAO–Unesco *Soil Map of the World* legend, US *Soil Taxonomy*, and the French classification, have all adopted the term Vertisol as one of their Major Soil Groupings, and so the name has become widely accepted for these soils, which cover some 340 million hectares of the world's surface.

The occurrence of Vertisols is mainly between latitudes 45°N and 45°S, with extensive areas in India, Sudan, Australia and southwest USA. In earlier soil classifications, they were called Tropical Black Clays, Vlei Soils, Black Cotton Soils or Gilgai Soils. Other localized folk names used for these soils include grumusols (USA), regur (India),

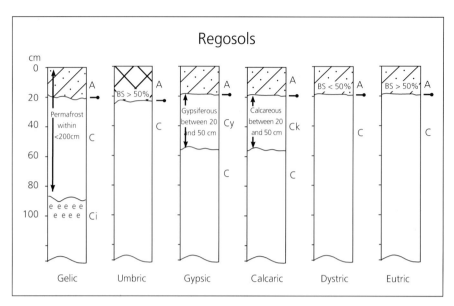

Fig. 6.6 Classification of Regosols.

badobes (Sudan), tirs (North Africa) and margalite (Indonesia).

Vertisols are defined as soils which have over 30 per cent clay in all horizons of their upper 50 cm. As the soil dries it develops cracks, from the surface downwards, which should be at least 1 cm wide to a depth of 50 cm. Vertisols also have one or more of the following features: wedge-shaped or parallelepiped structures and slickensides at some depth between 25 and 100 cm from the surface (Plate B5). These properties are described as **vertic** and are thought to result from the swelling and contracting of the clay as it wets and dries. Slickensides are the polished and striated ped faces, formed as the soil structures moved against each other; the term is borrowed from glacial geomorphology (Plates A22 and A23). The expansion–contraction of vertisols can be measured by the ratio of the difference between the moist length and the dry length of a clod to its dry length, $(L_m - L_d)/L_d$. This ratio is called the coefficient of linear extensibility (COLE).

When dry, these clay-rich soils have the property of shrinking and cracking widely, so that material from the topsoil can fall down the cracks. When the soil is rewetted and expands, there is too much bulk lower in the profile and so the soil heaves upwards to give a characteristic surface micro-relief, called 'gilgai' by Australian aboriginal people. Erosion of the mounds into adjacent hollows over

time results in the whole soil gradually inverting itself (Fig. 6.7). Smectite (montmorillonite) clays, which are capable of considerable expansion and contraction as they wet and dry, were originally thought to be responsible for the vertic properties. However, not all Vertisols have been found to be rich in this clay mineral: kaolinite, halloysite, mica, hydroxy interlayer vermiculites, chlorite and other mixed layer lattice minerals are also involved. Originally associated with a base-rich environment in strongly seasonal climatic conditions, acid vertisols are now known to occur, especially in former estuarine conditions where sulphidic materials have accumulated.

The smectite-rich Vertisols are an example of the formation of clay minerals in the soil. In a strongly alternating climatic regime, weathering products are washed from upland areas downslope into valleys or plains, but are not flushed completely out of the landscape. When the pH is above neutrality, and calcium, magnesium and silica are available in the soil solution, crystallization of smectite can occur as the soil dries.

Despite the pedoturbation, Vertisols are not as homogenized and uniform in their profile characteristics as was originally thought, so it has been necessary to adopt a more comprehensive concept and definition for these soils. The chief characteristic is the presence of slickensides and shearing

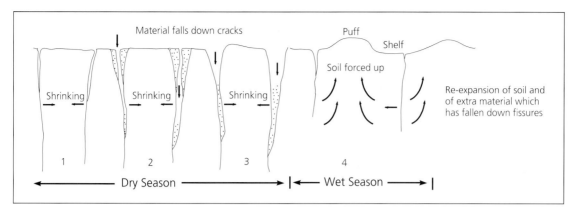

Fig. 6.7 Gilgai features in Vertisols. Shrinkage during the dry season allows material to fall down the cracks. Expansion when wetted forces the soil into a ridge (puff) whilst the area around the crack remains at a lower level (shelf).

within the subsoil. Cracking, gilgai micro-relief and high clay content are commonly associated with Vertisols, but these features are not exclusive to them. Recent views tend to associate the shrink–swell phenomenon with inter- and intra-particle pore volume changes rather than with particle repulsion by the diffuse double layer as drying and rehydration of clay layers occurs, as has been invoked in the past.

During the dry season, some Vertisols have a granular structure and hard consistency, but in the wet season they are very sticky, plastic and become impassable to traffic. Other Vertisols have a massive surface horizon in which it is very difficult to prepare a seed bed. As a result of the cracking the initial hydraulic conductivity is high, but as the soil becomes wet (upwards from the bottom of the deep cracks) the hydraulic conductivity is reduced to extremely low rates as the clays expand. Leaching cannot be strongly developed in these slowly permeable clays, which often have a low base saturation. In some cases this probably results from the original composition of the clay.

Classification of Vertisols in the FAO–Unesco *Soil Map of the World* legend was originally based on colour: black ones (Pellic Vertisols) with chromas of less than 2, and those with stronger colours (Chromic Vertisols). In the revised FAO–Unesco *Soil Map of the World* legend, it has been found necessary to recognize other Soil Units in

the Vertisols (Fig. 6.8). These are: **Gypsic Vertisols**, which have a gypsic horizon; **Calcic Vertisols**, which have a calcic horizon; **Dystric Vertisols**, which have a base saturation of less than 50 per cent; and **Eutric Vertisols**, which have a base saturation of more than 50 per cent. Recent proposals have made a case for adding Thionic, Salic, Sodic and Chromic units to the Vertisols.

Vertisols normally occupy the lower parts of the landscape, often on extensive, level alluvial plains as in Sudan, or on gently sloping piedmont or plateau sites where parent materials of high base status occur at the surface, as in southeastern Ghana. Dystric Vertisols can be seen on the inland sides of tropical swamps on the island of Trinidad, but in arid climates Vertisols may be associated with

Fig. 6.8 Classification of Vertisols.

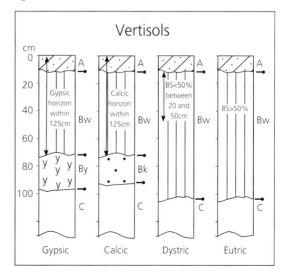

Profile of a Calcic Vertisol (Udic Chromustert) from near Nagpur, Maharashtra State, India

ISRIC Profile IN 12
(Parent material: basalt)
Diagnostic criteria: ochric A horizon; cambic B horizon; calcic horizon; vertic properties.

Ah	0–32 cm	Very dark greyish-brown (10YR 3/2) silty clay with coarse angular blocky structure; sticky, plastic; very firm; moderately porous; many fine roots; non-calcareous
Bk₁	32–48 cm	Very dark greyish-brown (10YR 3/2) clay with moderate medium angular blocky structure; sticky, plastic; very firm; continuous slickensides on structure faces; slightly porous; many fine roots; frequent medium hard irregular calcareous concretions; strongly calcareous
Bk₂	48–60 cm	Very dark greyish-brown (10YR 3/2) clay with moderate medium subangular blocky structure; sticky, plastic; firm; continuous slickensides on structure faces; slightly porous; many fine roots; frequent irregular hard calcareous concretions; strongly calcareous; wavy boundary
BCk	60–135 cm	Dark brown (10YR 3/3) clay loam with massive to weak coarse subangular blocky structure; sticky, plastic, firm, hard; continuous slickensides; slightly porous; few fine roots; frequent irregular hard calcareous concretions; few strongly weathered basalt fragments; strongly calcareous

Selected analyses

Horizon	Ah	Bk1	Bk2	BCk
Depth (cm)	0–32	32–48	48–60	60–135
Clay (%)	50	34	27	29
pH H₂O (1:2.5)	7.8	8.0	8.2	8.1
Org. C (%)	—	—	—	—
CEC	64	61	54	54
Base sat. (%)	sat.	sat.	sat.	sat.

Comment: very dark greyish-brown clayey soil with deep wide cracks during the dry season. Gilgai surface features and slickensides are present, and an accumulation of calcium carbonates places the soil in the Calcic Vertisols.

Solonchaks and on higher ground, Gypsisols or Calcisols. In West Africa and India, black Vertisols form the lower members of a catena, with red Acrisols or Lixisols higher upslope.

Cryosols

These soils are influenced by permafrost and occur on 1800 million hectares of the northernmost parts of Eurasia, Canada and the ice-free areas of Greenland and Antarctica. This soil grouping does not occur on the FAO–Unesco *Soil Map of the World*, but later publications by FAO have indicated the limits of permafrost and a proposed revision of the legend includes a grouping for soils with permanently frozen subsoils (Plate B32).

The alternate freezing and thawing of the surface layers above an impermeable frozen subsoil of ice and mineral material causes saturation throughout the summer months, and during the winter the whole soil is frozen. The low temperatures retard decomposition of the debris from the tundra vegetation and so Cryosols have organic-rich surface layers of weakly decomposed mosses and lichens.

Below the soil surface, Cryosols are subject to cryoturbation, the churning effect produced by differential growth of ice masses within the soil. As the ice masses grow, the soil material is forced to move, resulting in involutions or swirling patterns in the subsoil (Fig. 6.9). Other characteristic features are the development of ice wedges and layers, often arranged in a polygonal pattern (Fig. 6.10). The frozen layer commonly has between 30 and 70 per cent by volume of ice, and is impermeable. Material

Fig. 6.9 The effect of a periglacial climate can be seen in features known as involutions or festoons.

Fig. 6.12 Ibyuk Hill, a pingo in the delta of the Mackenzie River, Canada.

Fig. 6.10 Frost polygons. Freeze–thaw activity pushes coarser material into a polygonal pattern.

between the frozen surface and the permanently frozen layer can become thixotropic when under pressure and saturated. It can then move downslope in the process called 'solifluction'. The downslope movement of coarser soil materials produces stripes of stones on steeply sloping land and a polygonal pattern on level or slightly sloping land (Fig. 6.11). The polygonal structures often have raised centres resulting from mud being squeezed upwards by the freezing ice masses (Plate A28). Sections through these features show complex mixing of the soil materials.

In the deltas of rivers in the tundra regions, large mounds, up to 45 m in height (average 27 m), can develop as a result of thixotropic muds being forced out to form a soil blister or 'pingo'. Two types of pingo are recognized. In a closed system pingo, such as Ibyuk Hill in the Mackenzie River delta, Canada, material from between the freezing surface layers and the permafrost is squeezed up into the mound (Fig. 6.12). The other type is referred to as an open system pingo in that hydrostatic pressure developed down a valleyside slope breaches the surface frozen layer, and material is again forced out to form a mound. In the latter case, when the ice content melts, an almost circular mound is left, the centre of

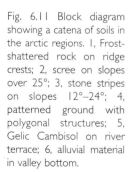

Fig. 6.11 Block diagram showing a catena of soils in the arctic regions. 1, Frost-shattered rock on ridge crests; 2, scree on slopes over 25°; 3, stone stripes on slopes 12°–24°; 4, patterned ground with polygonal structures; 5, Gelic Cambisol on river terrace; 6, alluvial material in valley bottom.

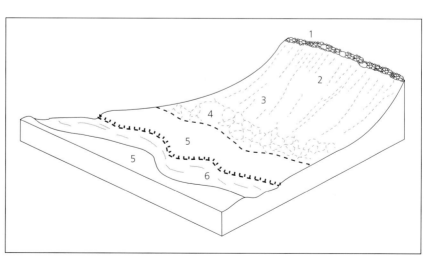

which becomes filled with peat. Fossil examples of this type occur in central Wales (Fig. 6.13).

Evidence of fossil Cryosols extends much further south than the present areas influenced by permafrost. During the Pleistocene, tundra conditions affected much of Europe north of the Alps and also much of North America. It is common to find remnants of frost action in the subsoils and parent materials of soils unaltered by the current soil-forming processes. An understanding of Cryosols is necessary to interpret the features seen in many European and North American soils, and they provide an excellent example of the effect of climate change on soil development.

Cryosols are provisionally defined as soils having permafrost within 100 cm of the soil surface and which are saturated with water during the period of thaw. They show features of cryoturbation at the surface or in the solum. No diagnostic horizons other than a histic or ochric A horizon are present.

Two Soil Units are proposed for the Cryosols: **Histic Cryosols**, which have a histic horizon; and **Thixotropic Cryosols**, which become liquid when saturated with water under pressure.

Associated with the Cryosols are Gelic Histosols, which develop in the hollows between the raised mounds of patterned ground. Gelic Cambisols may occur on freely drained sites, and Gelic Gleysols in poorly drained locations.

Fig. 6.13 A fossil pingo. The ice core has melted and the centre collapsed, leaving a circular mound filled with peat.

Further reading

Andriesse, J.P., 1988. *Nature and Management of Tropical Peat Soils*. FAO Soils Bulletin No. 59, FAO, Rome.

Driessen, P.M. and Dudal, R., 1991. *The Major Soils of the World*. Agricultural University Wageningen and Katholieke Universiteit, Leuven.

Dudal, R., 1965. *Dark Clay Soils of Tropical and Subtropical Regions*. FAO Agricultural Development Paper No. 83, FAO, Rome.

FAO, 1993. *World Soil Resources: an Explanatory Note on the FAO World Soil Resources Map at 1:25,000,000 Scale*. FAO, Rome.

Krolikowski, L., Kowalinski, S. and Trzcinski, W. (eds.), 1986. *Album Gleb Polski*. Polish Soil Science Society, Warsaw.

Misota, C. and Van Reeuwijk, L.P., 1989. *Clay Mineralogy and Chemistry of Soils formed in Volcanic Material in Diverse Climatic Regions*. Soil Monograph No. 2, ISRIC, Wageningen.

Shoji, S., Namzyo, M. and Dahlgren, R.A., 1993. *Volcanic Ash Soils: Genesis, Properties and Utilization*. Developments in Soil Science No. 21, Elsevier, Amsterdam.

Tarnocai, C., Smith, C.A.S. and Fox, C.A., 1993. *International Tour of Permafrost Affected Soils: The Yukon and Northwest Territories of Canada*. Centre for Land and Biological Resources Research, Agriculture Canada, Ottawa.

Tedrow, J.C.F., 1977. *Soils of the Polar Landscapes*. Rutgers University Press, New Brunswick.

Thompson, C.H., 1992. Genesis of Podzols on coastal dunes in southern Queensland. 1. Field relationships and profile morphology. *Australian Journal of Soil Research* **30**:593–613.

Thorp, J. and Smith, G., 1949. Higher categories of soil classification: order, suborder and great group. *Soil Science* **67**:117–26.

Wilding, L.P. and Puentes, R. (eds.), 1988. *Vertisols: their Distribution, Properties, Classification and Management*. Technical Monograph No. 18, Soil Management Support Services, Texas A&M University.

7 Soils conditioned by topographic position or limited by their age

Many soils throughout the world possess topsoil, A horizons and subsoil, B horizons, which on morphology, chemical and physical analysis appear to be only moderately changed from the original parent material. They are interpreted either as soils in which the full development of the profile has been retarded by the balance of erosion exceeding soil formation or by the influence of the topographic position in which they have developed, or simply as soils on fresh parent materials. Four Major Soil Groupings are considered in this chapter: Leptosols, Fluvisols, Gleysols and Cambisols.

The Major Soil Grouping of **Leptosols** was created by bringing together all the shallow soils which have an A horizon lying directly upon the parent rock material. It is an amalgamation of the soils described in the 1974 legend and represented on the *Soil Map of the World* as Lithosols, Rendzinas and Rankers. **Fluvisols** are developed on alluvial materials and in some cases, where empoldering and drainage have occurred, may have had time for the development of a B horizon. Soils developed in saturated conditions are referred to as **Gleysols**. In the **Cambisols** an A horizon enriched with organic matter, which usually qualifies as an ochric or umbric A horizon, has developed. The B horizon has been changed slightly by soil-forming processes, but it has not received any illuvial additions, therefore it is a cambic B horizon. These soils are frequently interpreted as relatively young soils and so their profile development is limited by their age, insufficient time having elapsed since soil formation began for the profile to have acquired more mature or complex pedological features.

In earlier classifications, these soils were referred to as **intrazonal** or **azonal** as they can occur almost anywhere on the Earth's surface and are not confined to any particular climatic zone. Leptosols are associated with strong relief and youthful landscapes. Fluvisols are associated with fluvial deposition in valleys and deltaic plains. Gleysols also are often associated with landscapes of low relief, especially low-lying areas or level, plateau-like topography with a covering of fine-grained parent materials influenced by a high level of ground-water, or having horizons with restricted permeability.

Leptosols

The name Leptosols first appeared in the 1988 revision of the FAO–Unesco *Soil Map of the World* legend. The soils which now bear this name were previously known as Lithosols, Rankers (in part) and Rendzinas. Therefore, to trace the origin of the Leptosols, it will be necessary to look briefly into the background of these former soil units to appreciate their position in the current classification.

Although Leptosols are shallow, they have a great extent and are of significance in the soil mantle as they are, in many cases, young or weakly developed soils of the other Major Soil Groupings. So the maximum development of these soils will often be the minimum criteria necessary for acceptance into one of the other Major Soil Groupings.

Leptosols are one of the most widespread Major Soil Groupings, covering an area of approximately 1655 million hectares. These soils occur in all parts of the world, from the tropics to the cold polar tundra and from sea level to the tops of the highest mountains. Lithic Leptosols, in which hard rock occurs at shallow depth, are the largest subgroup, forming the most extensive soils in mountainous regions, and covering 545 million hectares (Plate B4). Their greatest concentration is in the mountains of east and central Asia and South America. Leptosols of the deserts occupy 420 million hectares, mainly in Africa, Asia and Australia, and 345 million hectares of tundra regions such as the Ungava peninsula of northern Canada and the Alaskan mountains.

Thorp and Smith (1949) were the first to use the word Lithosol to denote an azonal group of soils having an incomplete solum or no clearly expressed soil morphology, and consisting of a freshly or incompletely weathered mass of hard rock or hard rock fragments. The term 'Lithosol' originates from the Greek word *lithos* (stone), and implies soils with hard rock at shallow depth. It has been used in many soil classification systems, including those of the USA and France, and the 1974 legend of the FAO–Unesco *Soil Map of the World*. The adjective 'lithic' persists in numerous other soil classifications, including the FAO–Unesco *Soil Map of the World* legend and USDA *Soil Taxonomy*, but only in an adjectival form, not as a group name. On the FAO–Unesco *Soil Map of the World*, the term Lithosol is defined as a very shallow soil that has continuous hard rock within a depth of 10 cm, which is sufficiently coherent and hard when moist to make hand digging impracticable.

Rankers are defined as soils that have a dark-coloured surface horizon, are rich in organic matter with a low base status, and directly overlie unconsolidated siliceous material exclusive of alluvial deposits, or hard rock. The word 'Ranker' stems from an Austrian word meaning steep slope; it is indicative of soils developed from siliceous parent materials. The name was used by Kubiena (1953) in *The Soils of Europe*, and it has also been adopted by several national soil survey organizations. In the 1974 legend of the FAO–Unesco *Soil Map of the World*, the Ranker is broadly defined; it is not necessarily a shallow soil but it may not have hydromorphic properties within 50 cm. The term has been given more restricted meanings in various European classifications, for example in the French classification and the German classification (Muckenhausen, 1977).

As first used by Sibirtzev in 1901, the name Rendzina was originally assigned to intrazonal soils on calcareous rocks (Plate B3). The word 'Rendzina' originates from a Polish word, suggesting the noise a plough makes as it passes over shallow, stony ground. The name was publicized by Kubiena (1953) in *The Soils of Europe*, and the idea of a shallow soil on limestone has been used in many soil classification systems. On the FAO–Unesco *Soil Map of the World*, Rendzinas are defined as soils that have a dark-coloured surface horizon, are rich in organic matter with a high base status, and directly overlie a highly (>40 per cent) calcareous rock or sediment.

Essentially, all Leptosols are shallow or very stony soils overlying rock or partially altered rock or strongly calcareous material within 30 cm. Full descriptions and analyses of Leptosols are uncommon as the majority of representative profiles described in soil surveys are chosen from deeper soils which may be utilized for agriculture or forestry. The shallower soils, often under scrub or rough grazing and interspersed with rock outcrops, are not considered as important and so descriptions are not made nor samples taken of them. However, from the point of view of genesis, the Leptosols are a significant group of soils as they can demonstrate the initial phases in the process of soil development. They are important in terms of classification for they include those soils which have insufficiently developed subsoil characters to qualify as diagnostic horizons, and only their A horizons can be used in classification.

Leptosols are defined either as soils which are limited in depth by continuous hard rock within 30 cm of the surface or by highly calcareous materials within the same depth, or as very stony soils which have within the first 75 cm less than 10 per cent fine earth by weight, and no diagnostic horizons other than a mollic, umbric, ochric or vertic horizon (Fig. 7.1).

At the Soil Unit level of classification, and in order of identification in the key, Leptosols which have continuous hard rock at 10 cm are **Lithic Leptosols**. Leptosols with permafrost within 200 cm of the surface are **Gelic Leptosols**. Leptosols with a mollic horizon which contains free carbonates or which overlies a calcareous material with a calcium carbonate equivalent of more than 40 per cent are **Rendzic Leptosols**. In recent redefinitions, rendziniform soils developed over continuous cemented layers (calcretes) are now specifically excluded from this group as the calcareous pan is an integral part of a deeper soil profile development (i.e. Calcisols).

Leptosols with a surface horizon which qualifies as a mollic A horizon are **Mollic Leptosols**; similar soils with a base saturation of less than 50 per

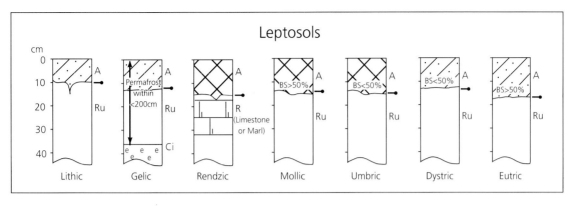

Fig. 7.1 Classification of Leptosols.

cent are **Umbric Leptosols**. Those Leptosols which fail to meet the colour criteria for mollic or umbric horizons and have a base saturation of less than 50 per cent are **Dystric Leptosols**. The parent material for these soils will commonly be sandstones and shales in exposed situations, such as on the crest of escarpments and steep slopes in humid environments. Where the balance of soil formation is exceeded by leaching and erosional losses, these

soils may even form over calcareous-rich rocks. Any remaining Leptosols are placed in the final unit, **Eutric Leptosols**.

Fluvisols

The concept of a group of soils developed from alluvial sediments has been a consistent feature of soil classification throughout the 20th century, and many systems of soil classification have had a category of alluvial soils. Their presence as a discrete physiographic grouping can be observed in all continents and in all climatic regimes. These soils are widely distributed, particularly along major river valleys and in deltas. Fluvisols are usually of high fertility and with water supplies available; they are one of the most important soil groups used for the growth of food crops. Altogether, it is estimated by FAO that there are 355 million hectares of alluvial soils, slightly less than 3 per cent of the world land area, of which the greater part (297 hectares) occurs in the developing countries of the world.

By definition, Fluvisols occur on materials deposited in sedimentary environments, specifically the inland fresh-water fluvial and lacustrine conditions, the truly marine environment and the coastal brackish-water environment. In all three cases, deposition has been controlled by fluvial processes which have normally sorted the material into distinct particle sizes and, more often than not, laid it down in distinct sedimentary layers. Young alluvial soils retain this stratification in the subsoil, but on older terraces it is gradually disrupted by soil-forming processes, and many soils on terraces come to resemble major soil groups on adjacent interfluvial areas.

Profile of a Rendzic Leptosol (Rendoll) from Kije, Poland (after Krolikowski et al., 1986)

(Parent material: Cretaceous siliceous marl)

A₁	0–30cm	Dark grey humus horizon, containing rock fragments, firm with coarse structure
A/C	30–60cm	Transition zone, light grey, stony with high content of parent rock fragments
C	60+cm	Siliceous marl

Selected analyses

Horizon	A	AC	C
Depth (cm)	0-20	20-30	30+
Clay (%)	29	31	–
pH H₂O (1:2.5)	7.6	8.0	8.0
Org. C (%)	1.77	1.26	–
CaCO₃ (%)	13.2	55.3	66
CEC	17.7	15.2	10.6
Base sat. (%)	sat.	sat.	sat.

Comment: as the name Rendzina comes from Poland, it is perhaps appropriate that an example is chosen from that country. The profile is developed on a hard, siliceous calcareous marl with a CaCO₃ content of about 66 per cent.

The many different landforms associated with river floodplains provide an immediate key to the nature of the materials in which Fluvisols develop. Some alluvial soils of the backswamp areas of floodplains are poorly drained or even peaty, but others, on levées or terraces, are imperfectly or freely drained. Most soils of alluvial areas have been subject to intense human activity throughout historical time and so many Fluvisols are considerably altered from their natural state through embankment, mixing, irrigation, warping and paddy-field construction. These situations will be dealt with in the section on Anthrosols (Chapter 8).

Soil scientists distinguish Fluvisols by the presence of **fluvic properties** in the soil profile (Plate A19). Fluvic properties refer to fluvial, lacustrine or marine sediments which receive fresh additions of material at regular intervals, are stratified, and have an irregular content of organic carbon with depth (Plate B6). Normally, the stratification can be seen, but in fine-grained sediments which have accumulated very slowly, the layering is not clear and so it is necessary to use the variation in organic carbon content to identify the fluvial properties. Problems of classification have arisen where Fluvisols have been embanked to stop flooding. Subsequent cultivation destroys the stratification, and development of a B horizon brings them into a more developed

soil group. Thus, for positive identification the layering must be within 25 cm of the soil surface. Fluvisols may have an ochric, mollic, histic or umbric A horizon, but there are no diagnostic horizons in the subsoil other than perhaps a sulphuric horizon or sulphidic materials. The presence of the pale yellow potassium iron sulphate mineral jarosite is indicative of a sulphuric horizon. While sulphidic materials remain in reduced conditions jarosite cannot be formed.

Once a soil has been identified as a Fluvisol, it is then possible to allocate it to one of seven Soil Units (Fig. 7.2). Those soils with a sulphidic horizon or sulphidic materials are separated as **Thionic Fluvisols.** Those with a mollic or umbric A horizon can be allocated to **Mollic** or **Umbric Fluvisols,** respectively, and those which are calcareous are **Calcaric Fluvisols.** Where the base saturation is less than 50 per cent and the soil does not qualify as an Umbric Fluvisol it reverts to a **Dystric Fluvisol,** and if it has salic properties it is a **Salic Fluvisol;** otherwise it is a **Eutric Fluvisol.**

Gleysols

Poor drainage can be observed in some soils in most regions of the world, and as such represents one of the most extensive and common soil conditions. According to FAO, Gleysols occupy 720 million hectares, of which about one-third are in

Fig. 7.2 Classification of Fluvisols.

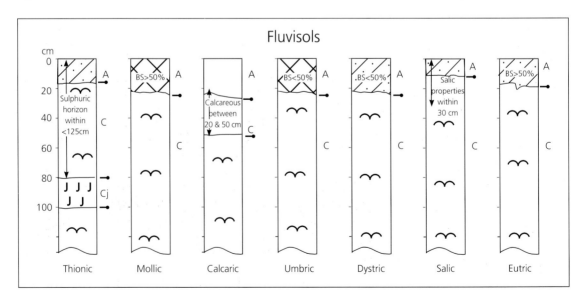

Profile of a Thionic Fluvisol (Typic Sulfaquent) from Guangzhou Province, China

ISRIC Profile CN 33
(Parent material: alluvium)
Diagnostic criteria: stratified clayey alluvium; irregular organic carbon profile; gleyic properties and sulphidic materials.

Ap	0–10 cm	Dark yellowish-brown clay with weak coarse prismatic structure breaking to subangular blocky; very sticky, very plastic; firm; common distinct mottles; common pores; common fine roots; earthworm channels; clear smooth boundary
Ag₁	10–25 cm	Dark brown (10YR 4/3) clay with very weak coarse prismatic structure breaking to weak coarse angular blocky; very sticky, very plastic; very firm; many fine distinct mottles; few pores; common very fine roots; few earthworm channels; gradual smooth boundary
Ag₂	25–45 cm	Dark brown (10YR 4/3) clay with very coarse prismatic structure breaking to coarse angular blocky; very sticky, very plastic; very firm; many distinct strong brown mottles; few pores; few very fine roots; few worm channels; clear wavy boundary
Cg₁	45–68 cm	Greyish-brown (2.5Y 5/2) clay loam with very weak prismatic structure breaking to coarse angular blocky; very sticky, very plastic; firm; many prominent strong brown mottles; few pores; few very fine roots; abrupt smooth boundary
Cg₂	68–110 cm	Light olive-brown (2.5Y 4/1) sandy loam, structureless; slightly sticky, slightly plastic; few fine prominent mottles; few pores; few very fine roots.

By auger: continuing to 200 cm as light olive-brown sandy loam.

Selected analyses

Horizon	Ap	Ag	Cg1	Cg2
Depth (cm)	0–10	10–45	45–68	68–110
Clay (%)	37	20	25	11
pH H_2O (1:2.5)	5.6	6.5	3.1	4.8
Org. C (%)	2.7	1.7	2.2	1.4
CEC	17.9	17.9	12.6	8.9

Comment: layered nature of the parent material is not very clear but irregular organic carbon confirms alluvial origin. Mottling and strongly acidic sulphidic material between 45 and 68 cm place this profile as a Thionic Fluvisol. This soil is also known as an acid sulphate soil.

the tropics and about half lie in the tundra regions of northern Eurasia and North America. They are seen as the lowest members of catenary sequences, often occupying the lower slopes where water is received from upslope. They also occur on plateau sites where drainage vertically through the soil profile is slow.

Gleysols, or Hydromorphic Soils, are unlike freely drained soils as they are permanently or periodically saturated with water, and it is in these conditions that the process of gleying operates. Gleysols can be found in association with almost all other soils, in places where water can gather in the soil in sufficient volume and for sufficient time to produce the morphological effects of gleying.

The process of gleying is concerned with the alternate reduction and oxidation of soil material, which is evident from the state of iron and manganese compounds and their distribution in the soil profile. Grey colours (reductomorphic features) are common on structure faces and linings of pores where iron compounds have been reduced and/or removed. Such conditions occur in soils which are permanently saturated. When water saturates a soil, filling all pore spaces and driving out the air, oxygen in the water is soon consumed by the microbial population and the soil becomes anaerobic. In the absence of oxygen, iron and manganese compounds become chemically reduced from the trivalent ferric and manganic forms to the divalent ferrous and manganous state. In the divalent state, both are more soluble, and in association with organic molecules they can pass into solution. Removal of iron, in particular, gives Gleysols their characteristic grey–blue coloration under continuously reducing conditions (Plate B9). Intermittent saturation causes the mottling associated with alternate oxidation and reduction.

Where reducing conditions alternate with oxidizing conditions, soil materials have brighter colours associated with the presence of iron minerals (oximorphic features): reddish-brown is associated with ferrihydrite, yellowish–brown with goethite and lepidocrocite, and a conspicuous pale yellow with the mineral jarosite, occasionally present as a weathering product of pyrite and potassium silicates (Plate B8). Movement of the solubilized compounds in reducing conditions is balanced by redeposition in oxidizing conditions to form mottles and concretions in the lower horizons, and sheaths of iron oxides on grass roots in the A horizon.

Gley soils can be subdivided into those soils which have **gleyic properties** (Plate A17) caused by a periodic high ground-water level, and those which have **stagnic properties** (Plate A18) resulting from temporary periods of saturation caused by slow permeability in the soil. Generally, this division distinguishes permeable soils, with a permanent water table within the profile, from those which have a slowly permeable horizon upon which water collects as it passes down the profile. Pedologists in Germany and France have referred to the former as Gley Soils and the latter as Pseudogley Soils, whereas in the UK these have been called Ground-water Gley and Surface-water Gley Soils, respectively.

Surface-water Gley Soils, also called Stagnogley Soils, develop the grey colours caused by gleying above an impervious or very slowly permeable subsoil horizon (Fig. 7.3). In well-developed examples, an albic Eg horizon is produced, overlying a mottled Btg horizon with well-developed stagnic properties. If a pit is dug in such soils, water can be seen to seep from the sides of the pit. The slowly permeable horizon often has an increased clay content and other characteristics which qualify it as a gleyed argic horizon. These include marked grey colours on structure faces, but the inner parts of the peds have sufficient oxygen to remain aerobic and so bright orange colours dominate. Soils with stagnic properties may occur in Plinthosols, Solonetz, Phaeozems, Alisols, Luvisols and Lixisols, but they are an essential feature of Planosols. Thus, by definition, soils with stagnic properties are excluded from the Gleysols, but are clearly related to them by the process of soil formation which is operating.

Ground-water Gley Soils are those influenced by a water table within the profile of the soil (Fig. 7.4). The lower parts of the profile are permanently wet, but the upper parts are subject to aeration as the level of the water table rises and falls according to the balance of rainfall and evapotranspiration. Usually these soils form from rather permeable parent materials, such as alluvial sands and gravels, which in turn overlie an impermeable substratum upon which the water rests. Therefore, these Ground-water Gley Soils occupy the lowest parts of the landscape and are often transitional to Histosols. If a profile pit is dug in these soils, water

Fig. 7.3 Diagrammatic profile of a Surface-water Gley Soil.

Fig. 7.4 Diagrammatic profile of a Ground-water Gley Soil.

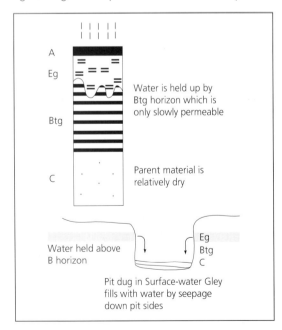

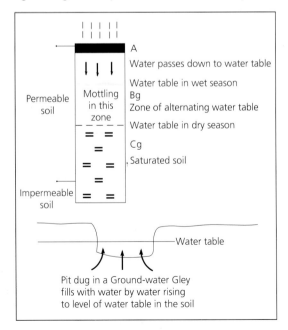

wells up through the floor of the excavation, and it is therefore wise to describe and sample the lower horizons first!

Having ascertained that a soil is not coarse-textured and has the appropriate gleyic properties within 100 cm of the surface, that it does not have any diagnostic horizons other than an A horizon, histic H horizon, cambic B horizon, a calcic or a gypsic horizon, and that it lacks plinthite, the soil is a Gleysol. Gleyic properties may also occur at depth in Major Soil Groupings other than Gleysols. In this case they are classified as a gleyic soil unit (e.g. Gleyic Luvisol).

Subsequent classification to Soil Unit level, in strict order of precedence of the key (Fig. 7.5), is first to identify soils with permafrost within 200 cm of the surface: these are **Gelic Gleysols**. Soils with a sulphuric horizon or sulphuric materials at less than 125 cm from the surface are **Thionic Gleysols**. Where soils have andic properties as well as gleyic properties they are **Andic Gleysols**. Soils with organic-rich A horizons are **Mollic** or **Umbric Gleysols**, according to base saturation. **Calcic Gleysols** have a calcic horizon within 125 cm of the soil surface. Those soils with ochric A horizons and a base saturation of less than 50 per cent are **Dystric Gleysols**, and other soils are **Eutric Gleysols**.

Fig. 7.5 Classification of Gleysols.

Cambisols

The name Cambisols is given to moderately developed soils with A and B horizons (from Latin *cambiare*, to change). These soils cover about 925 million hectares throughout the world, and are the second largest grouping on the FAO–Unesco *Soil Map of the World*. Essentially soils of the temperate regions, Cambisols are less common in the tropics, where weathering and soil formation have been operating for much longer periods compared with the regions outside the tropics. Cambisols are common on young parent materials which resulted from Pleistocene glaciations, such as tills and outwash materials, but these soils also occur where moderate weathering and a climate with summer rains has limited the effects of eluviation, so there is an absence of any accumulation of soil constituents in the B horizon.

The soil-forming processes operating in Cambisols include leaching of carbonates, which are removed from the A and B horizons; however, some may still remain in the parent material or be present in the topsoil of arable soils as added agricultural lime. The profile is normally neutral to moderately acid, with base saturation and pH rising with depth in the profile. Most Cambisols contain weatherable minerals in the sand and silt fractions, and feldspars are being changed into clay. Normally freely drained, there is sufficient moisture for hydrolysis of these primary minerals, which release

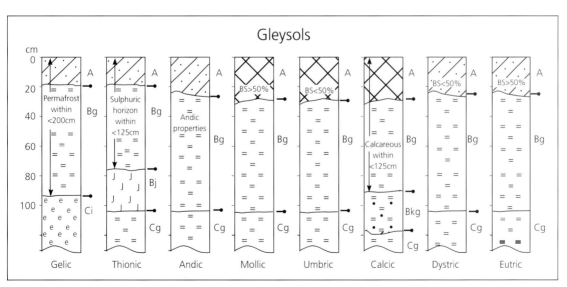

Profile description of a Eutric Gleysol (Typic Tropaquept) from Maung Sing Buri district, Thailand

ISRIC Profile TH 04
(Parent material: alluvium)
Diagnostic features: ochric A horizon; fluvic properties.

Apg	0–13 cm	Dark greyish-brown (10YR 4/2) clay with very weak coarse subangular blocky structure; sticky; plastic; slightly porous; common fine roots; non-calcareous; gradual smooth boundary
Bw	13–53 cm	Dark grey (10YR 4/1) clay with weak to moderate fine angular blocky structure; sticky; plastic; porous; many medium distinct mottles (7.5YR 4/4); pressure cutans; few very fine roots; non-calcareous; diffuse smooth boundary
BC	53–113 cm	Dark grey (10YR 4/1) clay with weak to moderate fine angular blocky structure; sticky; plastic; firm; porous; many medium distinct mottles (10YR 5/6); few very fine roots; non-calcareous; abrupt smooth boundary
2C	113–123 cm	Grey (10YR 5/1) sandy clay with moderate fine subangular blocky structure; slightly sticky; slightly plastic; porous; many coarse distinct mottles (9YR 5/8); few very fine roots; frequent mica fragments; non-calcareous

Selected analyses

Horizon	Apg	Bw/BC	2C
Depth (cm)	0–15	15–115	115–125
Clay (%)	73	70	31
pH H$_2$O (1:2.5)	5.0	6.2	6.6
Org. C (%)	1.46	0.56	0.21
CEC	30.2	27.2	12.9
Base sat. (%)	65	90	95

Comment: a poorly drained clayey soil used for rice cultivation. It has a base saturation of over 50 per cent so qualifies as a Eutric Gleysol.

---

iron in the ferrous state. This iron is then oxidized to ferric oxides and hydroxides. In this state it coats most of the sand and silt particles, giving the soil a warm brown colour. This is particularly obvious in the B horizon, but in the A horizon it is masked by organic matter accumulation. The composition of the clay fraction, as shown by the silica:sesquioxide ratio, should be uniform throughout the profile. Except for Gleyic Cambisols, the Cambisol profile is freely drained and the organic horizons on the soil surface are often of the mull type, although they may range from calcareous mull to moder or even mor in soils transitional to the Gleysols and Podzols. The nature of the parent material also has a strong influence on the type of humus developed.

Cambisols are identified by the presence of a **cambic B horizon** (Plate A7). In the past, there has been a tendency for the cambic B horizon to be negatively defined, that is it included those characteristics which were left after all the other diagnostic soil characters had been used to allocate soils within the classification. It may be noted that the Cambisols are the last Major Soil Grouping in the key for the FAO–Unesco *Soil Map of the World*. Recently, there has been a more positive attitude to the definition of the cambic B horizon, although its definition still retains exclusions for the argic B, spodic B and natric B diagnostic horizons. In the field, a cambic horizon must have a texture which is sandy loam or finer (which separates them from Arenosols) and it must be at least 15 cm thick and have its base at least 25 cm below the surface of the soil. The progress of soil formation is such that soil structure is present in at least half the horizon (i.e. rock structure is subordinate or absent) and the horizon must show a stronger chroma or redder hue than the underlying horizon, or there must be evidence of removal of carbonates. An absence of cementation and the brittle consistency of a fragipan is required (Plate B31).

In the key for classification, Cambisols are the soils which remain when all those profiles with clear diagnostic characteristics have been allocated to their correct position in the classification system. Thus the Cambisols include many soils which do not quite qualify for inclusion in other Major Soil Groupings. However, this point of view does not give a true picture of this important major group of soils and a preferred definition of Cambisols is soils having an ochric or umbric A horizon overlying a cambic B horizon. If a mollic A horizon is present, it has a B horizon with a base saturation of less than 50 per cent in some part within 125 cm of the surface. The cambic B horizon is recognized by changes in colour and structure of the horizon which lies between the topsoil and the relatively unaltered parent material. There is little or no evidence for the accumulation of illuvial clay, iron, aluminium or humic material and this debars these soils from the Luvisols or Podzols (see Chapter 9). The Cambisols are excluded from Ferralsols by the requirement that they should have a medium to high CEC (i.e. $>16\,cmol_c\,kg^{-1}$).

Because Cambisols are soils with only moderate development of pedological characteristics, and as they occur in different climatic regions throughout the world, there are many Soil Units in the Cambisols which may represent youthful versions of profiles, insufficiently mature for inclusion in other Major Soil Groupings (Fig. 7.6). Cambisols with permafrost within 200 cm of the soil surface are **Gelic Cambisols**; these may be found in sub-

arctic regions. Imperfectly drained Cambisols, transitional to Gleysols, where gleyic properties occur within 100 cm of the soil surface are classified as **Gleyic Cambisols**. If the soil possesses vertic properties it is a **Vertic Cambisol**, and if there is an umbric A horizon the soil unit is a **Humic Cambisol**. Where Cambisols retain calcium carbonate in the B horizon, **Calcaric Cambisols** are recognized. Although rarer in the tropical regions, Cambisols with ferralic properties and those with bright-coloured B horizons are transitional to Ferralsols and are recognized as **Ferralic** and **Chromic Cambisols**, respectively. In humid temperate environments **Eutric** and **Dystric Cambisols** develop, dependent upon the base status of the cambic B horizon.

Cambisols are used intensively for a wide range

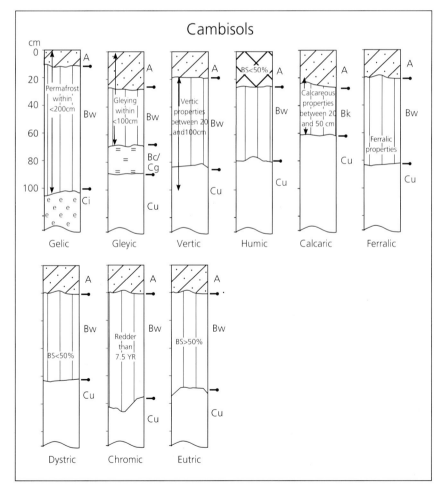

Fig. 7.6 Classification of Cambisols.

of activities. They often occur on flat and gently undulating topography where they are cultivated widely, and Cambisols are among the world's most productive soils. On more steeply sloping land, Cambisols are used for forestry or grazing. Many Gleyic Cambisols have been converted into paddy soils; elsewhere in the tropics, Cambisols provide soils which are more fertile than Nitisols, Acrisols, Alisols and Ferralsols.

Profile of a Dystric Cambisol (Dystrochrept) from West Glamorgan, Wales

Profile SK 19/6010 Soil Survey of England and Wales (Parent material: Coal Measures sandstone)
Diagnostic criteria: ochric A horizon; cambic B horizon.

O	0–3 cm	Black (10YR 2/1) stoneless thin organic layer; weakly developed subangular blocky structure; friable; common woody roots; clear smooth boundary
Bw_1	3–23 cm	Dark yellowish-brown (10YR 4/4) slightly stony clay loam; fragments of tabular sandstone; moderate fine subangular blocky structure; friable; common fine woody roots; clear smooth boundary
Bw_2	23–46 cm	Dark yellowish-brown (10YR 4/6) moderately stony clay loam with weakly developed fine subangular blocky structure; common fine woody roots; clear smooth boundary
BC	46–80 cm	Olive brown (2.5YR 4/4) very stony sandy loam with large tabular sandstone fragments; common fine fibrous roots; non-calcareous
R	80+ cm	Soliflucted sandstone rubble

Selected analyses

| Horizon | O | Bw1 | Bw2 | BC |
Depth (cm)	0–3	3–23	23–46	46–80
Clay (%)	–	29	26	16
Org. C (%)	24	3.5	1.7	1.0
pH H_2O (1:2.5)	3.9	3.9	4.2	4.2

Comment: profile is acid throughout, structure and colour indicate a cambic B horizon below an ochric A horizon. Although CEC is not given, presence of O horizon and acidity indicate a Dystric Cambisol.

Further reading

Bridges, E.M. and Creutzberg, D., 1994. Leptosols and Fluvisols. Commission V Symposia, *Transactions of the 15th World Congress of Soil Science*, Volume 6a:868-872, Acapulco, Mexico.

Driessen, P.M. and Dudal, R., 1991. *The Major Soils of the World.* Agricultural University Wageningen and Katholieke Universiteit, Leuven.

FAO, 1993. *World Soil Resources: an Explanatory Note on the FAO World Soil Resources Map at 1:25,000,000 Scale.* FAO, Rome.

Krolikowski, L., Kowalinski, S. and Trzcinski, W. (eds.), 1986. *Album Gleb Polski.* Polish Soil Science Society, Warsaw.

Kubiena, W.L., 1953. *The Soils of Europe.* Murby, London.

Muckenhausen, E., 1977. *Entstehung, Eigenschaften und Systematik der Boden der Bundesrepublik Deutschland.* 2nd edition, DLG-Verlag, Frankfurt am Main.

Rudeforth, C.C., Hartnup, R., Lea, J.W., Thompson, T.R.E. and Wright, P.S., 1984. *Soils and Their Use in Wales.* Bulletin No. 11, Soil Survey of England and Wales, Harpenden.

Spaargaren, O.C. (ed.), 1994. *World Reference Base for Soil Resources.* ISSS, ISRIC, FAO, Wageningen/Rome.

Thorp, J. and Smith, G., 1949. Higher categories of soil classification: order, suborder and great group. *Soil Science* **67**:117–26.

8 Soils strongly influenced by human activity

Early soil classifications, based on natural soils, virtually ignored the influence of human beings on soil formation; Jenny, in *Factors of Soil Formation* (1941), included human beings as just one of the many organisms which influenced soil formation. Within the past 15 years it has become obvious that the influence of human beings upon soils has increased tremendously, sometimes for good, but often, regrettably, with disastrous results. Recent studies have drawn attention to the significance of human activities which impinge upon the soil in so many different ways. A major problem faced by soil scientists is to convince policy-makers, other scientists and the general public that soil is an important natural resource which must be used carefully now in order to conserve it for the use of succeeding generations. History teaches the lesson that neglect of their soils has eventually resulted in the downfall of several civilizations.

Level terrain with deep, well-drained soils is a highly valuable resource which is in great demand for all types of land-use. As well as being suitable for growing crops, such areas are sought after for high-return economic activities as well as for housing and recreational purposes. Urbanization throughout the world has resulted in the loss of many thousands of hectares of the most agriculturally productive land, as cities expand, motorways and airports are constructed, and new 'out of town' commercial and industrial enterprise zones are created from 'greenfield' sites.

The loss of soil through urbanization is of concern in many European countries; a recent report to the European Assembly stated that 120 hectares are being lost daily in Germany through expansion of urban areas. In Austria the daily loss is 35 hectares, and in Switzerland, a country with a small reserve of flat land, it is 10 hectares per day. Although these examples are drawn from Europe, the loss of land and soils to urbanization is occur-

ring worldwide. Except for a few outstanding examples, most governments have yet to show much interest in protecting soils from losses, or in diverting urbanization onto soils with low agricultural potential.

Soils in which human activities have resulted in a profound modification of the profile are classified as **Anthrosols**. These soils have been estimated by FAO to occupy about 0.5 million hectares in Europe alone, with areas present in all continents, but their scattered nature does not enable them to be shown on a small-scale map. The definition of Anthrosols does not include the many millions of hectares of soils modified by the normal agricultural practices of human beings. The Anthrosols were not recognized as a separate major soil unit in the 1974 legend of the FAO–Unesco *Soil Map of the World*, but in the revision of 1988 they emerged as a Major Soil Grouping.

Although human activities are concentrated mainly in cultivating the surface horizons or topsoil, heavy equipment developed during the 1950s has enabled some soils and soil materials to be completely mixed so that the processes of soil formation have to begin again, effectively with a new parent material. In some instances, natural soils have had their surface horizons greatly thickened by human activity, and industrial activities have led to soil contamination and the accumulation of waste materials, some of which also form new soil parent materials.

Anthrosols are defined as soils in which human activities have resulted in profound modification or burial of the original soil horizons through removal or disturbance of surface horizons, cuts and fills, secular additions of organic and mineral materials, long-continued irrigation, etc. The impact of human actions upon soils has been referred to as 'metapedogenesis' and the results may be considered to be both beneficial and deleterious.

Beneficial activities include deep cultivation, intensive fertilizer applications, sedimentary additions during irrigation, drainage, checking soil erosion, additions of organic materials, and creation of poor drainage for wet cultivation of rice. Although these activities have modified soils drastically, in general they have enhanced soil productivity and not caused soil degradation.

Deleterious practices include the removal of plant nutrients in crops without replacing them, addition of toxic materials, acceleration of erosion, the burning of organic layers, reduction of organic matter content, destruction of soil structure, compaction by farm machinery, and acidification. These activities have had the effect of lowering soil fertility and, in the worst cases, complete loss of the soil resource has occurred.

Classification

Considerable discussion is still taking place about the definition of Soil Units within the Anthrosols, and no consensus is currently available. The 1988 revision of the *Soil Map of the World* legend introduced the **fimic horizon** (Plate A5), a diagnostic horizon defined as *a man-made layer 50 cm or more thick, produced by long-continued manuring with earthy admixtures*. This concept included such features as the **plaggen horizons**, first recognized in northwestern Europe, and the **anthropic epipedon**, both of which were included in the *Soil Taxonomy* system of classification. Brief definitions of these are given in the following paragraphs. Currently, the only established subsurface horizon resulting from human activity is the **agric horizon** of *Soil Taxonomy*, which is the result of cultivation and the washing of suspended silt, clay and humus into the horizon immediately below the plough layer, where these materials form thick lamellae, lining pores and structure faces.

Russian pedologists have suggested a genetic classification in which several types of anthropogenic soils are recognized, including Agrozems, Irrigational Soils and Anthropogenic-accumulative Soils. In China, where there is a long history of soil use and modification, Chinese soil scientists have recognized Anthrosols at the highest level in their (1990) system of soil classification.

In the current groupings of the legend of the *Soil Map of the World*, four Soil Units are recognized (Fig. 8.1): **Aric Anthrosols** show remnants of former diagnostic horizons disturbed by deep cultivation; **Fimic Anthrosols** have a fimic horizon as defined previously; **Cumulic Anthrosols** have evidence of an accumulation of fine sediment from the long-continued practice of irrigation; and **Urbic Anthrosols** have mine waste, town refuse and other fill materials to a depth of more than 50 cm (Plate B2).

Even more significant than the soils with features relating to a long period of soil use are the soils which have been modified in paddy fields for growing rice. In 1988 FAO–Unesco introduced the idea of an **anthraquic phase** of soils, with features caused by human-induced soil waterlogging for the production of rice. However, many soils are only slightly modified by the activity of agriculturalists, and in this account these soils will be discussed first, followed by those which have been changed to an increasing extent from their natural state.

Fig. 8.1 Classification of Anthrosols.

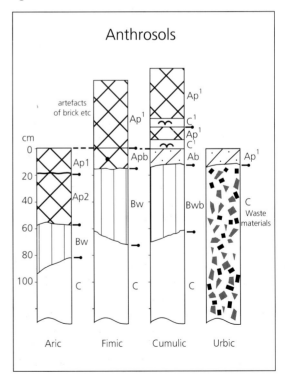

Soil modification by agriculture

In the humid temperate climate of western Europe, agriculturalists have modified soils over at least the last 2000 years by cultivation, addition of lime and dung, and by drainage. In the last 100 years, fertility has been enhanced by the addition of chemical fertilizers.

When a soil has had its natural vegetation removed and it is to be used for growing crops, it is usually cultivated to provide satisfactory germination and rooting conditions for crop plants. Cultivation mixes the surface horizons, spreading the superficial organic materials through 20 or 30 cm of what has become 'topsoil' or an Ap horizon. In freely drained soils this process encourages oxidation of the organic matter, which gradually decreases in amount as few or only limited additions of fresh organic matter are added subsequently.

Soil amendments

From the Middle Ages until the present day, addition of organic manure to the fields has been accomplished by penning animals on the cultivated fields after harvest, and placing the cleanings of stables and cowsheds on the fields in an attempt to delay the exhaustion of the soil's fertility. It is still a convenient system, as benefit is obtained from the nutrients contained in the manure, and the organic content helps to maintain the organic matter status of soils.

It has been recognized since Roman times that marl (chalky clay) spread on acid soils improves their fertility, bringing the pH value to between 6 and 7, which suits most food crops. Many fields in the eastern counties of England (Norfolk, Suffolk and Essex) contain a pit, 15 to 20 m in diameter and 10 to 15 m deep, in which calcareous marl (chalky boulder clay) was dug from below cover sands and placed on the soil surface. The lime raised the pH, and the clay helped with moisture and plant nutrient retention. This practice was widely used during the 18th century by the pioneers of the English 'Agricultural Revolution' but lapsed in the 20th century with the availability of agricultural lime.

Since the invention of superphosphate fertilizers by Sir John Lawes in 1842, and with the use of natural nitrate and potash ores, it has been possible to increase soil fertility by adding chemical nitrogen, phosphate and potash to soils rather than relying upon their natural inherent fertility. The use of artificial fertilizers has increased rapidly since the 1950s and has enabled agriculturalists both to raise the content of available plant nutrients in the soil and to greatly increase crop yields.

The general effect of these activities is to produce modified soils that have a dark-coloured topsoil which is neutral or slightly acid, and has high fertility. The profiles are freely drained and resemble the Eutric Cambisols, and the Haplic or Luvic Phaeozems. Very old, deep, long-cultivated, agricultural soils are identified by an **anthropic epipedon** (USDA) which has a citric-soluble phosphate content of more than 250 ppm P_2O_5; otherwise, these long-cultivated topsoils conform closely to the appearance of the mollic epipedon of *Soil Taxonomy* or the mollic A horizon of the FAO–Unesco system.

Drainage

With the exception of rice, roots of the common agricultural crops do not like to grow into a saturated soil. Removal of excess moisture from the soil enables plant roots to exploit a greater volume of soil in their search for nutrients. Drainage also permits easier access to the land for vehicles, so cultivations can begin earlier in the year, and a freely drained soil warms more rapidly in the spring, encouraging early growth of crops.

On poorly drained soils, from the medieval period onwards, the land surface was ploughed into a series of ridges and furrows (selions), usually with a wavelength of about 1.5 m and an amplitude of about 50 cm. Such disturbance thoroughly mixed the upper soil horizons, but it provided an insurance of good grazing on the ridge tops when there was a wet season, or in the furrows when there was a long dry season. These ridge-and-furrow patterns can still be seen in many old pastures throughout the Midlands of England.

Where arable soils are poorly drained, a system of land drains may be installed to remove excess water from the soil and to increase the depth of soil that plant roots can exploit. These may take the form of open ditches around the fields, or a system of underground tile drains may be installed at regular intervals across the field. Open drains would seriously interfere with agricultural activities, so a system of underground drains is preferred. Tubular earthenware or plastic tiles are laid end to end in the bottom of trenches below plough depth, covered with a permeable fill (gravel) which transmits the water to the drain without washing the soil in with it, and finally the topsoil is replaced. In soils where the texture is suitable, mole drains are often made at intervals between the tile drains, and at an angle to them. They are made by drawing a cylindrical plug (the mole) through the soil below plough depth but deep enough to intersect with the permeable fill and to make a network of channels along which excess water can flow out of the soil.

Drainage of organic soils has brought a large area of highly productive land into cultivation, particularly in the temperate regions of the world. Drainage of peats causes shrinkage, so the level of the land subsides, and oxidation of the organic matter eventually results in the disappearance of the peat, leaving a dark-coloured, humus-stained mineral soil.

Paddy soils

An extremely important group of soils in mid- to low latitudes contains soils modified for the production of rice in flooded conditions. Although upland or dry rice is grown, the greater part of the 125 million hectares devoted to rice cultivation is on soils which are flooded during the growing season. The term 'paddy soils' includes mainly soils on alluvial parent materials, but irrigated terraces on the hillsides are also modified for rice crops, so a wide range of soils comes into this grouping of Anthrosols.

Characteristics which develop in paddy soils are generally associated with hydromorphism and compaction resulting from cultivation. The appearance of paddy soils may change greatly during the dry season, when the soil is allowed to dry out. For classification purposes, proposals have been made for the introduction of a **hydragric horizon sequence** which consists of the puddled surface layer, a plough-pan and a subsurface illuvial layer (Fig. 8.2). The puddled layer has grey colours of

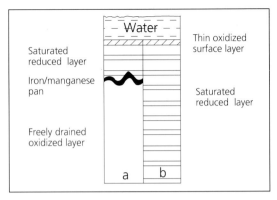

Fig. 8.2 Diagrammatic profiles of paddy soils: (a) freely drained at depth; (b) in ground-water gley conditions.

reduction with mottles of low hues, and iron and/or manganese cutans occur on ped faces and pore walls. Cultivation in wet conditions creates a massive plough-pan with a platy structure, which is compact and has a low hydraulic conductivity. Reddish-brown or brown mottling occurs along cracks and root channels. The underlying illuvial layer shows evidence of accumulation of iron and manganese. Below the illuvial horizon in alluvial soils, the profile may be saturated, with permanent reducing conditions. In contrast, on terraces and upland soils devoted to rice, the subsoil may be freely drained, with oxidizing conditions, even though the surface horizons have been chemically reduced by puddling and saturation (Fig. 8.3).

Fig. 8.3 Paddy fields in Sri Lanka.

ISRIC Profile CN 03

(Parent material: clayey alluvium)

Diagnostic criteria: ochric A horizon; argic B horizon;
stagnic properties (hydragric horizon sequence).

Ap_1	0–21 cm	Brown (10YR 4/3) clay with massive structure; slightly sticky, slightly plastic; faint mottles; common pores; common fine roots; abrupt smooth boundary
Ap_2	21–27 cm	Dark greyish-brown (10YR 4/2) clay with massive structure; sticky, plastic; common clear yellowish-brown mottles; few pores; common fine roots; abrupt smooth boundary
Bg_1	27–52 cm	Brown (10YR 4/3) clay with weak medium angular blocky structure; slightly sticky, slightly plastic; common distinct mottles; common pores; few fine roots; clear smooth boundary
Bg_2	52–65 cm	Brown (10YR 4/3) clay with medium angular blocky structure; slightly sticky, slightly plastic; few distinct mottles; patchy cutans; common pores; soft manganiferous concretions; clear smooth boundary
Bg_3	65–102 cm	Brown (10YR 5/3) clay with moderate coarse angular blocky structure; firm; many distinct mottles; patchy cutans; common pores; frequent soft and hard ferruginous and manganiferous concretions; clear wavy boundary
Cr	102–120 cm	Dark grey (10YR 4/1) clay with massive structure; slightly sticky, slightly plastic; friable; many fine and medium mottles; few pores

Selected analyses

Horizon	Ap1	Ap2	Bg1+2	Bg2
Depth (cm)	0–21	21–27	27–65	65–102
Clay (%)	26	25	26	41
pH (H_2O)	7.2	7.5	7.8	8.2
$CaCO_3$ (%)	–	2.7	2.0	3.7
Org. C (%)	1.11	0.77	0.44	0.28
CEC	16.1	15.1	14.9	18.1
Base sat. (%)	sat.	sat.	sat.	sat.

Comment: deep poorly drained soil in which submergence and puddling have produced a structureless topsoil abruptly overlying a massive plough-pan. Solution of iron and manganese has occurred with reprecipitation below the pan. A waterlogged paddy soil.

Constructed soils

In several parts of the world, soils have been thickened by soil materials gathered from the surrounding countryside. An accumulation of successive additions of earthy material has raised the surface of the soil above the level of the surrounding lands.

The classic method of raising the soil surface was to cut turves from the heath or the forest, which were used in stables and cowsheds and then spread on the arable fields; examples of this can be seen on the very poor sandy soils of northwest Europe where the **plaggen soils** occur. Some soils with plaggen horizons have been so thickened over several centuries that the surface has been raised by up to a metre. The distinctive nature of the plaggen soils resulted in the identification of a diagnostic plaggen epipedon in *Soil Taxonomy*. This is described as a man-made surface layer, 50 cm or more in thickness, which has been produced by long-continued manuring. Within the plaggen epipedon, marks of digging can be seen, fragments of brick or pottery may be found, and occasional thin layers of sand occur, assumed to be the result of the rain beating on an exposed, cultivated soil surface.

In Ireland, mixtures of seashore sand, dung and seaweed have been used to form Anthrosols up to 80 cm deep (lazy beds), and in southwest England ancient rights exist for the use of sea sand for bedding in cowsheds and for liming soils. In Israel, artificial soils have been created by placing desert sand over rocky pediments in the southern rift valley near Eilat, for the production of horticultural crops. Before the colonial period in New Zealand, the Maori people cultivated crops on a mound-and-pit system. Mound systems of cultivation are also widespread in Africa.

An interesting, locally significant area of soils around the head of the Humber estuary in England has been created by a process of 'warping'. River floodwaters containing fertile silts have been allowed to flood certain areas in a controlled manner so that the sediment is deposited and the water runs off slowly. After many flooding and sedimentation episodes, the new fluvial deposit is ready for conversion into a productive soil. Although a homogenized topsoil is produced by cultivation,

Fig. 8.4 A constructed 'warp' soil, Lincolnshire, England.

below 20–30 cm the individual layers produced by the warping process can still be seen (Fig. 8.4).

Constructed soils also occur in urban areas in what have been described as 'amenity soils'. Interest in the soils of urban areas has only arisen during the past few years, mainly through concern about the accumulation of toxic metallic elements which might pose a hazard to public health. It has been established that certain plants absorb more metallic elements than others, and that safe limits in vegetables for human consumption can be exceeded. However, human diet is very varied and in any case the plant acts as a screen: if it is exposed to excessive amounts of toxic substances, it dies and will not be available for either human or domestic animal consumption. Many constructed soils in our cities are made of fresh soil material brought in from construction sites, or even from outside the urban area, to serve as a growth medium for ornamental shrubs which enhance the appearance of the built environment. However, their situation in an urban area means that the soils are subject to continual chemical fallout and dust from vehicles containing lead and zinc, as well as from smoke and dust from industrial and domestic coal-burning fires, which also contain toxic metals.

Soil degradation

In many parts of the world, particularly in the developing countries, small farmers have insufficient capital to be able to replace plant nutrients

88

removed from the soil by their crops. The result is a chemically degraded, exhausted soil with steadily declining fertility and increasingly poor crop returns. At the same time, increasing population numbers force small farmers onto steeper land, unsuitable for cropping, where the natural vegetation once protected the soil. When cultivated, erosion on the steep slopes strips the soil. The cycle of poverty is thus reinforced, the soil is lost and the landscape devastated.

Similar problems are encountered with overgrazing. In semi-arid regions in particular, there is a great temptation for farmers to increase herd sizes in wet periods, a tendency which is encouraged by the provision of wells where previously none existed. But in a drought period the grazing is insufficient, the plants are grazed to extinction and trampling leaves the bare soil in a state where wind or water can easily erode it.

Although soil science can identify these problems and recommend ways of avoiding or overcoming them, it is quite obvious that social and economic conditions take precedence over soil conservation and the soils suffer degradation. Recognition and measurement of soil degradation is not straightforward, but the problem may be approached by considering the percentage of topsoil eroded and with it, the percentage of plant nutrients lost.

Loss of organic-rich topsoil also results in a decrease of the water-holding capacity of soils, limiting the amount available for growing crops. This loss is accompanied by a reduction in the buffering capacity – the ability of the soil to provide nutrients for the plant and to resist further chemical degradation. The solution to the problem of how to use soils in a sustainable system of agriculture, as proposed by the 1992 United Nations Conference on Environment and Development (UNCED) held in Rio de Janeiro, requires the eradication of rural poverty, and comprehensive co-operation is needed from all strata of society, from the government to the individual farmer, for success to be achieved.

Modern society has still not accepted, or fully recognized, the significance of the problem of excessive soil erosion. Whilst heavy rainstorms on freshly cultivated land cause obvious destruction,

with the development of gullies, the insidious loss of a few millimetres of topsoil each year tends to pass without remark. A recent study in the USA demonstrated that significantly lower yields of maize occurred on severely eroded soils compared with only slightly eroded ones. The reduction in yield was up to 34 per cent and was significant at the 5 per cent level. However, it is not easy to eliminate all the contributing factors in crop response, and further studies are needed to reinforce the seriousness of erosion on crop yields. A recent study of crop productivity on eroded soils in Africa suggests that yield is reduced by 2 to 5 per cent for each millimetre of soil lost, and that overall yield reduction caused by past erosion stands at 9 per cent in Africa as a whole. If erosion continues at the present rates, yield reduction by 2020 is estimated as 16.5 per cent (Fig. 8.5).

Worldwide, 1094 million hectares of soil have suffered erosion by water and a further 548 million hectares erosion by wind. All the evidence points to the continued increase of erosion on cultivated lands, although the technology to limit its impact has been available for the last 60 years, and traditional methods for much longer. The loss of 1 cm ha^{-1} of topsoil is a loss of between 100 and 150 tonnes of soil, and each 100 tonnes of soil lost per hectare represents a total loss of 2000–2500 kg of humus, 200–300 kg of nitrogen, 100–200 kg of phosphate and 500–1000 kg of potash. These nutrients have to be replaced if yields are to be maintained.

Erosion of soil from the crests and slopes of hills causes thinning of the soil profile in these areas and deepening of the profile at the foot of the slope. Movement of material downslope is a normal process and results in thicker colluvial phases of soils, but where catastrophic erosion has occurred, lower-slope soils may be completely buried under redeposited material. Downstream, the eroded material causes sedimentation in rivers, lakes and reservoirs, inflicting further costs upon society.

Peatlands alongside rivers are fertile, and have given rise to intensive agricultural and horticultural activities. These land-uses require drainage, and the subsequent oxidation of the peat results in the loss of organic matter and the lowering of the land surface.

Fig. 8.5 Example of soil erosion, New Zealand.

Salinization is a potential problem for all soils where irrigation is practised. Irrigation is required when the climate is dry and evapotranspiration greatly exceeds rainfall. However, evaporation of the water from the soil and transpiration through plants leaves the salts in the soil, and careful management is required to prevent salinization. There should be adequate soil drainage to ensure that salts can be washed out of the profile in the cool season. The world area of salinized soils is in the region of 76 million hectares, 53 million hectares of which occurs in Asia (Fig. 8.6).

Soils can also suffer physical damage by compaction caused by the use of heavy machinery when the soil contains too much moisture. Compaction results in the breakdown of soil structure, loss of porosity and moisture-holding capacity, and loss of permeability.

Soil pollution

Contaminants affecting soils may be in the form of solids, liquids or gases. Soils are composed of mineral and organic substances which vary in concentration and content both geographically and vertically down the soil profile. Therefore, it is not always easy to establish a threshold concentration of a contaminant below which a contaminated soil may be considered safe. All soils are to some extent contaminated by naturally occurring harmful or toxic elements, but not all soils are polluted. Also, pollutants react with soil materials in different ways. The most common toxic soil pollutants include metallic elements and their compounds, asbestos, organic chemicals, oils and tars, pesticide residues, explosive and asphyxiant gases, and radioactive materials. These substances often arrive in the soil as a result of intentional disposal under the mistaken dictum that 'the solution to pollution is dilution'. They may also arrive as seepages from designated or unofficial landfill sites, from spillages,

Fig. 8.6 Salt efflorescence, southern Tunisia.

and from atmospheric fallout. Broadly speaking, soil pollution can be discussed in terms of dispersed and concentrated pollution.

Dispersed pollution

Two of the most common forms of dispersed chemical soil pollution result from acid deposition and from radionuclide fallout from the atmosphere. Soils with acid organic surface horizons, shallow profiles and a low buffering capacity, such as occur widely on the uplands of Britain and the Scandinavian countries, have little resistance to acidification. Soil acidification is not a visually obvious feature, but when it occurs it affects plant life, and waters draining from the soils contain toxic concentrations of exchangeable aluminium; this has serious impacts on river life and possible effects on human life, if the link between aluminium and Alzheimer's disease is correct. Values of pH have been recorded to fall by two units over 30 years on land continuously cropped with sisal in East Africa, and by half a unit in soil under permanent grass in England. However, because of the greater efficiency of trees in intercepting acid deposition, the fall of pH value in woodland areas may be as much as three units. Only 16 per cent of the soils of England and Wales have a high neutralizing capacity, and 38 per cent have little or no capacity to counter acidification.

Fallout of radioactive elements results from a combination of atomic weapons testing and accidental releases, such as the Chernobyl nuclear power station disaster of 1986. There is sufficient radioactive caesium in soils now for it to be used as a tracer in erosion studies. Theoretical predictions that radioactive elements would become locked in the lattice of clay minerals may have been correct for mineral calcareous soils, but acid organic soils in Wales and the English Lake District allowed the radioactive elements to remain available for uptake by plants and hence find their way into the food chain via grazing animals. The highest concentrations occur in organic-rich flush sites, where movement of water through the soil has concentrated the polluting radionuclides. This has been observed in sites in England and Wales, as well as in the Pripet marshes near Chernobyl.

The major radionuclides in soils are caesium (^{134}Cs and ^{137}Cs) and strontium (^{89}Sr and ^{90}Sr). The caesium isotopes have a relatively long half-life (2 and 30 years, respectively) but, as they are trapped by adsorption on clays, danger of entering the food chain only occurs on very peaty soils. Strontium isotopes have a shorter half-life (measured in days) but it acts chemically like calcium and is a cause of concern because it can be passed from soils to plants and animals, and finally to humans. It is not possible to give concentrations of these elements in soils as they decay at different rates and therefore persist for variable lengths of time, but soils, particularly the upper few centimetres, are becoming a reservoir of radionuclides. These elements can be resuspended by wind or rain and become stuck to the outside of leaves and so brought into the food chain.

Concentrated pollution

Concentrated areas of soil pollution are more of an urban problem, but not exclusively so. Redevelopment of urban areas has brought to light many plots of land formerly associated with the mining and working of metals, chemical works, pharmaceutical works, gas works, pesticide manufacture, explosives manufacture, oil and petroleum refining, asbestos, integrated circuit and semiconductor manufacture, scrapyards, sewage works and waste-disposal sites, which are very strongly polluted. In rural areas, soil pollution has occurred at sites where arsenical pesticides have been used, and many vineyards are polluted with copper sulphate.

There are techniques available for cleaning contaminated soils but they are expensive, and in many cases some form of containment has been resorted to, which does not necessarily solve the problem. The cost of rehabilitating strongly disturbed land can be in the region of £25,000 per hectare (1985–1990 prices), but where soils are polluted as well this cost can rise to £100,000 per hectare. Surveys have shown that there are many badly polluted sites in all industrial countries, but official sources are very reticent about the area involved and about the availability of funds to rehabilitate these badly damaged lands.

The uptake of toxic elements (Cu, Pb, Zn, Cd, As) by plants from soils is influenced by depth of

Metals	Concentration (mg kg⁻¹ dry weight)
Cr	100
Co	20
Ni	50
Cu	50
Zn	200
As	20
Cd	1
Pb	50

Table 8.1 Common standards adopted for metallic soil contaminants

rooting, nutrient status, pH and the presence of other toxic metals, as pollutants rarely occur singly. Soil-particle size, organic matter content, pH and redox state are all relevant to the mobility and availability to plants of many metal contaminants of soils.

Researchers have attempted to set threshold values for metallic content of soils below which they can be safely used for food production. Because soils naturally contain very variable amounts of toxic metals, which are available in widely differing amounts, such general values are not always helpful. However, there is a degree of agreement that soils should not contain more than the values indicated in Table 8.1.

Human activities have made, and continue to make, considerable impact on the soils of the world. A survey published in 1991 found that water erosion is the most significant type of human-induced soil degradation in all continents except for western Asia and Africa, where water and wind erosion are of almost equal importance. Almost 50 per cent of

land affected by salinization is situated in western Asia, and almost equal areas occur in southeast Asia and Africa. Over-grazing is of particular importance in Africa and Asia, and poor agricultural practices have adversely affected soils in all continents (Table 8.2).

Table 8.2 represents a 'snapshot' of the situation of world soil degradation at a particular time (1989), but in reality soil degradation is a very dynamic problem. The impact of land-use on different types of soil degradation may change dramatically in a very short time, dependent on the vulnerability of soils. The heterogeneous nature of soils means that they vary greatly in their ability to withstand maltreatment. To enable sustainable development to take place in all countries of the world, it is necessary to have a co-ordinated policy for soil conservation. The sad situation prevailing is that no international policy exists, even though FAO (1982) has published a *World Soil Charter* outlining the importance of soils and the ways in which they can be conserved. UNEP (1982) has published a *World Soils Policy* document, while the Council of Europe (1972) has published the *European Soil Charter*, the clauses of which are reproduced in the list on page 93 (from *Naturopa* **65**, 1990).

It would be incorrect to leave the reader with the impression that mankind's actions concerning soils were all negative. In many cases, steep landscapes have been terraced to arrest soil erosion, and elsewhere the depth, drainage and fertility of soils has been improved. In this chapter it has been observed that soils can be created where none existed previously, and improvements can be made to soils with

	World	Asia	Africa	America	Europe	Australia
Water	1094	440	227	229	114	83
Wind	548	222	187	82	42	16
Nutrient decline	135	14	45	72	3	+
Salinization	76	53	15	4	4	1
Pollution	22	2	+	+	19	–
Acidification	6	4	2	–	+	–
Compaction	68	10	18	5	33	2
Waterlogging	11	+	4	9	1	–
Subsidence	5	2	+	+	2	–
Total	1965	747	494	402	218	102

Table 8.2 Types of human-induced soil degradation: figures in million hectares (after Oldeman et al., 1990)

1 Soil is one of humanity's most precious assets. It allows plants, animals and man to live on the Earth's surface.

2 Soil is a limited resource which is easily destroyed.

3 Industrial society uses land for agriculture as well as for industrial and other purposes. A regional planning policy must be conceived in terms of the properties of the soil and the need of today's and tomorrow's society.

4 Farmers and foresters must apply methods that preserve the quality of the soil.

5 Soil must be protected against erosion.

6 Soil must be protected against pollution.

7 Urban development must be planned so that it causes as little damage as possible to adjoining areas.

8 In civil engineering projects, the effects on adjacent land must be assessed during planning, so that adequate protective measures can be reckoned in the cost.

9 An inventory of soil resources is indispensable.

10 Further research and interdisciplinary collaboration are required to ensure wise use and conservation of the soil.

11 Soil conservation must be taught at all levels and be kept to an ever-increasing extent in the public eye.

12 Governments and those in authority must purposefully plan and administer soil resources.

a low potential for crop production. The cost of these improvements is the removal of the natural ecosystem related to the soil and the substitution of an agricultural ecosystem in its place. Unlike the natural soils and plants which have been displaced, these man-modified soils require continual maintenance to sustain them. Unless the message of soil conservation contained in the *European Soil Charter* is adopted, current rates of soil degradation will be a major threat to future peace and prosperity.

Further reading

Alloway, B.J. (ed.), 1990. *Heavy Metals in Soils.* Blackie, Glasgow.

Bidwell, O.W. and Hole, F.D., 1965. Man as a factor in soil formation. *Soil Science* **99**:65–72.

Bridges, E.M., 1978. Interaction of soil and mankind. *Journal of Soil Science* **29**:125–39.

Bridges, E.M., 1989. Soils of the urban jungle. *Geographical Magazine* **61** (9) Analysis Supplement: 1–3.

Bridges, E.M., 1989. *Surveying Derelict Land.* Oxford University Press, Oxford.

Bullock, P. and Gregory, P.J. (eds.), 1991. *Soils in the Urban Environment.* Blackwell, Oxford.

Council of Europe, 1972. *European Soil Charter.* Naturopa, Centre Européen d'information pour la Conservation de la Nature, Strasbourg.

Craul, P.J., 1992. *Urban Soil in Landscape Design.* John Wiley, New York.

Davidson, D.A., 1982. Soils and Man in the past. In: Bridges, E.M. and Davidson, D.A. (eds.) *Principles and Applications of Soil Geography.* Longman, Harlow.

FAO, 1982. *World Soil Charter.* FAO, Rome.

Kosse, A., 1990. Diagnostic horizons in Anthrosols. In: Rozanov, B.G. (ed.) *Soil Classification. Report on the International Conference on Soil Classification.* Centre for International Projects, USSR State Committee for Environmental Protection, Moscow.

Lal, R., 1995. Erosion–crop productivity relationships for African soils. *Soil Science Society of America Journal* **59**:661–7.

Logan, T.J., 1990. Chemical degradation of soil. *Advances in Soil Science* **11**:187–221.

Oldeman, L.R., Hakkeling, R.T.A. and Sombroek, W.G., 1990. *World Map of the Status of Human-induced Soil Degradation.* International Soil Reference and Information Centre, Wageningen.

Russell, J.S. and Isbell, R.F., 1986. *Australian Soils: the Human Impact.* University of Queensland Press, Brisbane.

UNEP, 1982. *World Soils Policy.* UNEP, Nairobi.

Yaalon, D.H. and Yaron, B., 1966. Framework for man-made soil changes – an outline of metapedogenesis. *Soil Science* **102**:272–7.

9 Soils of the mid-latitudes: oceanic areas

Four Major Soil Groupings can be considered to be typical of the cool, temperate, humid regions of the world: Luvisols, Podzoluvisols, Planosols and Podzols. Although there is considerable climatic variation in the mid-latitude areas, there is sufficient precipitation (500 to 1500 mm) to maintain an overall downward movement of soil moisture and with it, any soluble soil constituents. The minimum length of growing period is taken as 135 days for this soil–ecological zone, but the average of the maximum temperatures of the six warmest months remains below 25°C.

Throughout this soil–ecological zone, the prevailing climate has encouraged the natural growth of coniferous forests in the northern part and deciduous forests in the south, but in western Europe most of the natural vegetation has been removed, much of it in early historical times. Except for a few small forested areas, arable or pastoral agriculture has replaced the natural vegetation and the soils have been modified to a variable extent.

Human influence on the soils of this zone has been considerable, and some have been sufficiently changed to qualify for a position in the Anthrosols, areas of which are widely scattered throughout this zone.

The landscapes on which the soils of this region have developed include areas that were formerly glaciated, or were peripheral to the glaciers, where till, fluvio-glacial outwash and loess were deposited during the Pleistocene. Much of this soil–ecological region in Europe and North America is dominated by gently undulating plains, interrupted by low mountain ranges. Often the Pleistocene deposits contain weatherable minerals and the depth of soils is rarely more than a metre. However, a few pockets of deeper weathering have survived the passage of glaciers, and these strongly suggest palaeosols formed in the warmer climate of an interglacial period.

The major processes controlling soil development are leaching, eluviation, podzolization and gleying. Accumulation of organic matter as peat takes place in lowland basins, where a high water table inhibits organic decomposition, as well as upon uplands, where saturation of the soils is maintained by regular and heavy rainfall.

In the northern areas of Europe, Asia and North America, the length of time during which soil formation has been taking place is limited to about 10,000 years, but outside the areas influenced by the Pleistocene glaciations and periglacial conditions, a longer period has been available for the development of specific features in the profiles of soils. Different parent materials also influence the speed of soil formation, so there is a considerable diversity of soils. Climate changes in the Holocene have also left their imprint upon soils.

Luvisols are characterized by the presence of an argic B horizon resulting from eluviation of clay from the surface horizons. They commonly occur on fine-textured parent materials, predominantly in the more southerly regions of the mid-latitudes, typically in the Mediterranean areas. **Podzoluvisols** have a strongly developed bleached E horizon which tongues deeply into an argic B horizon. **Planosols** are characterized by an abrupt change of texture between the eluvial and illuvial horizons, which results in a slowly permeable B horizon. The **Podzol** is typical of more northerly areas where it is associated with the boreal forests; however, Podzols may be seen in more southerly areas where heath plants occupy sandy or gravelly areas. Some very deep Podzols occur in the tropical regions, but by definition these would normally fall within the Arenosols.

Throughout this soil–ecological zone, the soils discussed in this chapter are accompanied by Histosols, Leptosols, Cambisols, Gleysols and, to a lesser extent, Andosols.

Luvisols

Luvisols are most extensive south of the Great Lakes in North America and in the inter-montane basins of the Rocky Mountains. In South America they occur on both sides of the southern Andes in Chile and Argentina. They are extensive in northern Europe, extending from the British Isles, France, Belgium and Germany, Poland, northern Ukraine and Russia as far as the Urals. They are also common throughout the countries of the Mediterranean basin, Portugal, Spain and Greece, where they are associated with Leptosols and Cambisols. There are limited areas of Luvisols in South Africa, China, India and New Zealand, but they are extensive throughout eastern Australia from Queensland to Victoria. It is estimated by FAO that there are 650 million hectares of Luvisols worldwide.

The name 'Luvisols' has been adopted for well-developed soils on decalcified, fine- or medium-textured weathering residues from sedimentary rocks, loess, plateau drifts, ancient alluvia and glacial till, that have an argic B horizon with an increased clay content (Plate B29). Following the removal of calcium carbonate from the fine earth, it would appear that bases are leached from the clay–humus complex leading to a decrease in the pH value to between 5.5 and 7.0. As the depth of leached soil increases and the flocculating effect of calcium ions is reduced, a movement of clay-sized particles through the soil begins, referred to as 'eluviation'. Three phases of this eluvial process may be recognized: first the clay must be mobilized, then transported, and finally precipitated from suspension in the soil solution. Mobilization of the clay is controlled by rainfall and pH, then the clay particles are washed from the A and E horizons into the B horizon, where they are deposited on, and lie parallel to, the ped faces as a result of a combination of flocculation and filtration (Fig. 9.1). By these means, the B horizon gradually has its clay content increased at the expense of the upper horizons. The B horizon comes to have a strongly developed prismatic or blocky structure which contrasts with the weaker blocky structures of the overlying A and E horizons. The clay is not broken down chemically during eluviation, but is washed physically down the pores and cracks, particularly after a period of summer drying when shrinkage cracks are widest.

On pervious parent materials, such as loess and limestones, these soils remain freely drained, but over time the argic B horizon, having fewer cracks that are partly infilled with clay, will impede the movement of water through the soil profile. Consequently, with clayey parent materials on level sites, and particularly in older landscapes, features of gleying are apparent and the Luvisols merge laterally into analogous Gleysols or Planosols. In south-eastern England, the eluviation of clay is not so intense and pedologists have classified these soils as Argillic Brown Earths, but across the Channel in France, the process is more strongly developed and French authors have identified a group of 'Sols Lessivés'. Further south, in the zone of Mediterranean climate, the soils are subject to eluviation during the winter rains, but in summer the soils dry and iron compounds oxidize to the

Fig. 9.1 Thick clay skin lining a pore and thin skins on ped faces.

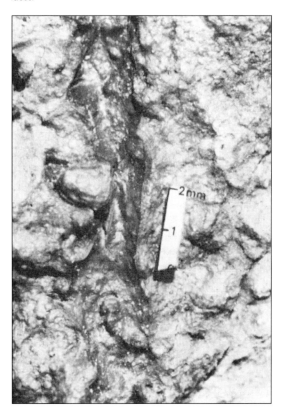

hematite state, giving the lower horizons, in particular, a bright red colour. Where erosion has revealed these horizons at the surface, the term 'Terra Rossa' has been used to describe them (Fig. 9.2).

Having decided that a soil belongs to the Major Soil Grouping of Luvisols, there is a choice of eight Soil Units into which a soil may be classified (Fig. 9.3). First, those soils with gleyic properties within 100 cm of the surface are **Gleyic Luvisols**. If stagnic properties are present within 50 cm of the surface, the soil is a **Stagnic Luvisol**. The presence of an albic E horizon indicates an **Albic Luvisol**. If the soil has vertic properties it is a **Vertic Luvisol**. The presence of a calcic horizon or powdery lime gives a **Calcic Luvisol**. In warmer climates, the presence of ferric properties keys a soil as a **Ferric Luvisol**, and if the B horizon has a strong brown to red colour (hue of 7.5YR and a chroma of more than 4 or a hue redder than 7.5YR), the soil is a **Chromic Luvisol**. Finally, if the soil does not meet any of these requirements it is classified as a **Haplic Luvisol**.

Podzoluvisols

As the name suggests, these soils have a combination of features which they share with both Podzols and Luvisols. The environment in which they develop is in the colder areas of the mid-latitude regions

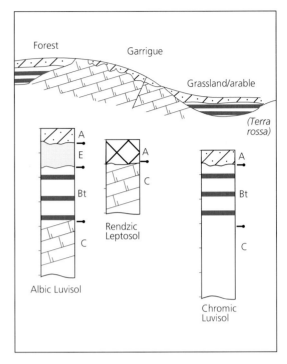

Fig. 9.2 Catena of soils in the Mediterranean zone.

where rainfall is evenly distributed and amounts to between 500 and 1000 mm per annum. The natual vegetation of these areas is boreal forest. The parent

Fig. 9.3 Classification of Luvisols.

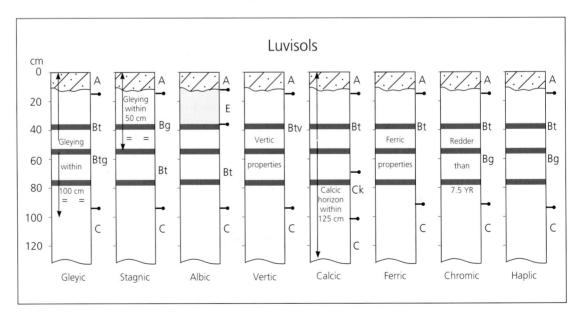

Profile of a Calcic Luvisol (Hapludalf) from near Thessaloniki, Greece

ISRIC Profile GR 03

(Parent material: river terrace deposits)

Diagnostic criteria: argic B horizon; calcareous within 125 cm; colour redder than 7.5YR

Ap	0–17 cm	Brown (7.5YR 4/4) slightly gravelly sandy loam with moderate fine subangular blocky structure; slightly sticky, slightly plastic; many fine pores; many fine roots; non-calcareous; abrupt smooth boundary
A	17–26 cm	Strong brown (7.5YR 4/8) slightly gravelly sandy clay loam with weak fine subangular blocky structure; slightly sticky, slightly plastic; many fine pores; many very fine roots; non-calcareous; abrupt smooth boundary
Bt₁	26–72 cm	Yellowish-red (5YR 4/8) slightly gravelly sandy clay loam with strong medium prismatic structure; sticky, plastic; continuous moderately thick clay cutans; many fine pores; many fine roots; non-calcareous; abrupt wavy boundary
Bt₂	72–97 cm	Reddish-brown (5YR 4/4) sandy clay loam with strong coarse prismatic structure; sticky, plastic; continuous moderately thick cutans; common very fine pores; common fine roots; non-calcareous; abrupt irregular boundary
Btk	97–138 cm	Strong brown (7.5YR 5/6) slightly gravelly clay loam with moderate coarse prismatic structure; sticky, plastic; moderately thick clay cutans; common very fine pores; common very fine roots; strongly calcareous; clear irregular boundary
BC	138–213 cm	Strong brown (7.5YR 5/6) slightly gravelly silt loam with weak coarse prismatic structure; sticky, plastic; moderately thick clay cutans; few fine pores; few fine roots; few small hard calcareous inclusions; strongly calcareous

Selected analyses

Horizon	Ap	Bt1	Bt2	Btk	BC
Depth (cm)	0–26	26–72	72–97	97–138	138–213
Clay (%)	16	31	25	28	11
pH H₂O (1:2.5)	7.5	6.9	7.4	8.5	8.4
CaCO₃ (%)	0	0	0	8.2	2.8
Org. C (%)	1.12	0.32	0.16	0.14	0.11
CEC	15.3	23.9	18.6	19.6	22.3
Base sat. (%)	93	99	109	127	125

Comment: freely drained, sandy loam over sandy clay loam; presence of increased clay content and clay skins confirm argic B; calcareous within 125 cm, so the profile is a Calcic Luvisol.

materials which give rise to Podzoluvisols are mainly unconsolidated materials of Pleistocene and Holocene age: glacial till, lacustrine deposits and loess. These soils occur from Poland through Russia and into Siberia in Eurasia; in North America they extend westwards from Hudson Bay to the Rockies. Worldwide, they are estimated to cover 320 million hectares, but they have not been identified in the southern hemisphere.

The Podzoluvisols are subject to strong leaching in which humus breakdown products complex with metals from the soil as they are washed down through the profile (Plate B23). The loss of iron compounds from the horizon immediately below the surface leads to an albic E horizon, the clear development of which is facilitated by the low amount of biological activity. Saturation, especially following snowmelt over a still-frozen subsoil, produces gleyic properties which intensify the effect of leaching. As the soil solution follows preferential paths through the soil, there is a strong tendency for these soils to have tongues of bleached albic material penetrating deep into the B horizon beneath. It is this tonguing that distinguishes these soils from the Albic Luvisols, which are widespread in Canada, and a good case exists for these two Soil Units to be amalgamated. Like the Luvisols, these soils have an argic B horizon resulting from the eluviation of clay from the upper horizons.

After it has been established that a soil has an albic E horizon which tongues deeply into the argic B horizon, it is possible to separate the soils into five Soil Units (Fig. 9.4). Those soils which have permafrost within 200 cm of the surface are **Gelic Podzoluvisols**. Where there are gleyic properties within 100 cm the soil is a **Gleyic Podzoluvisol**, and if the gleying is of the stagnic nature within 50 cm of the surface, the soil is a **Stagnic Podzoluvisol**. Finally, a distinction is made between those soils with a low base saturation, **Dystric Podzoluvisols**, and those with base saturation over 50 per cent, **Eutric Podzoluvisols**.

Planosols

Planosols are somewhat similar to Luvisols and Podzoluvisols, but with an extremely dense B horizon separated from the overlying horizons by an

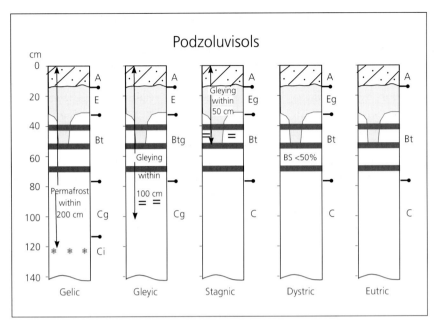

Fig. 9.4 Classification of Podzoluvisols.

abrupt textural change. Lack of permeability in the B horizon restricts the downward movement of water, resulting in stagnic properties and the development of a well-developed albic E horizon. These soils develop in temperate and sub-tropical climates where the environmental conditions are such that

---

Profile of a Stagnic Podzoluvisol (Fragiaqualf) from Bois de Hingues, France

ISRIC Profile FR 11
(Parent material: loess)
Diagnostic criteria: ochric A horizon; albic E horizon; albic tonguing; argic B horizon.

O	6–0 cm	Undecomposed leaves becoming slightly decomposed with depth
Ah₁	0–7 cm	Black (10YR 2/1) humic silt loam with large and moderate crumb structure; friable; many roots; clear boundary
Ah₂	7–21 cm	Very dark brown (10YR 2/2) humic silt loam with massive structure; many roots; clear boundary
AE	21–24 cm	Greyish-brown (10YR 5/2) silt loam with coarse angular blocky structure; many roots; clear boundary
E	24–35 cm	Pale brown (10YR 6/3) silt loam with weak very coarse angular blocky structure; tubular voids; irregular boundary tonguing into horizon below
Bgt₁	35–72 cm	Pale brown (10YR 6/3) with mottles (2.5YR 6/8) silt loam with medium angular blocky structure; frequent tubular voids; diffuse boundary

Btg₂ 72–110 cm Pale brown (10YR 6/3) with mottles (2.5Y 7/2) silt loam with medium angular blocky structure; iron/manganese concretions from 86 cm; diffuse boundary

Bgtx 110+ cm Pale brown (10YR 6/3) with mottles (2.5Y 7/2) silt loam with medium angular blocky structure; iron/manganese concretions; fragipan

Selected analyses

Horizon	O1	Ah	AE	Bgt1	Bgt2	Bgtx
Depth (cm)	6–0	0–21	21–35	35–72	72–110	110–128
Clay (%)	–	39	34	30	24	24
pH H₂O (1:2.5)	4.3	4.3	4.6	4.6	4.9	5.2
Org. C (%)	–	9.28	1.75	0.65	0.25	0.28
CEC	–	46.3	8.2	14.7	13.8	14.7
Base sat. (%)	–	2	1	3	9	49

Comment: below the forest litter and ochric A horizon is a pale brown albic E horizon which tongues into horizon below. The argic B horizon restricts water movement so that a perched water table rests on its upper surface. Mottling starts at 35 cm and iron/manganese concretions occur below 86 cm from the mineral soil surface.

there is low relief, strongly alternating wet–dry seasons, and scrub vegetation in which growth is suppressed by the hydromorphic nature of the upper soil horizons and the compact nature of the subsoil. There are about 130 million hectares of these soils in the world; they are extensive in Brazil, northern Argentina, South Africa, eastern Australia and Tasmania, and smaller areas occur in the USA, Turkey and Romania (Plate B17).

In these areas, soil formation takes place under the influence of a strongly seasonal climate in which the soil is alternately saturated, with chemical reducing conditions, or aerated, with oxidizing conditions. In the process of **ferrolysis**, anaerobic conditions develop as the soil is saturated and free iron is reduced to the ferrous state. The ferrous iron displaces cations from the exchange positions on the clays, and the cations are partly leached away during the early part of the wet season. The structure of the clay minerals is also attacked by the hydrogen ions, and aluminium, magnesium and other ions are released from the edges of the clay lattice.

As the soil dries, oxidation causes iron hydroxides to change from ferrous to ferric, liberating hydrogen ions. These hydrogen ions then begin another cycle by displacing cations and attacking the lattice structure of the clay minerals. The result of this process of ferrolysis is the formation of a seasonally wet, grey, unstable, silty or sandy soil with a low clay content and a very low cation exchange capacity.

Once the critical features of an albic E horizon and the abrupt textural change have been identified, it is possible to allocate these soils to one of five Soil Units (Fig. 9.5). Planosols that occur in areas where there is permafrost within 200 cm of the soil surface are **Gelic Planosols**. Planosols with a mollic A horizon are **Mollic Planosols**; similarly when there is an umbric A horizon the soil is an **Umbric Planosol**. Finally, a distinction is made between those soils with a base saturation of less than 50 per cent, **Dystric Planosols**, and those with a high base saturation, **Eutric Planosols**.

Podzols

Traditionally, these soils are characterized by the presence, just below the soil surface, of an ashy-coloured horizon from which they derive their Russian peasant name (*pod*, under and *zola*, ash). On world soil maps Podzols are shown as extending in a circumpolar belt approximately from the arctic circle southwards to the latitude of St Petersburg in Europe, and to the northern shores of the Great Lakes in North America. Podzols occur south of this zone, but only where a combination of parent material, vegetation and climate are favourable for their development. Podzols are rare in the southern continents, occurring in southern

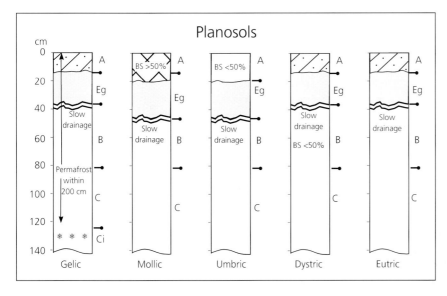

Fig. 9.5 Classification of Planosols.

Profile of a Dystric Planosol (Albaqualf) from Nambour, Queensland, Australia

ISRIC Profile AU 31

(Parent material: sandstone (lateritic))

Diagnostic criteria: albic E horizon; abrupt textural change; argic B horizon.

Ah$_1$	0–5 cm	Dark grey (10YR 5/1 dry) sand with weak fine subangular blocky structure; firm; many medium distinct mottles; porous; few very fine roots; clear boundary
Ah$_2$	5–10 cm	Light brownish-grey (10YR 6/2 moist) sand with massive structure; extremely firm, porous; few very fine roots; clear boundary
A/E	10–20 cm	Light grey (10YR 7/2) loamy sand with massive structure; extremely firm, porous; few very fine roots; clear boundary
E(g)	20–50 cm	White (10YR 8/1) loamy sand with massive structure; extremely firm, porous; few very fine roots; abrupt boundary
B(g)	50–55 cm	Light grey (10YR 7/1) fine sandy loam with weak coarse columnar structure; firm, porous; gradual boundary
Bt(g)	55–63 cm	Grey (10YR 6/3) fine sandy loam with weak subangular blocky structure; firm, porous; coarse prominent mottles (10YR 5/8); clear boundary
Btg$_1$	63–91 cm	Grey (10YR 6/1) sandy clay loam with weak subangular blocky structure; firm, porous; common coarse prominent mottles (10YR 5/8); diffuse boundary
Btg$_2$	91–110 cm	Light grey (2.5YR 7/0) sandy clay with moderate coarse angular blocky structure; plastic, porous; common medium prominent sharp mottles (7.5YR 5/6 and 2.5YR 4/8); non-calcareous

Selected analyses

Horizon	Ah1/2	A/E	E(g)	B(g)	Bt(g)	Btg1	Btg2
Depth (cm)	0–10	10–20	20–50	50–55	55–63	63–91	91–110
Clay (%)	3	4	5	8	14	26	31
pH H$_2$O (1:2.5)	5.9	5.7	5.6	5.3	4.7	4.4	4.8
Org. C (%)	0.5	0.27	0.14	0.03	0.03	0.05	0.06
CEC	2.5	1.8	1.7	3.0	3.9	7.9	9.5
Base sat. (%)	124	106	65	30	46	62	34

Comment: the profile is non-calcareous throughout and a seasonal perched water table develops on the abrupt textural change to give the Planosol character to this soil. Mottling occurs throughout the profile and this soil is a Gleyed Podzolic Soil according to the *Handbook of Australian Soils.*

Argentina and Australia only. A form of deep tropical Podzol occurs in several parts of the tropics, South America, Africa and Australia, but because of the way these soils are defined and the structure of the classification, these are classified as Arenosols.

Within the main Podzol zone of the northern hemisphere, large areas of the Earth's surface are mantled by Pleistocene glacio-fluvial deposits. Although podzolization proceeds most rapidly upon permeable sands and gravels, soils with a Podzol profile may be found on a wide range of different parent materials including sandstone, siltstones, clays and, in certain circumstances, even in soils formed over limestones.

The climates associated with Podzol development have long cold winters and short mild summers. In European Russia, these soils are frozen for at least 5 months of the year and during the brief summer, temperatures only reach to between 15 and 19°C. In this typically cool continental climate, winter precipitation is mainly in the form of snow and about half the annual rainfall occurs as summer rain. The total amount of precipitation is not great: 500–550 mm is stated as average for the Eurasian area, but up to 1000 mm may occur in North America. Podzols are found predominantly in Köppen's 'cold zone', which may experience temperatures of over 10°C in the warmest month and below −33°C in the coldest month. This corresponds to the humid micro-thermal climates (Dfa, Dfb, Dwa and Dwd), as well as the subarctic climates (Dfc, Dwc and Dwd) and marine west coast climate (Cfb). Freezing conditions in the colder areas inhibit the soil-forming processes, but with the snowmelt of spring, considerable moisture becomes available and strong leaching and gleying of the soil profile occur.

The vegetation associated with Podzols is the coniferous boreal forest or 'taiga'. In Europe this forest is composed of spruce, pine, larch and birch; in Siberia the Dahurican larch is dominant in the areas of most extreme climate, and in the Far East, fir becomes co-dominant with spruce. The number of tree species in the American forests is greater, with spruce and fir growing on the better-drained soils and black spruce and tamarack on the poorly drained areas. Burnt areas are colonized by jack pine, birch and aspen, while western forests are dominated by lodgepole pine and alpine fir. As the ecotone with the tundra is approached, the boreal forest thins and a discontinuous cover of crowberry, bilberry and lichens, such as *Cladonia*, is characteristic. South of the main Podzol zone, these soils are restricted to heath plants which have colonized sandy and gravelly parent materials. In association with archaeological evidence, it has been proposed that the formation of Podzols in sandy parent materials may have been initiated by human clearance of lightly wooded areas, allowing heath plants to dominate and begin the podzolization process.

Although the original Russian definition of a Podzol emphasized the bleached E horizon (Plate A6), the trend of modern classifications has been to identify soils by their subsoil horizons. In the case of Podzols, this is the **spodic horizon** (Plate A10), where amorphous compounds, consisting of organic matter and aluminium with or without iron and other cations, have accumulated. The process whereby these materials have been mobilized, transported and finally deposited in the B horizon is called **podzolization** (Plate B13). Loss of material from the eluvial horizon results in the bleached albic E horizon, and the accumulation in the spodic B horizon can be demonstrated by increased amounts of iron and aluminium in combination with organic matter, and the presence of coatings of organic matter and aluminium on sand grains.

The process of podzolization has interested many soil scientists, and studies on the subject have been published throughout the past 100 years. For the development of a bleached E horizon and the accompanying spodic (Bh and Bs) horizon, several closely interrelated processes are in operation. First, organic breakdown products are released from the acid, decomposing plant debris. These substances include fulvic acid, which is capable of forming a temporary linkage with both aluminium and iron, chemically referred to as 'chelation'. Also, soluble polyphenolic compounds, washed off the vegetation and fresh organic matter, have the ability to convert iron and aluminium into soluble forms.

Controversy exists about the manner in which iron and aluminium are transported from the eluvial to the illuvial horizons of Podzols. Movement

---

Profile of a Haplic Podzol (Orthod) from Derbyshire, England

Soil Survey of England and Wales
(Parent material: Bunter pebble beds)
Diagnostic criteria: albic E horizon and spodic B horizon.

Ol		Litter of beech, oak and larch leaves
Of	4–2.5 cm	Comminuted, darkened and partly decomposed leaves
Oh	2.5–0 cm	Black amorphous organic matter with a scatter of bleached sand grains
Ah	0–13 cm	Very dark grey (10YR 3/1) structureless, humus-rich sand with bleached grains slightly stony; merging boundary
E	13–30 cm	Grey (10YR 5/1) structureless slightly stony sand with bleached grains and low organic matter content; abrupt boundary
Bh	30–31 cm	Black (10YR 2/1) sand and stones, firm, compact with organic matter and iron; abrupt boundary
Bfe	31–32 cm	Dark brown (7.5YR 3/2) thin indurated iron pan; narrow boundary
Bs	32–40 cm	Reddish-yellow to strong brown (7.5YR 6/6–5/6) very stony compact structureless sand; gradual boundary
C/R	40+ cm	Bunter pebble beds

Selected analyses

Horizon	Ah	E	Bh	Bs
Depth (cm)	0–13	13–30	30–32	32–40
Clay (%)	15	11	–	15
pH H$_2$O (1:2.5)	3.6	4.0	4.5	5.5
CEC	12.7	5.2	17.1	7.1
Base sat. (%)	5	12	9	27

Comment: the profile has developed with a mor humus form and a pronounced albic E horizon. The spodic B horizon has three parts: a humic B horizon (Bh) overlies a thin iron pan or placic horizon (Plate A27) (Bfe), and the iron-rich lower B horizon. The lower part of the profile is normally freely drained, but decreased permeability is associated with the thin iron pan.

---

as ions, colloids, metal and organic complexes, and the formation of transient soluble minerals have been proposed. Many of the simpler answers to the problem have been shown to be inadequate to explain the complex chemistry behind the development of the characteristic Podzol profile.

It has been demonstrated that organic compounds are capable of mobilizing, transporting and precipitating sesquioxides, and many investigators favour an explanation which directly involves their activity. Organic acids are washed down through the soil profile, and sesquioxides are picked up by chelation and transported downwards, only to be redeposited. Further organic acids, cascading downwards, redissolve the uppermost organo-metallic precipitates until they too are saturated, when precipitation occurs again. Microbial activity frees the iron and aluminium which is taken up by the downward-cascading organic acids. Lower in the B horizon, microbial action releases aluminium which combines with SiO_2 to form allophane and imogolite. The iron released forms ferric oxihy-droxides. In this way the B horizon is gradually deepened and also differentiated into an upper Bh and a lower Bs horizon. The differentiation is explained by the stronger complexing ability of iron, which is carried further down the profile leav-ing an aluminium maximum in the upper part of the B horizon. The organic and aluminium-rich upper part of the B horizon does not form as a later accumulation on top of an already existing iron-rich Bs horizon, as has been suggested in the past. Although the mineral imogolite is present in Podzol B horizons, it does not play an essential role in the podzolization process.

Alternatively, the theory of movement as an inorganic substance revolves around the presence of imogolite/allophane-type minerals in Podzols.

From the presence of deep, allophane-cemented Bs horizons in Scotland, it has been argued that the allophane and iron oxides were deposited from a mixed, negatively charged, Al_2O_3–Fe_2O_3–SiO_2–H_2O sol which passed through the E horizon and was precipitated on the positively charged, sesquioxide-coated surfaces in the B horizon.

The presence of a spodic B horizon is the diag-nostic property for the Major Soil Grouping of Podzols. Once it has been recognized, considera-tion of the Soil Units within the Podzols can pro-ceed by elimination (Fig. 9.6). If there is permafrost within 200 cm of the surface it is a **Gelic Podzol**. If there are gleying properties within 100 cm of the surface, the soil is a **Gleyic Podzol**. Where there is an accumulation of organic matter but insufficient iron to turn red on ignition, the soil is a **Carbic Podzol**. If the ratio of free iron to organic carbon is greater than six, the soil is classified as a **Ferric Podzol**. Where a spodic hori-zon is present but no albic E horizon, and no part of the B horizon is visibly enriched with organic carbon, the soil is a **Cambic Podzol**. Any other soils with a spodic B horizon fall into the **Haplic Podzols**.

Associated soils

There are a number of variations of the Podzol profile which may be seen in the field. On lowland

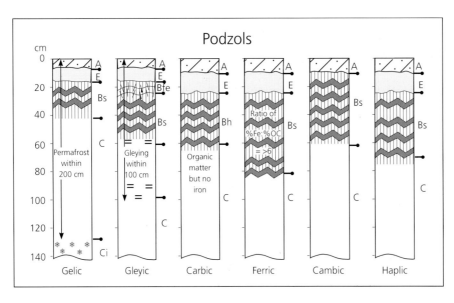

Fig. 9.6 Classification of Podzols.

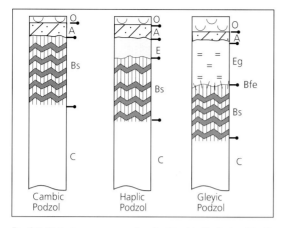

Fig. 9.7 Maturity sequence of soils: Cambic Podzol – Haplic Podzol – Gleyic Podzol (after Mackney, 1961).

increased, organic material was arrested by it and so accumulated mainly above the iron-rich Bs horizon, where it forms a Bh horizon. Examples of this sequence can be seen by judicious selection of sites in northwest Europe. However, some parent materials lacking in iron cannot develop an Iron–Humus Podzol profile, and some dune deposits in The Netherlands have spodic horizons composed entirely of humic material; these are Carbic Podzols.

Where a high ground-water level occurs in a pervious parent material undergoing podzolization, the normal processes are modified. A Gleyic Podzol (Ground-water Podzol) with an albic E horizon and a mottled B horizon develops (Fig. 9.8). Oxidation and reduction conditions, caused by alternate aerobic and anaerobic conditions, result in the development of weakly cemented patches of orange-brown sand. In the Podzol zone, where wet conditions coincide with impervious parent materials, Gleysols and Histosols usually result on lowland sites.

It should be noted that the Russian concept of a Podzol includes many soils which pedologists elsewhere would classify as Hydromorphic Soils, hence the great extent of Podzols in northern Russia. In many parts of the world the Podzol is considered to be a freely drained soil which occurs predominantly

sites it has been suggested that some of these variations may be linked in a maturity sequence (Fig. 9.7). This begins with a Cambic Podzol (Acid Brown Soil) with a weakly developed Bs horizon, continues with a Haplic Podzol (Iron Podzol under old oak woodland) and culminates in the most mature soil, a Gleyic Podzol (Humus–Iron Podzol under heathland). In this developmental sequence, it has been suggested that as the iron content

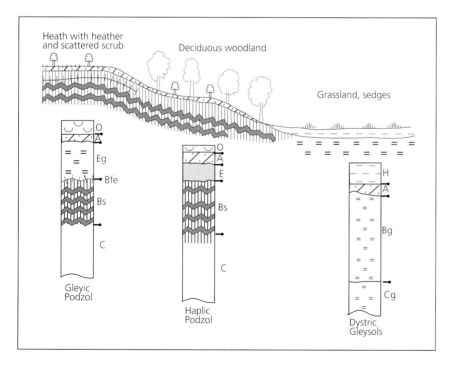

Fig. 9.8 Catenary position of lowland Podzols.

on sandy parent materials, frequently associated with heathland.

Strong leaching and podzolization also occur on the uplands of western Europe, where a form of Podzol has developed in a high-rainfall regime. In an environment which has greater cloudiness and a decreased rate of evapotranspiration, accumulation of an acid organic mat is encouraged. Gleying develops beneath the mat and an Eag horizon is produced. As a result of the removal of iron from the Eag horizon, a thin iron pan, or placic horizon, resembling a walnut shell in section, develops below the Eag horizon. Water perched upon this iron pan emphasizes the gleying effect of the saturated surface horizons, and it can become quite convoluted as it gradually migrates downwards. This profile, a Placic Podzol, figured in the earlier versions of the legend of the *Soil Map of the World*, but it was amalgamated into the Gleyic Podzols in the 1988 revision.

Further reading

Anderson, H.A., Berrow, M.L., Farmer, V.C., Hepburn, A., Russell, J.D. and Walker, A.D., 1982. A reassessment of podzol formation processes. *Journal of Soil Science* **33**:125–36.

Avery, B.W., 1990. *Soils of the British Isles*. CAB International, Wallingford.

Bridges, E.M., 1966. *The Soils and Land Use of the District North of Derby*. Memoir of the Soil Survey of England and Wales, Harpenden.

Bullock, P. and Clayden, B., 1980. The morphological properties of Spodosols. In: Theng, B.K.G. (ed.) *Soils with Variable Charge*. Soil Bureau, Lower Hutt, New Zealand, pp. 45–65.

Buurman, P., 1984. *Podzols*. Van Nostrand-Reinhold, New York.

Buurman, P. and Reeuwijk, L.P., 1984. Proto-imogolite and the process of soil formation: a critical note. *Journal of Soil Science* **35**:447–52.

Davidson, D.A., 1987. Podzols: changing ideas on their formation. *Geography* **72**:122–8.

De Coninck, F., 1980. Major mechanisms in the formation of spodic horizons. *Geoderma* **24**:101–23.

Driessen, P.M. and Dudal, R. (eds.), 1991. *The Major Soils of the World*. Agricultural University of Wageningen and Katholieke Universiteit, Leuven.

Farmer, V.C., Russell, J.D. and Berrow, M.L., 1980. Imogolite and proto-imogolite allophane in spodic horizons: evidence for a mobile aluminium silicate complex in podzol formation. *Journal of Soil Science* **31**:673–84.

Mackney, D., 1961. A podzol development sequence in oakwoods and heath in central England. *Journal of Soil Science* **12**:23–40.

Muir, A., 1961. The podzol and podzolic soils. *Advances in Agronomy* **13**:1–56.

Ranney, R.W. and Beatty, M.T., 1969. Clay translocation and albic tongue formation in two Glossoboralfs in west-central Wisconsin. *Soil Science Society of America Proceedings* **39**:1177–81.

Spaargaren, O.C. (ed.), 1994. *World Reference Base for Soils*. ISSS, ISRIC, FAO, Wageningen/Rome.

Stace, H.T.C., Hubble, G.D., Brewer, R., Northcote, K.H., Sleeman, J.R., Mulcahy, M.J. and Hallsworth, E.G., 1968. *A Handbook of Australian Soils*. Rellim Technical Publications, Glenside.

Stobbe, P.C. and Wright, J.R., 1959. Modern concepts of the genesis of podzols. *Proceedings of the Soil Science Society of America* **23**:161–4.

Thompson, C.H., 1992. Genesis of Podzols on coastal Dunes in Southern Queensland. 1. Field relationships and profile morphology. *Australian Journal of Soil Research* **30**:593–613.

Vepreskas, M.J. and Wilding, L.P., 1983. Deeply weathered soils in the Texas coastal plain. *Soil Science Society of America Journal* **47**:293–300.

Walker, P.H. and Chittleborough, D.J., 1986. Development of particle size distribution in some Alfisols of southeast Australia. *Soil Science Society of America Proceedings* **32**:97–101.

10 Soils of the mid-latitudes: continental areas

Soil formation in the mid-latitudes is conditioned by a wide range of climates with many transitional zones and variations, but in general the climate is described as 'temperate'. Parent material, relief and vegetation are similarly variable, and especially in this zone, which is suitable for a wide range of crops, the impact of human beings upon soils has been profound.

The mid-latitude continental soil–ecological zone may be identified with the steppe, prairie or pampas regions. These formerly grassy plains all occur in continental locations with an environment which has a relatively low rainfall (250–600 mm per year), mostly falling in spring and early summer. Winters are long, with low to very low temperatures, and summers are short and hot.

An important soil parent material of these regions is loess (Fig. 10.1). In both Europe and North America, areas peripheral to the Pleistocene glaciations were arid or semi-arid tundra, where wind action on unconsolidated outwash deposits separated and blew away silt-sized material which was subsequently deposited as a blanket over original landforms further away from the glacial margins. In Europe, the loess cover increases eastwards from isolated patches in Britain and western France to deposits 40 m thick in eastern Europe, and in China it reaches over 300 m in thickness. Pauses in loess accumulation provided opportunities for soil formation to take place, and sections through the loess show several palaeosols, for example, in the cliffs at Constanta in Romania.

These areas were originally covered by natural grasslands maintained by grazing and fire, which restricted arboreal vegetation to steep slopes and river valley sides, but they are now extensively cultivated. The soils and climate are well suited for the production of grain crops, and since the

Fig. 10.1 World distribution of loess.

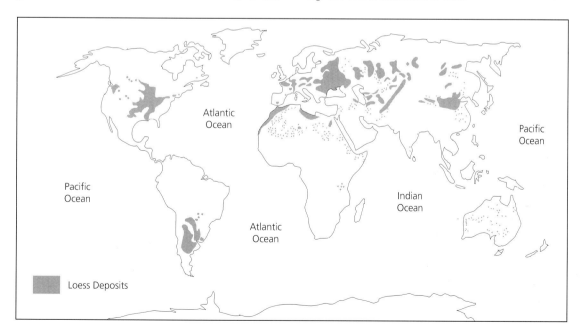

Atlantic Ocean

Pacific Ocean

Pacific Ocean

Indian Ocean

Atlantic Ocean

Loess Deposits

development of mechanized agriculture, cropping of wheat, barley and maize has become dominant, with the natural grasses restricted to special nature reserves.

Four Major Soil Groupings occur in these areas, all of which have the mollic A horizon as their chief diagnostic feature. The central member is the **Chernozem**, developed under grassland and noted for its deep, organic-rich A horizon and accumulation of calcium carbonate at depth in the profile. On the Ukraine–Russia border in Europe, and in the mid-western states of Iowa and Kansas, USA, the balance of the soil-forming environment changes to cooler, moister conditions and woodland gradually replaces the grasslands. In the soils, the carbonates are leached deeper in the profile and eluviation of clay can be seen, and **Greyzems** are recognized. As summer conditions become warmer and rainfall increases, leaching of carbonates occurs, leading to the recognition of a major group of **Phaeozems**. With increasingly dry conditions, organic returns to the soils are lower and there is less leaching, so a fourth major group of soils, the **Kastanozems**, can be identified between the Chernozems and the soils of the arid regions.

Chernozems

Southwest of Kiev in Ukraine, oriented in a northeast–southwest direction, lies a 500 km wide belt of Chernozems. To the west it extends into Moldova, Romania and Hungary, and to the east into Russia. East of the Ural Mountains it continues into central Asia as far as 100°E. In North America, the distribution of Chernozems lies west of 95°W, extending from the Arkansas River in the south into southern Alberta in Canada. Chernozems cover about 230 million hectares and are confined mainly to the northern hemisphere. Somewhat warmer conditions of similar climatic areas in the southern hemisphere, such as Argentina and Uruguay, favour development of Phaeozems rather than Chernozems.

In both continents where they are of major occurrence, Chernozems have developed on loessial parent materials. Outside the areas of the northern hemisphere which were glaciated during the Pleistocene, tundra conditions prevailed. In

summer, and when the continental glaciers finally melted, large quantities of meltwater carrying finely ground rock debris flowed across the sparsely vegetated outwash plains of the tundra. Winnowed by the wind, silt from the outwash plains was transported and redeposited as loess. The coarser sandy material remained nearer to the rivers as sandy river terraces (Fig. 10.2). On the plainlands, after some reworking as is evident from the deeper layers, the loess has formed the parent material of Chernozem soils, though loess is also found as a minor constituent of many soil parent materials elsewhere.

Climatic conditions of the continental interiors have a cold winter with temperatures between –7°C and –10°C, and the soil is frozen to a depth of 60 to 80 cm from November to April. The annual precipitation amounts to 550 to 600 mm, with a slight rainfall maximum in late spring and early summer; winter snow cover is not deep, but when it melts it can contribute to greater leaching in low-lying situations. Temperatures in July are in

Fig. 10.2 Relationship of Chernozems to the landscape.

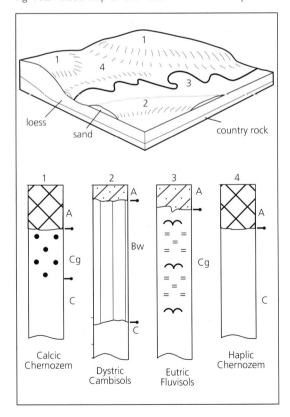

the range of 19°C to 21°C, and there is a period of 150 to 160 days in the year without a killing frost. As their formation depends upon a balance of temperature and moisture conditions, Chernozems occur in at least two of Köppen's climatic divisions: humid continental with short summer (Dwa) and humid continental with long summer (Cwa), extending into mid-latitude steppe (BSk).

Chernozems develop naturally beneath a grassland composed of a large number of genera including *Agropyron*, *Bouteloua*, *Buchloe*, *Poa* and *Stipa*. Herbaceous plants are common and patches of trees, including oak and lime, are characteristic of the ecotone of the forests to the north. This landscape, a gently undulating plain where grasses and small herbaceous plants once formed a dense ground cover, is now mainly cultivated.

The genesis of Chernozems depends largely upon the warm spring and summer temperatures with adequate moisture supply from snowmelt and early summer rains. The rapid growth of grasses and herbs produces a large quantity of roots and aerial shoots. The drought of late summer and the frosts of winter largely arrest the process of decomposition, and so losses of organic matter from the soil are minimized. Humus formation takes place in a neutral environment with calcium available, so the mull form of humus results; it is deeply incorporated by an active soil fauna including small vertebrates, whose presence is shown by their infilled burrows, known as 'krotovinas' (Fig. 10.3 and Plate

B20). Alternatively, Chernozems may have their origins in the tundra conditions during the Pleistocene, when organic accumulation took place followed by increasing faunal pedoturbation as the climate ameliorated, mixing the organic matter with the subsurface layers of calcareous loess to give the deep profile which exists today.

Fig. 10.3 Diagrammatic profile of a Chernozem.

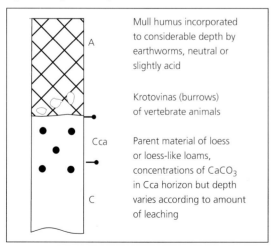

	A	Mull humus incorporated to considerable depth by earthworms, neutral or slightly acid
		Krotovinas (burrows) of vertebrate animals
	Cca	Parent material of loess or loess-like loams, concentrations of CaCO₃ in Cca horizon but depth varies according to amount of leaching
	C	

Profile of a Calcic Chernozem (Boroll) from near Kursk, Russia

ISRIC Profile SU 06
(Parent material: loess)
Diagnostic criteria: mollic A horizon; calcic horizon.

Ah₁	0–30cm	Black (10YR 2/1) silty clay loam with moderate medium crumb structure; friable; many roots; non-calcareous; gradual boundary
Ah₂	30–65cm	Very dark grey (10YR 3/1) silty clay loam with moderate medium subangular blocky structure; friable; porous; many roots; non-calcareous; gradual boundary
Ah₃	65–100cm	Very dark grey (10YR 3/1) silty clay loam with fine subangular to fine prismatic structure; friable; porous; many roots; gradual irregular boundary
ABk	100–150cm	Brown (10YR 5/2) silty clay loam with moderate fine prismatic structure; friable; porous; common calcareous concretions and pseudomycelia; some mixing of darker and lighter soil material by animal activity (krotovinas)
Bwk	150–180cm	Light yellowish-brown (10YR 6/4) silty clay loam with fine to medium prismatic structure; friable; porous
BCk	180+cm	Light yellowish-brown (10YR 6/4) silty clay loam with medium to coarse prismatic structure; friable; porous

Selected analyses (by Dokuchaev Institute, Moscow)

Horizon	Ah1	Ah2	Ah3	Bk/Ck
Depth (cm)	0–30	30–65	65–100	100–180
Clay (%)	32	32	30	33
pH H₂O (1:2.5)	6.7	6.7	6.7	8.0
Org. C (%)	4.7	2.9	1.6	0.5

Comment: under a natural grass steppe, this profile has a mollic A horizon and an accumulation of calcium carbonate in the lower A horizon between 100 and 150cm. Tunnelling and mixing by soil fauna causes the krotovinas.

Chernozems are defined as soils with a mollic A horizon, having a dark colour (a moist chroma of 2 or less) to a depth of at least 15 cm (Plate A2). These soils also have concentrations of soft powdery lime, a calcic horizon or a petrocalcic horizon within 125 cm of the soil surface (Plates A12, A13 and A26). A cambic B or argic B horizon is permissible, but in the central concept of Chernozems these are absent or only weakly developed. The presence of a natric horizon, salic properties and any of those properties which are specific to Vertisols, Planosols or Andosols will disqualify a soil from inclusion in the Chernozems.

At the Soil Unit level of classification, the following criteria are considered in strict order (Fig. 10.4). If gleyic properties are present the soil is a **Gleyic Chernozem**. If an argic B horizon has developed then the soil becomes a **Luvic Chernozem**. Where the mollic A horizon is seen to be tonguing into the cambic B horizon or the C horizon below, the soil is a **Glossic Chernozem**. Many soils in this Major Soil Grouping have a calcic or petrocalcic horizon, and these are **Calcic Chernozems**. Any remaining soils are placed in the **Haplic Chernozems.**

The deep, humus-enriched A horizon, 100 cm deep, with its well-developed crumb/fine angular blocky structure is characteristic of the Typical Chernozem of the Russian classification system.

The humus content ranges from 10 per cent at the surface to 2 per cent at the lower boundary of the A horizon. The ratio of carbon to nitrogen is in the range of ten to twelve, and the clay minerals are of the smectite type. The exchange capacity and fertility are both high, but the soil is slightly leached so the upper horizons are non-calcareous and are neutral or even slightly acid.

The passage of water through the profile is downward following the spring thaw and snowmelt. During the summer, evaporation from the soil surface and plant transpiration reverse the process, so the soil is rarely wetted below a depth of about 1.5 m. It is this mild leaching and re-evaporation which leads to the concentration of calcareous material in the middle and lower part of the soil profile, and which also retains the plant nutrients within the rooting zone. The calcic horizon in the example extends from 90 to 180 cm and has a maximum of calcium carbonate content between 120 and 130 cm. The upper part of the accumulation is characterized by the pseudomycelia, a filamentous form of carbonate deposition. In the zone of maximum accumulation, powdery concretions occupy former pores and cavities in the loess, and small hard nodules may be formed.

The Russian system distinguishes a Typical Chernozem, which has a maximum depth of the mollic A horizon, from Ordinary Chernozems,

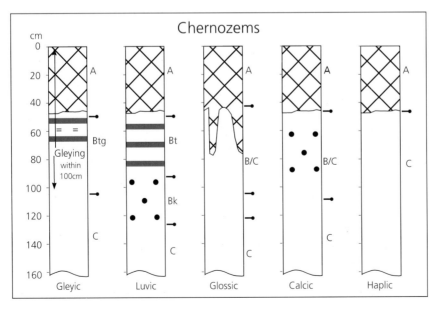

Fig. 10.4 Classification of Chernozems.

which have a maximum carbonate content in the upper part of the Cca horizon and even extending into the lower A horizon. Leached Chernozems have the maximum of carbonate accumulation lower in the Cca horizon. These variations in depth of leaching of the carbonates are related to minor differences in the rainfall or the micro-relief of the site, because during the spring snowmelt water is concentrated in low-lying positions in the landscape, where more leaching takes place compared with slightly higher areas. On the warmer, drier flank of the Typical Chernozems, Russian pedologists recognize Southern Chernozems, which have a shallower mollic A horizon but still retain the black to very dark grey colour in the surface.

The approach of the American system, contained in *Soil Taxonomy*, is to classify Chernozems as Mollisols, a soil order distinguished by the presence of a mollic epipedon and a base saturation of over 50 per cent. Moisture and temperature conditions are also important criteria for classification of Mollisols at the suborder level: Udolls are continually moist in the B horizon or the soil is dry for less than 60 consecutive days in 7 out of 10 years; Ustolls are dry for 90 days a year of which not more than 60 are consecutive; Xerolls are dry for more than 60 days each year in 7 out of 10 years. These three suborders include soils formed in environments with a mean annual temperature of more than 8°C, whereas the Borolls have formed with mean annual temperatures of less than 8°C.

Phaeozems

Soils of the wetter, warmer steppes and prairies are classified as Phaeozems (from Greek *phaios*, dusky and Russian *zemlja*, earth). It is estimated that there are about 155 million hectares of Phaeozems, situated on the prairies of North America, the pampas of Argentina and Uruguay, and the sub-tropical steppes of eastern Asia. These are soils of the 'tall grass prairie' with a very high biomass production. The Phaeozems were previously known as Prairie Soils or Brunizems. (The grouping in future will include soils formerly called Dark Grey Forest Soils or Leached and Degraded Chernozems in the Russian classification.)

Profile of a Calcaric Phaeozem (Aquic Hapludoll) from Schleswig-Holstein, Germany

ISRIC Profile DE 08
(Parent material: glacial till)
Diagnostic criteria: mollic A horizon; weak hydromorphic features.

Ap 0–18cm Black (10YR 2/1) silt loam with medium crumb structure; very friable; no mottles; no cutans; no inclusions; clear wavy boundary

Ah 18–50cm Black (10YR 2/1) slightly gravelly silt loam with moderate medium subangular blocky and medium crumb structure; friable; no mottles; moderately thick broken humus cutans in root channels and pores; clear smooth boundary

Bg₁ 50–70cm Olive (5Y 5/3) slightly gravelly silt loam with weak medium crumb and subangular blocky structure; friable; few medium distinct mottles (7.5YR 5/8); moderately thick broken humus cutans on ped faces; clear wavy boundary

Bg₂ 70–85cm Greyish-brown (2.5Y 5/2) slightly gravelly silt loam with moderate prismatic structure; friable; no mottles; continuous thick humus cutans in root channels and pores; clear smooth boundary

Cg 85+cm Greyish-brown (2.5Y 5/2) slightly gravelly silt loam with moderate medium prismatic structure; slightly sticky, slightly plastic; common medium distinct mottles (7.5YR 5/8); no cutans; ferruginous concretions and a few small manganiferous concretions (5YR 5/2)

Selected analyses

| Horizon | Ap | Ah | Bg | Bg/Cg |
Depth (cm)	0–18	18–50	50–70	70–85+
Clay (%)	12	13	22	21
pH H₂O (1:2.5)	7.3	7.9	8.5	8.3
CaCO₃ (%)	1.8	1.5	0.9	0.0
Org. C (%)	2.39	0.86	0.41	0.25
CEC	14.6	17.1	18.5	–
Base sat. (%)	100	90	81	–

Comment: mollic A horizon with 2.39 per cent organic carbon, weakly calcareous, so base saturation is over 50 per cent throughout the upper 125cm of the soil. Gleyic properties, resulting from decreased permeability at about 60cm, are not strongly expressed.

Phaeozems are defined as having a dark-coloured mollic A horizon, but there is no accumulation of calcium carbonate in the lower horizons of the soil profile (Plate B22). Although leached of free carbonates, the CEC remains more than 50 per cent saturated with bases, because an active soil fauna mixes the upper soil with lower, relatively unleached material. Cambic B and argic B horizons are allowed, and so are gleyic and stagnic properties, but characteristics which are diagnostic for Vertisols, Nitisols, Planosols and Andosols are not permitted. (Currently, there are proposals to amalgamate the Phaeozems and Greyzems; the main difference between these two groups is the presence of grains of silt and sand without any coatings in the Greyzems. Also, the concept of a completely leached soil will debar the present unit of Calcaric Phaeozems.)

At the second level of classification, there are currently five Soil Units in the Phaeozems (Fig. 10.5). First in the order of the key are those soils which have gleyic properties within 100 cm of the surface, **Gleyic Phaeozems**. If stagnic properties are present within 50 cm of the surface the soil is a **Stagnic Phaeozem**. If an argic horizon is present the soil is a **Luvic Phaeozem**. Phaeozems which are calcareous at least between 20 and 50 cm are **Calcaric Phaeozems**. Any other soils fall into the **Haplic Phaeozems**. (Proposals have been made to accommodate the present Major Soil Grouping of Greyzems as **Greyic Phaeozems**.)

Greyzems

This Major Soil Grouping appears on the FAO–Unesco *Soil Map of the World*, but occupies a very small area compared with other Major Soil Groupings. It is estimated by FAO that the extent of Greyzems is 34 million hectares. These soils occupy a zone in Russia and Canada on the wetter side of the Chernozems; they probably developed under a steppe vegetation which has since been invaded by trees under a moister climate regime.

The increased amount of moisture percolating through the soil profile has removed all free calcium carbonate from the profile, and grains of silt and sand in the A horizon have been stripped of their coatings of iron and organic matter. They therefore appear to be grey, giving the mollic A horizon of these soils a grey, speckled appearance. These soils are normally characterized by the presence of an argic B horizon.

Greyzems are defined as soils having a mollic A horizon with a moist chroma of 2 or less to a depth of at least 15 cm and showing uncoated silt and sand grains on ped surfaces (Plate B19). An argic B horizon is permitted as well as gleyic properties, but not the E horizon, nor the abrupt texture change and slowly permeable nature of the argic B horizon of the Planosols. There are only two Soil Units (Fig. 10.6): soils without gleyic properties are **Haplic Greyzems** and those which have gleyic properties are **Gleyic Greyzems**.

Fig. 10.5 Classification of Phaeozems.

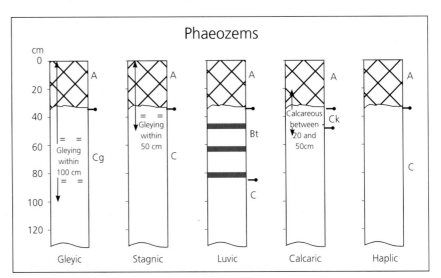

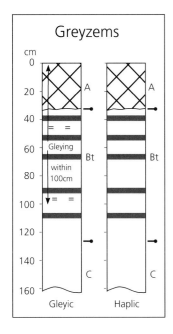

Fig. 10.6 Classification of Greyzems.

Profile of a Haplic Greyzem (Mollic Argiboroll) from Belgorod near Kursk, Russia

ISRIC Profile SU 05
(Parent material: loess)
Diagnostic criteria: mollic A horizon, argic B horizon

L&F	0–1 cm	Moderately decomposed leaves; abrupt boundary
Ah₁	1–10 cm	Very dark grey (10YR 3/1) silt loam with strong fine crumb to subangular blocky structure; friable; many very fine to coarse roots; clear boundary
Ah₂	10–17 cm	Greyish-brown (10YR 5/2) silt loam with moderate medium subangular blocky structure; friable; clear boundary
Bt(h)	17–27 cm	Greyish-brown (10YR 5/2) silty clay loam with strong medium subangular blocky structure; clear boundary
Bt₁	27–58 cm	Brown (10YR 5/3) silty clay loam with strong coarse blocky structure; patchy thin humus cutans on ped faces; gradual boundary
Bt₂	58–101 cm	Brown (10YR 5/3) silty clay loam with weak medium prismatic and subangular blocky structure; patchy thin humus cutans on ped faces; gradual boundary
B/C	101–150 cm	Loam with massive structure; calcareous pseudomycelia below 136 cm.

Selected analyses (by Dokuchaev Institute, Moscow)

Horizon	Ah	Bt1	Bt2	B3	BCk
Depth (cm)	0–27	27–50	50–100	100–135	135–150
Clay (%) (<0.001)	15	27	30	24	22
pH H₂O	7.0	5.8	5.2	5.6	8.1
CaCO₃ (%)	0	0	0	0	5.1
Org. C (%)	4.1	0.5	0.2	–	–

Comment: profile is developed under oak/maple woodland; mollic A horizon with dark colours extending below 15 cm and with evidence of uncoated silt/sand grains present; argic B horizon well developed.

Kastanozems

In both the USA and Ukraine, soils have been described from regions typified by short grass prairie or steppe; these soils have the name of Kastanozems. They occur in the drier, warmer climate areas, lying to the southeast of the Chernozems in Ukraine and extending eastwards along latitude 50° as far as the Irtysh river, and to the west of the Chernozems in North America, on the High Plains from the North Saskatchewan River southwards to the Llano Estacado of Texas. Similar soils occur in the warmer, arid parts of the pampas following the line of the Paraguay River. Earlier names given to these soils include Brown Chernozemic and Chestnut Soils. The name 'Kastanozem' (from Latin *castanea*, chestnut and Russian *zemlja*, earth) refers to the colour of the surface horizon which is very dark brown rather than the black of the Chernozems. Throughout the world there are 465 million hectares of these soils.

The parent material of these soils in southeast Russia and Ukraine is loess. The same parent material occurs in North America, but Kastanozems are also developed on calcareous glacial till parent materials in the USA–Canada border region of Montana and Saskatchewan. A natural vegetation of 'mixed prairie' grasses is characteristic of these grasslands, including the bunch grasses *Stipa*, as well as the lower-growing, more drought-resistant grasses of the species *Bouteloua* and *Aristida*. Salt-tolerant plants such as *Artemisia*, sagebrush and, in the USA, even cacti are components of the vegetation in the driest parts where Kastanozems occur.

Plant growth and biomass production are limited by the low rainfall and high summer temperatures. Although there is rainfall of 340 to 360 mm per annum, there is a high rate of evapotranspiration which limits the amount of available moisture. Temperatures of 25°C to 30°C are experienced during the summer, and in winter, freezing conditions may occur over much of the area where these soils occur. The supply of organic matter is less than in the Chernozems, but the humus form is still of the mull type.

Kastanozems have a mollic A horizon which is shallower than that found in the Chernozems (Plate B21); it is reduced in thickness to about 25 cm or less (Fig. 10.7). Although the production of biomass is limited by the climate, biological activity in these soils is still considerable, resulting in bioturbation and a good crumb structure. Argic B horizons are commonly developed and the accumulation of calcium carbonate occurs between 40 and 60 cm below the soil surface. Krotovinas are less frequent and less deep than in the Chernozems.

To qualify a soil for inclusion in the Kastanozems, the mollic horizon must be more than 15 cm deep and the soil must have soft powdery lime, a calcic, petrocalcic or a gypsic horizon within 125 cm of the soil surface. If a soil meets these criteria, there are then four Soil Units to which it can be allocated (Fig. 10.8). If there is a gypsic horizon, the soil is a **Gypsic Kastanozem**. If an argic horizon is present then the soil becomes a **Luvic Kastanozem**, but these may also be associated with a calcic horizon below the argic B horizon. With a calcic or petrocalcic horizon only, the soil is a **Calcic Kastanozem**. Any other Kastanozems are **Haplic Kastanozems.**

Associated soils

An interesting pattern of soil distribution may be seen on the drier steppes of southern Ukraine in the zone dominated by Kastanozems. This pattern is related to the micro-relief. Broad, shallow depressions occur in an otherwise flat landscape, and these receive water following snowmelt and spring rains. Saturation by water can lead to gleying and, in the warm dry climate, to the accumulation of salts. According to the amount of water received, the additional leaching achieved in these depressions can take the salts to different levels in the soil, migrating up and down with the season. This has led to the formation of a whole range of Gleyic Solonetz and Solodized Solonetz soils with associated halomorphic and hydromorphic features.

Fig. 10.7 Soil relationships in the Kastanozem zone of southern Ukraine.

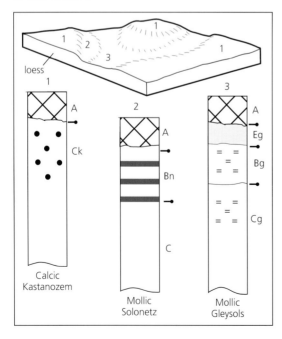

Fig. 10.8 Classification of Kastanozems.

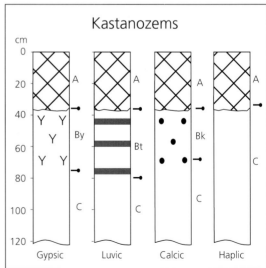

Profile of a Haplic Kastanozem (Haplustoll) from Kokkumber, Tien Shan, Kyrgyzstan

FAO–Unesco *Soil Map of the World* profile
(Parent material: old river terrace deposit)
Diagnostic criteria: mollic A horizon

A	0–15 cm	Grey heavy loam having chestnut shade (of colour) with granular structure; numerous roots; numerous earthworms; slightly compact
AB	15–25 cm	Grey heavy loam with granular structure; numerous roots; numerous earthworms; fungal mycelia; scattered stones
B$_1$	25–45 cm	Light grey medium loam with massive structure; porous; compact; common roots; scattered stones
B$_2$	45–90 cm	Pale medium loam with massive structure; compact; carbonate concretions
C	90+ cm	Gravelly loam

Selected analyses

Horizon	A	AB	B1	B2
Depth (cm)	0–15	15–25	25–45	45–90
Clay (%) (<0.001)	18	18	15	13
pH H$_2$O	8.2	8.4	8.1	8.4
Org. C (%)	3.5	2.7	2.0	1.1
CaCO$_3$ (%)	2.1	7.0	20.5	30.0
CEC	31	26	20	13

Comment: although Munsell colours are not available, this profile has a lighter-coloured mollic A horizon than the Chernozems and the carbonate content increases steadily down the profile. The clay content is uniform and the soil keys out as a Haplic Kastanozem. In this example, the parent material is loamy and situated on a level, high river terrace.

Further reading

Afanasyeva, E.A., 1966. Thick Chernozem under grass and tree cenoses. *Soviet Soil Science* (June issue): 615–25.

McClelland, J.E., Mogen, C.A., Johnson, W.M., Schroer, F.W. and Allen, J.S., 1959. Chernozems and associated soils of eastern North Dakota: some properties and topographical relationships. *Soil Science Society of America Proceedings* **23**:51–6.

Smith, G.D., Allaway, W.H. and Riecken, F.F., 1950. Prairie soils of the upper Mississippi valley. *Advances in Agronomy* **2**:157–205.

Stace, H.C.T., Hubble, G.D., Brewer, R., Northcote, K.H., Sleeman, J.R., Mulcahy, M.J. and Hallsworth, E.G., 1968. *A Handbook of Australian Soils*. Relim, Adelaide.

Thorp, J., 1947. Practical problems in soil taxonomy and soil mapping in Great Plains states. *Soil Science Society of America Proceedings* **12**:445–8.

11 Soil development in arid regions

It has been estimated by FAO that 25 per cent of the Earth's surface, or approximately 3000 million hectares, has an arid climate. The extent of desert conditions varies considerably from continent to continent; according to one definition, Australia has the greatest proportion of desert lands, with 44 per cent, followed by Africa with 37 per cent and Eurasia with 15 per cent. Arid conditions occur in a broad zone across sub-tropical Africa and Arabia, extending into central Asia, and interrupted by mountain ranges which have their own special climatic conditions. Central and western parts of Australia and relatively smaller areas of North and South America are also arid or semi-arid. These arid regions of the world have a severe environment in which restricted conditions of weathering and soil formation prevail, and highly specialized plant and animal life has evolved. Throughout the history of soil science, almost all world classifications have distinguished a group of desert soils. The unique environmental conditions of these areas mean that the soils of the deserts remain as separate groupings in modern soil classifications.

The climate of deserts is characterized by a lack of cloud cover and an irregular and low amount of rain; a figure of 150 mm rain is often taken as a criterion for a desert climate, but effectively it is the combination of a dry atmosphere, high temperatures and strong evaporation which together make the desert climate. The dry atmosphere of arid regions ensures that the annual total of evapotranspiration is in excess of rainfall, although rainfall may exceed evapotranspiration for short periods in winter. Consequently, there is little percolation of water through the soil. Light rainfall is rapidly evaporated and heavy showers quickly run off the dry surface without infiltrating the soil, causing flash-floods in otherwise dry wadis. Generalizing, it is estimated that the length of growing season is less than 75 days. These areas are climatically classified by Köppen as mid-latitude desert (Bwk) and low-latitude desert (Bwh).

The arid regions of the world have been affected by many climatic changes which date back to well before the Pleistocene; these have included, for example, drier phases between 20,000 and 13,000 BP and wetter phases between 12,000 and 8000 BP. Such changes are significant in the development of soils in these regions: the wetter phases have provided the environmental conditions suitable for clay migration to form argic B horizons, conditions which do not exist at the present time. Moister conditions would also leach soluble soil constituents, reducing the extent of those soils which contain soluble salts. In other cases, carbonates from calcareous dust would be dissolved and carried into the subsoil to reprecipitate as petrocalcic or petrogypsic horizons. The argic B horizons and the petrocalcic horizons remain in many desert soils as evidence of former climatic conditions.

Except for the rocky and salt-dominated areas, deserts are not completely lacking in plants; where they occur, they are usually well-adapted to drought, with small leaves, often reduced to sharp spines, and extensive deep root systems. The plants are also physically well-separated from each other, leaving areas of bare ground below which the roots lie in wait for any moisture. The roots are important as a source of organic matter for soil development, but the above-ground parts tend to contribute less to the soil's organic matter content. All the same, in arid and semi-arid areas, destruction of the plant cover by over-grazing may have disastrous results, as soil degradation can quickly follow.

Landforms, soils and plants have a close relationship in desert areas. In desert conditions, and in the absence of plant cover, any weathered material on upland areas is eroded by wind and water leaving bare rock surfaces, and soil development is inhibited. Large amounts of eroded material are washed into wadis by the irregular rainfall and transported to lower-lying land, where pediments are constructed at the foot of steeper lands (Fig. 11.1). On emerging from the uplands and the confines of the wadi, weathered debris is laid down in strict order of its particle size: first the gravels, then the sands, followed by the silts and clays. The clays and silts crack when they dry and curl into flakes, which subsequently become incorporated into the soil profile. Continual changes in direction of flow on detrital fans at the mouth of the wadis, as well as sheet-floods on plain surfaces, have combined to produce very long, low-angle slopes (*glacis* in French literature) of accumulated debris in front of mountain ranges. Dissected by changes in base level of the wadis, a succession of landsurfaces has been developed, carrying soils of different ages and morphology. Some excellent examples of these glacis landforms and related soils may be seen in central Tunisia and Algeria.

In enclosed basins (playas or salinas), which are found in many desert areas, the water containing clay particles and dissolved salts flows to the lowest part where it eventually evaporates, precipitating salts in concentric areas in order of their solubility: calcium carbonate then calcium sulphate, followed by chlorides, sulphates and nitrates. Although the mineral constituents of desert soils are fairly well sorted by fluvial processes, the wind also plays its part: sands are blown into dunes or sand sheets, and silts may be whipped up by the wind and blown outside the desert areas to form loess deposits. The salts may also be returned to the upland areas from the playa floors by wind action, as occurs with gypsum precipitated on the floor of the Chott Lakes of Tunisia. When a mixture of clay and salt on the

surface of a playa dries, the growing salt crystals may force the clay particles into silt-sized aggregates which can then be blown by the wind. This phenomenon can give rise to clay dunes, such as those seen in the Medjerda valley of northern Tunisia and the 'parna' described in the Murray-Murrumbidgee valley of Australia (Fig. 11.2).

On lowland (alluvial) areas, where a saline ground-water lies sufficiently near the surface, the soil is wetted by capillary rise of water containing salts. An accumulation of salt occurs in the soil as the water evaporates, and a saline crust often develops on the soil surface.

On upland areas, winnowing of the fine soil particles leaves a layer of stones on the desert floor forming a **desert pavement**. This process of development undoubtedly takes place, but another theory suggests that upward movement of stones through the soil during wetting and drying cycles forms these stony desert surfaces. In other cases, for example the 'gibbers' of Australia, the stones may remain as a lag deposit, a relict from a former silcrete (Plate A29). In Israel, the name of 'reg' is given to these soils with stony surfaces.

The stones constituting many of these desert pavements are covered on their upper surface with a dark manganese/iron coating up to 0.1 mm thick, while the lower surface remains a rusty brown colour. The origin of this **desert varnish** is thought to be biogenic, as bacteria, dependent upon the dew for moisture, trap wind-blown dust containing iron and manganese. Although their origin has not been proven, some of these coatings have been dated as more than 300,000 years old.

A thin layer of firm, stoneless, fine sand frequently underlies the desert pavement and contains

Fig. 11.1 Relationships of soils and landforms in deserts:
1 Regosols with desert pavement;
2 Fluvisols and Solonchaks;
3 Calcisols on glacis;
4 Arenosols on sands;
5 Leptosols on steep slopes;
6 bare rock upland surfaces.

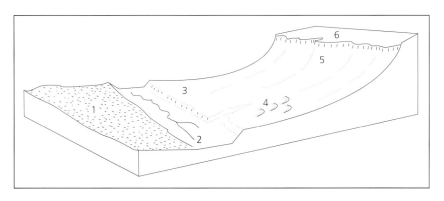

Fig. 11.2 Clay dune in the Medjerda delta, Tunisia.

numerous round vesicles, which are thought to have been formed by entrapped air on the rare occasions when the soil has become saturated. Other common features of desert soils include the infilling of desiccation cracks with sand from the surface.

It should of course be noted that desert conditions also occur through extreme cold, as in Antarctica. Biological activity is confined to mosses, lichens and algae, which occupy sheltered crevices or live below the soil surface. Soils in Antarctica usually have a stone pavement which, in older soils, is polished by attrition and stained with desert varnish. Below the surface, soil-forming processes take place slowly. There is virtually no organic matter present, but salts, including calcite and gypsum, are frequently present, concentrated by the freeze–thaw process. Freeze–thaw and the growth of salt crystals are important physical actions in the weathering processes contributing to the formation of these soils.

Classification

Classification of the soils of the arid regions, as in other areas, began with the assumption that the special features of an arid climate resulted in a particular group of soils, often lacking features observed in soils elsewhere. The name Raw Mineral Soils has often been applied to the weath-ered desert detritus which mantles the surface of many arid regions. Russian pedologists placed desert soils with some profile development in a grouping called Sierozems (Grey Desert Soils). The compilers of the FAO–Unesco *Soil Map of the World* perceived the soils of arid regions in terms of the development of the A horizon: those with a weakly developed A horizon were **Xerosols**, and those with very weakly developed features, **Yermosols**. These categories are shown on the maps produced between 1971 and 1981, but this division was more apparent than real, so in the 1988 revision of the legend these major groupings were dispensed with. However, the term **yermic** has been retained to emphasize the truly arid soils as a phase difference, and will also be used at the third level of classification when this is introduced. Another term, **takyric**, is used in the description of massive, fine-textured surface horizons on desert alluvial plains which crack widely when dry (Plate A30). To take the place of Xerosols and Yermosols, new Major Soil Groupings of **Calcisols** and **Gypsisols** have been introduced to categorize soils with calcic or gypsic horizons. Soils with salts more soluble than gypsum are classified as **Solonchaks** or **Solonetz**. Materials which have only a weak ochric A horizon belong to the Leptosols, Regosols or Arenosols (see Chapters 6 and 7). Often the only processes operating in the soils of the arid regions are the accumulation and migration of soluble salts.

Concentration of soluble salts occurs in the soils of arid regions where aerosols from sea-spray are carried inland and deposited on the soil surface. Up to $50\,gm^{-2}$ has been measured falling on soils near the coast of Israel.

American soil scientists have adopted a slightly different approach in *Soil Taxonomy*. In the first place, an Aridisol must have an aridic moisture regime 'dry in all parts more than half the time that the temperature is above 5°C and never moist in some or all parts for as long as 90 consecutive days'; secondly, it must have an ochric or anthropic A horizon; and thirdly, it may possess within 100 cm of the surface one or more of the following diagnostic horizons: argillic, calcic, cambic, gypsic, natric, petrocalcic, petrogypsic, and salic or a duripan. If salic, it may be saturated for one month in the year in any layer within 100 cm of the surface. In the original *Soil Taxonomy* there were two suborders: the Argids had an argillic horizon, and all other Aridisols were Orthids. Since revisions in 1994, there are now seven suborders: Cryids, Salids, Durids, Gypsids, Argids, Calcids and Cambids.

Calcisols

Accumulation of calcium carbonate within the profile is a characteristic feature of many soils in the semi-arid and arid regions, and this feature has been selected as a diagnostic property for the Calcisols. The presence of carbonates at shallow depth in the soil may be found in regions where the rainfall is below 500 mm, especially when this is combined with hot dry summers, as occurs in Algeria, Tunisia, Libya and Egypt. Similar soils also occur in the western states of the USA, southwest Africa, south and west Australia and the central Asian republics. Altogether, Calcisols occupy some 800 million hectares throughout the world.

In semi-arid regions, where rainfall is between 200 and 500 mm, leaching removes free calcium carbonate from the upper part of the soil profile and it is redeposited in the B or C horizons. Semi-arid regions also experience a considerable fallout of calcareous dust which, although sparingly soluble, is dissolved as calcium bicarbonate and carried down the profile when the soil is wetted. When the limit of wetting is reached, calcium carbonate begins to be precipitated (Plates A12 and A13). Precipitation is controlled by the concentration in solution and by the partial pressure of carbon dioxide in the soil air. In the soil pores, carbon dioxide is lost from the soil solution and calcium is precipitated as the mineral calcite (Plate B25). It has been estimated that a calcic horizon can be formed within a period of 4000 to 12,000 years.

Several forms of precipitated calcium carbonate occur as a result of pedogenesis. In seasonally dry climates, filamentous crystals of calcium carbonate, termed 'pseudomycelia' (so called because they resemble fungal mycelia), appear in the soil during the dry season, but they may be leached out in a subsequent wet season. Soft powdery lime must be seen to have some relation to the constituents of the soil fabric (Plate A26). It may disrupt the fabric of the soil matrix to form clusters of white crystals, termed 'white eyes', or it may be present as soft coatings on structure faces or in pores. The third form of carbonate accumulation is commonly seen as discrete nodular concretions of hard lime scattered through the B or C horizon (Plate B25). In arid, highly calcareous environments, these nodular forms can come to occupy a significant proportion of the soil matrix. In these cases there is probably more than 15 per cent calcium carbonate present, and if the horizon is more than 15 cm thick it conforms to the criteria of a **calcic horizon** (Plate A12).

When soils have carbonates at a depth of between 20 and 50 cm, remaining from the parent material and not formed by pedogenesis, they are described as 'calcaric'. Field tests would indicate slight to moderately calcareous (<5 per cent) conditions.

By the processes of accumulation and reprecipitation, the nodules eventually become cemented together in a massive layer of concretionary carbonates resembling limestone rock, referred to as 'calcrete' by geomorphologists. The rock-like appearance is increased by some reprecipitation of calcite in a laminar form on the upper surface of the calcrete. In pedological terminology, these are **petrocalcic horizons** (Plate A13); roots can only penetrate them through cracks, and they cannot be dug with a spade. The carbonate content can amount to 50 per cent or more of the horizon.

Profile of a Haplic Calcisol (Typic Calciorthid) from Jordan

ISRIC Profile JO 01
Diagnostic criteria: cambic B horizon; calcic horizon.

Ap	0–20 cm	Strong brown (7.5YR 5/6) gravelly loam with coarse subangular blocky structure; slightly sticky, non-plastic; friable; common fine roots; many gravel fragments; clear wavy boundary
Bw	20–35 cm	Strong brown (7.5YR 4/6) gravelly clay loam with weak medium subangular blocky structure; sticky and plastic; friable; common fine roots; few pores; strongly effervescent; clear wavy boundary
Bk	35–69 cm	Reddish-yellow (7.5YR 7/6) extremely gravelly clay, structureless; sticky and plastic; friable; few fine roots; violently effervescent; abundant gravel fragments; clear wavy boundary
Ck₁	69–96 cm	Reddish-yellow (7.5YR 7/6) extremely gravelly clay, structureless; sticky and plastic; firm; few fine roots; few pores; abundant gravel fragments; violently effervescent; clear wavy boundary
Ck₂	96–124 cm	Strong brown (7.5YR 5/6) extremely gravelly clay loam, structureless; sticky and plastic; friable; few pores; abundant gravel fragments; strongly effervescent; clear wavy boundary
Ck₃	124–150 cm	Strong brown (7.5YR 4/6) gravelly clay loam, structureless; sticky, plastic; friable; few pores; strongly effervescent

Selected analyses

Horizon Depth (cm)	Ap 0–20	Bw 20–35	Bk 35–69	Ck1/Ck2 69–124
Clay (%)	25	37	31	24
pH H₂O (1:2.5)	8.3	8.3	8.1	8.2
Org. C (%)	0.69	0.39	0.36	0.22
CaCO₃ (%)	32	55	62	44
CEC	15.3	12.6	10.4	10.1
Base sat. (%)	sat.	sat.	sat.	sat.

Comment: well-drained, moderately deep but gravelly loam over clay. Cambic B horizon recognizable below A and amount of CaCO₃ increases to maximum (62 per cent) in Ck₁ from 32 per cent in the A horizon, decreasing again in the Ck₂ horizon (44 per cent).

Many soils on older landsurfaces, especially in the semi-arid regions, have developed argic horizons during periods of cooler, wetter climate through eluviation of clay into the B horizon. A

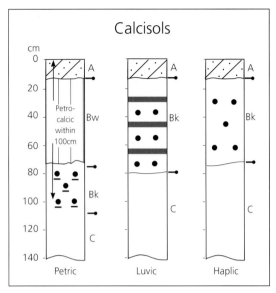

Fig. 11.3 Classification of Calcisols.

calcic horizon may occur in or below the argic horizon in which case they are Calcisols.

Calcisols are soils with an ochric A horizon; they may have a cambic B horizon or an argic B horizon permeated with calcium carbonate. A calcic horizon, a petrocalcic horizon or concentrations of soft powdery lime within 125 cm of the surface are essential characteristics. Calcisols are not allowed to have any vertic, gleyic or salic properties within 100 cm of the surface.

At present there are three Soil Units which are easily recognized in the field (Fig. 11.3). If there is a petrocalcic horizon, the soil is a **Petric Calcisol**; if there is an argic B horizon the soil is a **Luvic Calcisol**; any other Calcisol is a **Haplic Calcisol.**

Gypsisols

In arid regions that have less than 100–150 mm rain and a hot summer climate, in which virtually no leaching of the soil occurs, the possibility exists for the accumulation of pedogenetic gypsum. Usually, the presence of gypsum in soils is related to supplies of ground-water containing calcium sulphate. It is estimated by FAO that there are approximately 90 million hectares of Gypsisols in the world, and their main occurrence is in North Africa and the Middle East. These soils are well-represented around the Great Chott Lakes in southern Tunisia, and in the Middle East they are common on the Tigris–Euphrates plain. In Syria, they occupy terraces of the major rivers, and in Saudi Arabia and Bahrain they are associated with areas of upwelling ground-water. They are extensive between the Caspian and Aral seas and in Somalia, and also occur in southwest USA and central Australia.

Gypsum originates from beds of evaporite included in the Triassic, Jurassic and Cretaceous geological formations as gypsum or anhydrite. The gypsum is dissolved from these geological strata and is carried by surface- or ground-waters to low-lying lands associated with major river valleys or topographic depressions. The gypsum-rich water is drawn to the soil surface where the water is evaporated and the gypsum precipitated. An interesting feature observed with the development of gypsum crystals in soils containing both carbonates and gypsum is that their growth is preceded by a process of decalcification, so that the gypsum crystals grow unobstructed by other soil material. The calcite crystals, in contrast, form an intimate mixture with the other mineral soil material.

Several forms of gypsum are present in soils. Thin, filamentous forms, seen in association with pores and root channels, are similar to the pseudomycelia found in calcareous soils. Usually, this form is of relatively recent origin, and may be redissolved if the soil is wetted by rain. Secondly, compact, powdery gypsum accumulations with a sandy texture occur in soils with very high gypsum contents, associated with weathering over gypsum outcrops. Thirdly, coarser gypsum accumulations, as individual crystals, groups of crystals ('desert roses'), or as pendent crystals below pebbles, can be seen in many alluvial soils. These three forms may be found in **gypsic horizons** (Plate A14). Massive **petrogypsic horizons**, composed almost entirely of gypsum crystals, sometimes with a reprecipitated laminar surface, represent a fourth type (Plates A15 and B24).

Many gypsum-rich soils develop a thin, fluffy crust which, when trodden upon, feels like a deep carpet. Growth of the gypsum crystals makes this crust very uneven, as parts of the crust are forced upwards as the crystals grow. Massive, polygonal-shaped structures with up-turned edges develop on

gypsum-rich alluvial deposits, for example on the floor of the Chott el Djerid in southern Tunisia, and in the southwest sabkha of Bahrain.

The profile of Gypsisols typically has a yellowish-brown ochric A horizon overlying a cambic or argic B horizon onto which the gypsic features have been imposed. Where there is some effective rainfall, the gypsic features lie below the calcic features, but in truly arid areas the gypsic features may be seen from the soil surface downwards.

Gypsisols are soils having a gypsic horizon or a petrogypsic horizon, or both, within 125 cm of the soil surface. A gypsic horizon is enriched by gypsum over more than 15 cm, and it contains 5 per cent more than an underlying horizon; the thickness of the horizon multiplied by the percentage gypsum content should be more than 150 to qualify as a gypsic horizon. A petrogypsic horizon is cemented with gypsum to such an extent that plant roots cannot enter it and it does not slake if a fragment is placed in water. The content of gypsum in these horizons is usually in excess of 60 per cent.

Once it is agreed that a soil qualifies as a Gypsisol through the presence of a gypsic or petrogypsic horizon, it is then possible to proceed to place the soil in the appropriate Soil Unit (Fig. 11.4). **Petric Gypsisols** contain a petrogypsic horizon; where there is a calcic horizon the soil is a **Calcic Gypsisol**; if there is an argic horizon,

Fig. 11.4 Classification of Gypsisols.

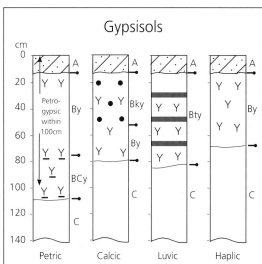

the soil is a **Luvic Gypsisol**; and any remaining soils with gypsic attributes are **Haplic Gypsisols**.

Gypsisols with less than 25 per cent gypsum can be used for growing crops without too many problems. Above 25 per cent, the uptake of water and nutrients by plants begins to be restricted. Under irrigation, solution in the subsoil can result in cavities in the soil, and subsidence may occur. The presence of gypsum and other salts in the soil can cause problems with the foundations of buildings if capillary rise of gypsum-rich solutions is not prevented. As the water containing the gypsum is evaporated, gypsum crystals grow and disrupt concrete and masonry.

Solonchaks

Saline soils were formerly classified as intrazonal soils, because they could appear in any area where the climate was dry enough for the salts to remain in the profile without being washed out by the rainfall. Consequently, they could be seen from cold polar regions to the hot, dry, tropical parts of the world. The Russian name, Solonchak, has been retained for these salty soils as it has become well-established in the literature of soil science. The environment in which these soils occur is one where seasonal or permanently waterlogged conditions prevail, and the water has a significant salt content. Secondary Solonchaks are formed where human activities have raised the water table so that salt accumulation occurs.

Solonchaks are mainly formed under the influence of neutral salts such as sodium chloride and sodium sulphate or calcium sulphate. Efflorescence of these salts on the soil surface gave the name White Alkali Soils (Fig. 11.5). Although sodium is present in these soils, they maintain a reasonable structure and pH values do not generally rise above 8.0.

Worldwide, there are 190 million hectares of Solonchaks. These soils occur in low-lying situations, particularly in semi-arid regions, and also in other climates where evaporation exceeds precipitation. They commonly occur on alluvial plains and are most common in North Africa, the Middle East and central Asia. In natural conditions, Solonchaks occur where a high ground-water level permits moisture to be drawn up to the soil surface and evaporated; any salts in the water are precipitated, leading to a high concentration of salts in the upper part of the soil profile. These soils are very common in old irrigated areas, and it is postulated that the downfall of the Mesopotamian and Indus valley civilizations of 2000 years ago was directly caused by mismanagement of irrigation and the salting of soils. Even today, irresponsible use of

---

Profile of a Haplic Gypsisol (Cambic Gypsiorthid) from Xinjiang, western China

ISRIC Profile CN 12
(Parent material: Pleistocene loess)
Diagnostic criteria: ochric A horizon; gypsic horizon.

A	0–6 cm	Brown (10YR 5/3 dry) silty clay loam with massive to weak platy structure; slightly sticky, slightly plastic; hard; many fine pores; few fine roots; clear smooth boundary
BC$_1$	6–36 cm	Brown (10YR 5/3 dry) silty clay loam with weak coarse columnar structure; slightly sticky, slightly plastic; hard; many fine pores; few fine roots; gradual smooth boundary
BC$_2$	36–77 cm	Brown (10YR 5/3 dry) silty clay loam with weak medium blocky structure; slightly sticky, slightly plastic; hard; many fine pores; few fine roots; gradual smooth boundary
C$_3$	77–160 cm	Brown (10YR 5/3 dry) silty clay loam with massive structure; slightly sticky, slightly plastic; friable and porous

Selected analyses

Horizon	A	BC1	BC2	C
Depth (cm)	0–6	6–36	36–77	77–160
Clay (%)	16	14	16	19
pH H$_2$O (1:2.5)	8.6	8.5	8.6	8.7
CaCO$_3$ (%)	3.6	3.5	2.5	3.0
Org. C (%)	0.73	0.27	0.14	0.15
CEC	7.6	7.4	7.2	6.3
Base sat (%)	sat.	sat.	sat.	sat.

Comment: very deep well-drained brown silt loam derived from loess. Surface of soil is a fragile, irregular crust formed as the crystals of gypsum have grown. The A horizon is weakly platy and low in organic matter; the BC horizon has weak columnar structure but was thought insufficient for a cambic B horizon; gypsum crystals were present in the BC$_2$ horizon.

Fig. 11.5 Salt (sodium sulphate) efflorescence on a Tajik cotton field.

water on crops and leaky irrigation canals are causing ground-water to rise until it can be drawn to the surface by capillary action and salts precipitated. Consequently, the area of Solonchaks continues to increase.

The soil above the water table through which moisture can rise by capillary action is called the 'capillary fringe'. Where the water table is deep within the parent material, the top of the capillary fringe lies below the soil surface, but with a shallow water table it (theoretically) can be above the soil surface. Any building placed upon such a site will have water drawn up into its walls, where salt pre-

cipitation causes disruption of the brick, stonework or mortar, as was described for Gypsisols.

Solonchaks are defined by the presence of **salic properties** within 30 cm of the soil surface. Salic properties are defined by an electrical conductivity of the saturation extract which exceeds 15 dS m^{-1} at 25°C at some time of the year, or of only 4 dS m^{-1} if the pH (H$_2$O) is more than 8.5. The Solonchak soil may have a mollic A horizon, a histic H horizon at the surface, and a cambic B, calcic or gypsic horizon lower in the profile, but no other diagnostic horizons are allowed (Plate B7).

To arrive at the correct Soil Unit within the

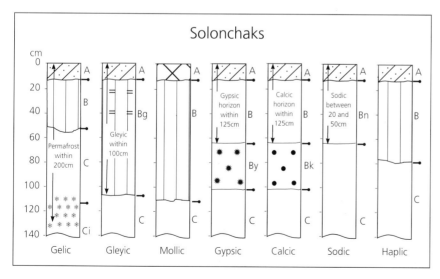

Fig. 11.6 Classification of Solonchaks.

Profile of a Sodic Solonchak (Salorthid) from Turpan Depression, Xinjiang, China

ISRIC Profile CN 14
(Parent material: colluvium)
Diagnostic criteria: ochric A horizon; salic properties; sodic properties; water table at 200 cm.

A	0–8 cm	Pale brown (10YR 6/3) sandy loam with crumb structure; friable; many fine to medium pores; common medium roots; slightly calcareous; abrupt wavy boundary
Azm	8–25 cm	White, hard salt pan; few roots in cracks; non-calcareous
Cz$_1$	25–44 cm	Brown (10YR 5/3) sandy loam with weakly coherent massive structure; slightly sticky, slightly plastic; very friable; few fine pores; few medium roots; slightly calcareous; clear smooth boundary
Cz$_2$	44–65 cm	Brown (10YR 5/3) sandy loam with weakly coherent massive structure; slightly sticky, slightly plastic; friable; few fine pores; few medium roots; slightly calcareous; diffuse smooth boundary
Cz$_3$	65–125 cm	Brown (10YR 5/3) sandy loam with weakly coherent massive structure; slightly sticky, slightly plastic; friable; few very fine pores; no roots; slightly calcareous

Selected analyses

Horizon	A	Azm	Cz1	Cz2	Cz3
Depth (cm)	0–8	8–25	25–44	44–65	65–125
Clay (%)	16	–	9	12	15
pH H$_2$O	8.7	8.6	8.5	8.9	8.5
CaCO$_3$ (%)	2.6	1.1	2.9	3.0	3.0
Org. C (%)	1.59	0.38	0.46	0.24	0.28
CEC	8.5	1.3	8.4	8.7	9.5
Base sat. (%)	sat.	sat.	sat.	sat.	sat.
EC (1:2.5)	39	59	14	8.9	6.0

Comment: profile from –80 m below sea level in the Turpan Depression. Imperfectly drained, brown saline sandy loam with a thick dirty white salt pan. The subsoil shows common white salt spots. pH is high and electrical conductivity (EC) is high.

Solonchaks, the soil scientist proceeds by eliminating, in strict order, those Solonchaks which have permafrost within 200 cm of the surface; these are **Gelic Solonchaks**. Then, if there are gleyic properties within 100 cm of the surface the soil becomes a **Gleyic Solonchak**; if there is a mollic horizon it is a **Mollic Solonchak**; if a gypsic horizon is present then it is a **Gypsic Solonchak**; similarly with a calcic horizon, the soil is a **Calcic Solonchak**; with sodic properties (>15 per cent CEC occupied by sodium ions) it is a **Sodic Solonchak**; any remaining soils are **Haplic Solonchaks** (Fig. 11.6).

Solonchaks may be used for cropping if the soluble salts are first washed out and the amount of irrigation water used is sufficient to keep the salts moving downwards and to stop salts from returning and recrystallizing in the soil horizons. At the same time, it is vital to ensure that the Solonchak has adequate drainage, otherwise the water table will simply rise until capillary rise again enriches the surface horizon with salts.

Solonetz

The total area of Solonetz is estimated to be in the region of 135 million hectares, and the world distribution is similar to that of the Solonchaks, with which they are closely associated. Solonetz are developed under the influence of sodium bicarbonate, sodium carbonate, sodium silicate and magnesium carbonate. In Solonetz, there is a loss of stability, the clay and organic materials become dispersed and pH values rise above 8.5. A former name given to these soils was Black Alkali Soils.

Unlike the Solonchaks, the Solonetz are usually fine-textured, and salt-affected mainly in their lower horizons. The A horizon may be rich in organic matter, but the presence of sodium on the exchange positions of the clay–humus complex means that the colloids are dispersed and the A horizon lacks structure, and it is described as massive, hard when dry, but fluid when wet. Moreover, the Solonetz have a natric B horizon that displays the typical columnar structure and is very dense and slow-draining. Development of Solonetz takes place on sodium-rich parent materials such as saline marine clays or alluvia.

The major diagnostic criterion for the Solonetz is that the soil should have a horizon which qualifies as a natric B horizon (Plates A9 and B18). This means that in addition to the properties of an argic B horizon, it has to have a columnar structure with tongues of the eluvial horizon containing uncoated sand or silt grains. Within the upper 40 cm it must have more than 15 per cent of the exchangeable capacity taken up with sodium. Also, if exchangeable sodium plus exchangeable magnesium amounts to more than exchangeable calcium plus exchangeable acidity within the upper 40 cm of the horizon, or if saturation with exchangeable sodium is more than 15 per cent in any sub-horizon within 200 cm of the soil surface, the soil qualifies as a Solonetz. Measurements of adsorbed sodium are given by the exchangeable sodium percentage (ESP) and the sodium adsorption ratio (SAR):

$$ESP = \text{exchangeable Na} \times 100 / CEC$$
$$SAR = Na^+ /[(Ca^{2+} + Mg^{2+}) / 2]^{0.5}$$

The Solonetz profile typically develops an eluvial horizon, containing uncoated silt or sand grains, which tongues down at least 2.5 cm into the natric B horizon.

There are six Soil Units within the Solonetz Major Soil Grouping (Fig. 11.7). The first unit to be identified includes Solonetz which have gleyic properties within 100 cm of the soil surface; these are the **Gleyic Solonetz**. Soils with gleyic properties only in the upper 50 cm are classed as **Stagnic Solonetz**. With a mollic A horizon, the soil is a **Mollic Solonetz**; and if there are gypsic or calcic horizons within 125 cm of the surface, the soils are **Gypsic** and **Calcic Solonetz**, respectively. Any remaining soils belong to the **Haplic Solonetz**.

Whilst the physical and chemical compositions of Solonetz are most unfavourable, in certain circumstances it is possible, with modern technology and capital input, to reclaim them for agriculture. Where carbonates are near to the surface, deep ploughing can bring the calcareous material to the surface, improve the structural stability and lower the pH. Other ameliorating substances which have been employed include ferric chloride and sulphuric acid, both of which are also effective in lowering the pH. Solonetz are very difficult soils to manage as they become very hard when dry and are very plastic when wet. Plant growth is severely limited by high pH (over 8.5) and by the presence in the soil of sodium carbonate and other salts. The salts in the soil result in an osmotic gradient from plant to soil, so that plants cannot draw moisture into their roots. Only plants with high osmotic pressure are able to survive in these soils. Normal agricultural crops cannot be grown, and grazing potential is limited.

Related soils

The low availability of moisture and lack of a vegetation cover leaves soils unprotected from the erosive effects of wind and water. There is a continual loss of finer soil particles, some of which are blown completely out of the arid areas, where they contribute to loess deposits. Larger soil particles, sorted and redeposited by flash-floods, can be mobilized by the wind into sand dunes. Fresh,

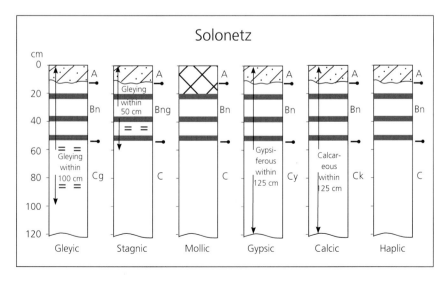

Fig. 11.7 Classification of Solonetz.

Profile of a Haplic Solonetz (Typic Natrustalf) from Alagoas, NE Brazil

ISRIC Profile BR 17
(Parent material: gneiss)
Diagnostic criteria: natric B horizon.

A	0–6 cm	Brown (10YR 5/3) sandy loam with very weak fine subangular blocky structure; non-sticky, non-plastic; friable; common fine pores; few fine roots; clear smooth boundary
E₁	6–20 cm	Yellowish-brown (10YR 5/4) sandy loam with very weak fine subangular blocky structure; non-sticky, non-plastic; common fine pores; few fine roots; clear wavy boundary
E₂	20–30 cm	Light yellowish-brown (10YR 6/4) very gravelly sandy loam, structureless; non-sticky, non-plastic; loose; abrupt wavy boundary
Btn	30–67 cm	Yellowish-brown (10YR 5/4) clay with columnar structure; very firm; very hard; pressure cutans on ped faces; few fine pores; clear wavy boundary
C	67–90 cm	Loamy sand, structureless; firm; frequent gneiss fragments

Selected analyses

Horizon	Ah	E	Btn	C
Depth (cm)	0–6	6–30	30–67	67–90
Clay (%)	10	9	41	6
pH H₂O (1:2.5)	5.0	5.7	7.9	9.4
Org. C (%)	1.49	0.74	0.23	0.05
CEC	6.9	4.4	13.6	5.8
Na⁺	6.0	4.1	23.5	7.5
Base sat. (%)	87	93	sat.	sat.

Comment: moderately deep poorly drained profile; E horizon variable in depth; abrupt texture change from sandy loam E to clay natric B horizon. Over 50 per cent of CEC is dominated by exchange sodium in the Btn horizon.

---

mobile dunes cannot be considered as soils and are normally placed in a category of miscellaneous land types. Dunes which have stabilized and have characteristics such as an ochric A horizon will normally fall into the **Arenosols** (Chapter 6).

The activities of wind and water in removing soil material from the landscape lead to the development of shallow **Leptosols**, where weathering and soil formation fail to keep up with erosional losses. Deeper surficial deposits may develop

Regosols (Chapter 6) or **Cambisols** (Chapter 7), depending upon the presence of a weathered B horizon.

Further reading

Alphen, J.G. and de los Rios Romero, F., 1971. *Gypsiferous Soils: Notes on their Characteristics and Management.* Bulletin No. 12, ILRI, Wageningen.

Buol, S.W., 1965. Present soil forming factors and processes in arid and semi-arid regions. *Soil Science* **99**:45–9.

Campbell, I.B. and Claridge, G.G.C., 1987. *Antarctica: Soils, Weathering Processes and Environment.* Developments in Soil Science No. 16, Elsevier, Amsterdam.

Dregne, H.E., 1976. *Soils of Arid Regions.* Elsevier, Amsterdam.

Dregne, H.E. (ed.), 1992. *Degradation and Restoration of Arid Lands.* International Centre for Arid and Semi-arid Land Studies, Texas Tech University, Lubbock.

Gile, L.H., Hawley, J.W. and Grossman, R.B., 1981. *Soils, and Geomorphology in the Basin and Range area of Southern New Mexico: Guidebook to the Desert Project.* Memoir No. 39, New Mexico Bureau of Mines and Mineral Resources, Sorocco.

Miller, D.E., 1971. Formation of vesicular structure in soil. *Soil Science Society of America Journal* **35**:635–7.

Nettleton, W.D. and Peterson, F.F., 1983. Aridisols. In: Wilding, L.P., Smeck, N.E. and Hall, G.F. (eds.) *Pedogenesis and Soil Taxonomy. II. The Soil Orders.* Elsevier, Amsterdam, pp. 165–215.

Nettleton, W.D., Witty, J.E., Nelson, R.E. and Hawley, J.W., 1975. Genesis of argillic horizons in soils of desert areas of the southwestern United States. *Soil Science Society of America Journal* **39**:919–26.

Yaalon, D.H. (ed.), 1981. *Arid Soils and Geomorphic Processes.* Catena Supplement No.1, Catena Verlag, Cremlingen.

12 Soils of the inter-tropical areas

The discussion of the factors of soil formation in Chapter 3 has already indicated that there is a theoretical possibility of deep, rapid weathering in the inter-tropical regions of the world. High soil temperatures and plentiful supplies of moisture encourage breakdown of rocks and rapid mineralization of organic matter. In contrast to the zones of warm and cool temperate climate, there has been no significant interruption of the warm, moist climate by conditions of either aridity or cold. As weathering and soil-forming processes have had a long period of continuous operation under optimum conditions, the average depth of regolith is greater than in temperate regions, with more than 30 m recorded in some places. The soils of inter-tropical regions often have deep profiles, but it is necessary to distinguish clearly between deep, weathered parent material and the actual soil. If the soil is thought of as that part of the Earth's crust influenced by current soil formation and exploited by plant roots, this helps to avoid, in part, the confusion between soil and parent material. However, in inter-tropical regions, as elsewhere, it is necessary to remember that conditions in the parent material may influence processes in the soil itself.

Many inter-tropical areas have been dry land for long periods of geological history, and the deposits upon them have been through several periods of weathering, erosion and deposition dating back to the Pliocene or Miocene. In the southern continents, geomorphologists have recognized a succession of plateau-like surfaces associated with cycles of erosion of different periods. These surfaces have upon them soils of different ages, with different profiles and properties. In many cases, there is evidence in the regolith of previous reworking of the materials before the current phase of soil formation. This results in a complicated pattern of soils, which can be understood only if the mode of origin of their parent materials is first deciphered. Concepts of erosional and depositional phases of soil materials, developed in Australia, have assisted greatly in elucidating the soil pattern found on these old continental areas (Fig. 12.1).

The presence of a pronounced stone layer is a characteristic feature of many tropical soils. These **stone lines** may occur at any depth within the soil or parent material. They may arise from an outcrop of a quartz vein: as the surrounding rock is weathered, the broken fragments of the quartz vein are moved gradually downslope by creep to form the stone line within the regolith. An alternative

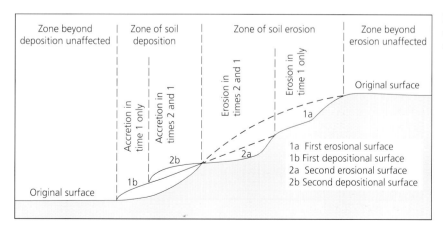

Fig. 12.1 Erosional and depositional phases of soils (after Butler, 1959).

125

suggestion is that the stones represent a former soil surface from which finer material has been winnowed by the wind or washed by overland flow, leaving the stones as a protective layer on the surface. The surface has subsequently been covered by additional colluviation from upslope. Moving of soil material by termites or other animals may also be responsible for the formation of a stone line.

Although this discussion has referred to the inter-tropical regions, these areas do not have a uniform climate. Equatorial regions are characterized by a continually moist environment with a pattern of two precipitation maxima, a total rainfall of 2000 mm or more, and a mean annual temperature of between 25 and 30°C, with only a slight annual and diurnal variation. This hot, humid climate has a length of growing period (LGP) of over 270 days and is classed as Af by Köppen. Towards the tropics (23°30'N and S), the rainy season becomes shorter and the dry season longer until there is only one rainy season. Rainfall varies considerably with location, from 600 to 1500 mm per annum, and although the average temperatures are similar to those of the equatorial regions, the range (up to 20°C) is much greater. Such climates are referred to as savanna (Aw) or monsoon climates (Am). The length of growing period in these areas is between 75 and 270 days, depending on the rainfall.

The climatic changes associated with the Pleistocene also affected the margins of the tropical areas. It is known from biogeographical evidence that the Sahara has been considerably moister than at present, and also that the present savanna has been subjected to a drier climate. During dry phases (inter-pluvial), restricted plant growth led to more rapid natural soil erosion; in wetter (pluvial) phases, the balance of vegetation was changed, with increased vegetation cover and greater soil stability.

The luxuriant tropical rain forest of the humid tropical regions does not always provide a good guide to the fertility of the soils. Most of the plant nutrients are contained in the vegetation and they are continually circulated as the leaves fall from the trees. A dense root mat efficiently captures most of the nutrients as they are released from the decaying plant litter and before they are lost in the drainage water. If this cycle of nutrients, from plant to soil

and back to the plants, is broken, a rapid decline in fertility occurs. Reserves of plant nutrients in many soils of the tropical regions are very low, as strong weathering and leaching over a long period of time have reduced them to very low concentrations. Virtually all the available plant nutrients are contained in the vegetation and litter.

Away from the continually humid regions, deciduous trees, which shed their leaves in the dry season, become more common, and eventually these give way to the savanna grasslands. On the margins of the forests and in the grasslands, fire can be a significant factor influencing the vegetation and the soils. Once the cover of vegetation has been burnt and the protective cover breached, the soils can easily be leached and eroded.

The strong leaching of soils in the humid tropics produces a moderately acid soil, but, because of the rapid circulation of the bases, strongly acid conditions do not develop in the surface horizons. In the warm, moist conditions, silica is more soluble than iron oxides and it is lost from the structure of the clay minerals. The iron and aluminium sesquioxides which remain are relatively insoluble. This process of relative enrichment with the sesquioxides is referred to as **ferrallitization**. Where these oxides form an obvious part of the soil B horizon, it is termed a **ferralic B horizon** (FAO) or an **oxic horizon** (USDA). The presence of the iron sesquioxides gives the soil a strong reddish or yellowish-brown coloration, which is characteristic of many freely drained tropical soils. The greater solubility of silica from the clay minerals is demonstrated by the composition of drainage waters from tropical rivers. Examples have been recorded where up to 50 per cent of the total solids carried by rivers in the tropics consists of silica, whereas the average content of all rivers only amounts to 12 per cent. Weathering studies of feldspars indicate that silica is lost in the first stage of rock weathering, while that which remains in the soil is predominantly in the form of quartz sand or the clay mineral kaolinite, both of which are relatively stable.

The long period of time required for soil formation and the greater mobility of soil constituents in tropical soils are reflected in the soil pattern and its relationship to the landscape. Movement of soil constituents downslope brings into being a sequence of soils, closely related to their position on slopes, known as a **catena** (Fig. 12.2). The soil relationships of the catena were first identified by Milne in the 1930s in East Africa, and the concept has since been found to be very useful in the interpretation of landscape–soil relationships in virtually all environments.

The character of the iron oxides remaining in the soil depends largely upon the water relationships of the soil. With freely drained conditions on the interfluves, the iron oxides remain dispersed throughout the profile, but if ground-water is in close proximity to the surface, then a grey soil with red mottles may develop. A process called **ferrolysis** has been proposed for the process of clay breakdown in hydromorphic conditions. This has been discussed in Chapter 4.

Movement and concentration of iron compounds in the process of soil formation can result in the production of coarse mottles with bright red colours and iron concretions in the form of nodules. When these features are present, a soil is said to have **ferric properties** (Plate A21) and is associated with Soil Units in the Luvisols, Alisols, Lixisols and Acrisols in humid tropical regions.

Many soils of the inter-tropical regions contain a humus-poor, iron-rich clayey mixture, which in some cases can harden on exposure to air. This property was exploited in former times in India and Cambodia, where these clays were dug out in a moist condition and blocks laid in the sun to dry. The blocks hardened to make very satisfactory bricks, hence the term **Laterite** (from Latin *later*, brick) has been used for this soil material (Fig. 12.3). In recent literature these irreversibly hardening clays have been called **plinthite** (Plate A24).

Where there is a large quantity of iron, the whole soil mass may become solidified where the air can reach it, forming a pisolitic, nodular or slag-like **ironstone** (Plate A25). These hardened ironstone formations often form the upper edge of escarpments, providing a mesa-like landscape typical of parts of Western Australia, West Africa and South America.

In the deep, freely drained, uniform conditions of many tropical soils, chemical and physical conditions are similar throughout the soil. Clay eluviation does occur in tropical soils, but in many cases

Fig. 12.3 Bricks cut from plinthite (laterite).

Fig. 12.2 A soil catena from East Africa: Itongo, Lusenye, Ibambasi, Itogoro-mbuga and Mbuga are colloquial soil names; murram is ironstone gravel (after Milne, 1935).

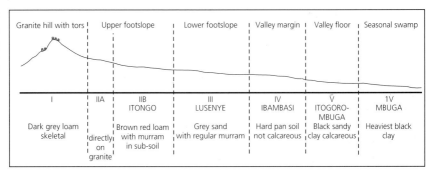

Granite hill with tors	Upper footslope		Lower footslope	Valley margin	Valley floor	Seasonal swamp
I	IIA	IIB ITONGO	III LUSENYE	IV IBAMBASI	V ITOGORO-MBUGA	1V MBUGA
Dark grey loam skeletal	directly on granite	Brown red loam with murram in sub-soil	Grey sand with regular murram	Hard pan soil not calcareous	Black sandy clay calcareous	Heaviest black clay

an increase in clay content in the B horizon of the profile reflects the intensity of weathering and clay formation, rather than clay migration. In soils which have formed in a climate with a marked dry season, silica may be deposited low in the profile.

Classification

There have been numerous approaches to the study and classification of soils in low latitudes. The early pioneers of soil science observed the development of red 'zonal' soils in tropical regions, and in more recent times Russian pedologists have identified Red Earths (Krasnozems) and Yellow Earths (Zheltozems) in the southern republics of the former Soviet Union. Within the inter-tropical areas, the use of the word Laterite, and its derivative Latosol, has bedevilled soil nomenclature for many years, and although the terms are still in occasional use, they are not employed in current soil classifications. Similarly, the use of the term 'tropical soils' is unhelpful as it implies that these soils have much in common, whereas there is a much greater variety of soils in the inter-tropical zone than in other areas of the world. Accumulation of the oxides of iron (Fe) and aluminium (Al) in tropical soils led the British soil scientist, Robinson, in the 1940s, to coin the term Ferallitic Soil, but it was in later classifications made by French pedologists that the concept was elaborated. Their grouping of soils without clay accumulation in the Ferrallitic Soils, and those soils with an argillic horizon into the Ferralsols or Ferruginous Soils, led directly to the present form of classification.

From these beginnings, it was a small step for the 1974 FAO–Unesco *Soil Map of the World* legend to have two similar groups: soils with ferralic B horizons, the Ferralsols, and soils with argic B horizons, the Acrisols and Nitosols. Subsequent redefinition in 1988 retained the Ferralsols and Nitosols (as Nitisols) but split the other soils with argic B horizons into four groupings: those with a higher CEC (more than $24 \text{cmol}_c \text{kg}^{-1}$ clay) and less than 50 per cent saturation, the Alisols; those with a higher CEC and more than 50 per cent saturation, the Luvisols (mostly extra-tropical); soils with a lower CEC (less than $24 \text{cmol}_c \text{kg}^{-1}$ clay) and low base saturation remain as Acrisols; and those with lower CEC and more than 50 per cent saturation by bases are the Lixisols.

Local variations in elevation and parent material, such as coarse siliceous sands, volcanic ashes, limestone, marine and fresh-water alluvia, all produce soils of different character which do not fit into the broad zonal pattern of soils identified by the late 19th- and early 20th-century pedologists, whose ideas were developed mainly on the plainlands of Africa. However, the early idea of tropical soils where weathering and soil-forming processes worked throughout the year and at greater rates than in the temperate parts of the world was substantially correct. Hence it is possible to retain an approximately zonal pattern for the discussion of these soils. Six Major Soil Groupings cover approximately 75 per cent of the humid tropical soil-ecological zone, of which Acrisols and Ferralsols are the most extensive, followed by smaller areas of Leptosols, Nitisols, Fluvisols and Gleysols.

Ferralsols

The long, uninterrupted period of soil formation in the inter-tropical regions has resulted in soils with uniform physical and chemical properties covering large areas of central Africa and Brazil. These soils are dominated by kaolinitic clays with low CEC, and by hydrated iron and aluminium sesquioxides which coat the clays, giving a yellowish-brown colour to the soil. Structure is moderately stable and there is a low content of water-dispersable clay. A micro-structure of pseudosand or pseudosilt is commonly developed, which disguises the actual clay content. There is an absence of weatherable minerals, but secondary accumulation of goethite or hematite and gibbsite may be present. Any rock structure remaining must be less than 5 per cent.

Typically, Ferralsols occupy flat or gently undulating surfaces of old peneplains below 2000m where the soil parent materials have passed through several phases of weathering, erosion and deposition, and so the parent material may be roughly stratified at depth in the profile. Soil formation is characterized by the slow and continual removal of silica, which leads to a relative accumulation of aluminium and iron oxides (the name 'Ferralsols' comes from the Latin *ferrum* and *alumen*, signifying a high content of sesquioxides). There is no clay accumulation in the B horizon, and as the iron hydroxides coat and bind together the clay particles in this soil, it is fairly stable. Ferralsols require careful clearance from virgin forest so that the topsoil is preserved, otherwise loss of organic matter and compaction will occur. Typically, Ferralsols have reasonable physical properties but are infertile because of the strong fixing powers for phosphate.

These soils cover about 745 million hectares worldwide, or about 6 per cent of the Earth's surface, mostly on the continental shield of South America in Brazil, and in the central African states of Zaire, Congo, western Angola, Guinea, part of Madagascar and the Central African Republic, and southeast Asia. Elsewhere, these soils develop only on easily weatherable basic rocks in warm humid climates.

The present Major Soil Grouping of Ferralsols has emerged from several previous groupings of soils in the humid tropics. These included Ferrallitic Soils, Latosols or Kaolisols. Similarly strongly weathered materials and soils occur on the savanna lands, having a low exchange capacity but lacking the strong leaching and acidity of the soils in the continually moist rain forest regions. Earlier attempts to classify these soils referred to them as Plateau Soils, Pallid Soils or as Weathered Ferrallitic

Soils. The position is now simpler as all these soils have been brought together in the major group of Ferralsols, which corresponds approximately to the Udox, Perox and Aquox suborders of *Soil Taxonomy*.

To belong to the Ferralsol Major Soil Grouping, a soil must have a **ferralic B horizon** (Plate A11). The ferralic B horizon must have a texture of sandy loam or finer with at least 8 per cent clay, and it must be more than 30 cm thick. The CEC has to be less than $16 \, cmol_c \, kg^{-1}$ and have less than 10 per cent weatherable minerals in the silt fraction, and there should be less than 5 per cent volume of the soil which has rock structure remaining. A Ferralsol has a silt:clay ratio of less than 0.2 and it contains less than 10 per cent water-dispersable clay. As there is a lack of clear horizon boundaries in Ferralsols, the profile appears to be very uniform from the surface to the parent material (Plate B16).

If a soil meets these criteria, then it could belong to one of the six Soil Units of the Ferralsols (Fig. 12.4). **Plinthic Ferralsols** are distinguished by the presence of plinthite. Those with very low CEC (less than $1.5 \, cmol_c \, kg^{-1}$) and a delta pH (pH KCl minus pH H_2O) of more than +0.1 are separated as **Geric Ferralsols**. Strongly humic soils with an umbric A horizon are **Humic Ferralsols**. Those with a strong red B horizon (redder than 5YR) are

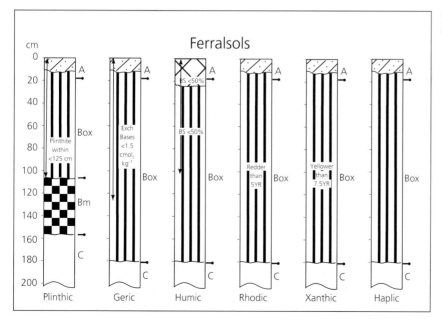

Fig. 12.4 Classification of Ferralsols.

Rhodic Ferralsols. Where there is a yellow B horizon (hue of 7.5YR or yellower) then the soil is a **Xanthic Ferralsol**. Any remaining soils with a ferralic B horizon are grouped together as **Haplic Ferralsols**.

Ferralsols are used under shifting cultivation in mixed cropping systems, growing crops such as cassava, yam, plantain, sweet potato and upland rice for human sustenance. Considerable areas, formerly appropriated under the colonial system, continue to be used as plantations, growing cash crops of coffee, rubber, cocoa, oil palm and coconut, often in agroforestry systems of management. Ferralsols require liming to counteract low pH and aluminium toxicity, and as they strongly fix phosphates, fertilizers should be given in split applications.

Nitisols

Many soils of the tropical regions possess an argic B horizon, and in the past these soils have been referred to as Ferruginous Soils, Ferrisols, Krasnozems, Zheltozems or Red-yellow Podzolic Soils. In the 1974 legend of the FAO–Unesco *Soil Map of the World*, these soils were brought into two Major Soil Groupings, the Nitosols and the Acrisols. However, in the subsequent revision of the legend in 1988, it was proposed that further subdivision was desirable, and the Nitosols were more closely defined as the Nitisols.

The Nitisols (from Latin *nitidus*, shiny) are some of the most valuable and productive soils of the tropical regions. These deep, dark red, freely drained soils are formed over base-rich parent materials, and in many volcanic areas may be rejuvenated from time to time by further additions of volcanic ash. They have a stable structure and so are naturally resistant to erosion. These soils occur on much younger landscapes than the Ferralsols, and the parent materials may contain weatherable minerals. In the profile, the diagnostic features are the clay-enriched argic B horizon with the presence of a characteristic angular blocky structure with shiny ped faces, and horizons which merge gradually into those above and below. The origin of the shiny ped surfaces is thought to be a combination of clay eluviation followed by pressure developed when the soil is wet, resulting in the orientation of clays on the ped surface.

There are approximately 200 million hectares of Nitisols throughout the world, with major occurrences in Brazil and the east African countries of Kenya, Tanzania and Ethiopia, and scattered areas in Central America, the western coast of India and in the southeast Asian countries of Indonesia, China and the Philippines.

Profile of a Xanthic Ferralsol (Typic Haplorthox) from near Yangamibi, Zaire

ISRIC Profile ZR 01
(Parent material: Pleistocene aeolian deposits)
Diagnostic criteria: ochric A horizon; ferralic B horizon.

O	2–0cm	Leaves, becoming more decomposed with depth
Ah	0–11 cm	Dark brown (7.5YR 3/2) loamy sand with moderate fine crumb to subangular blocky structure; slightly plastic and sticky; very friable; few faint mottles; abundant roots; clear wavy boundary
BA	11–32cm	Dark brown (7.5YR 4/4) sandy loam with fine crumb to weak fine subangular blocky structure; sticky, plastic; very friable; common faint mottles; many fine pores; common fine roots; smooth gradual boundary
Bo₁	32–80cm	Dark brown (7.5YR 4/5) sandy loam with weak coarse angular blocky to fine subangular blocky structure; sticky, plastic; very friable; common medium faint mottles; common fine roots; many pores; gradual smooth boundary
Bo₂	80–150cm	Strong brown (7.5YR 5/6) sandy clay loam with weak to moderate coarse subangular blocky structure; sticky, plastic; very friable; few medium faint mottles; many pores; few fine roots; gradual smooth boundary

Selected analyses

Horizon	Ah	BA	Bo1	Bo2
Depth (cm)	0–13	13–34	34–82	82–150
Clay (%)	19	22	25	28
pH H₂O (1:2.5)	3.9	4.2	4.4	4.3
Org. C (%)	1.5	0.4	0.3	0.2
CEC	5.7	3.5	3.7	3.5
Base sat. (%)	5	11	0	6

Comment: very deep, well-drained, yellowish-brown soil with an ochric A horizon and a ferralic B horizon.

In the legend for the FAO–Unesco *Soil Map of the World*, the Nitisols are defined as having an argic B horizon together with **nitic properties** (Plate A20). To be a Nitisol a soil must have more than 30 per cent clay, with a moderate or strong angular blocky structure, often referred to as polyhedric or 'nutty', the surfaces of which have characteristic shiny ped faces. Soils with nitic properties must have more than 0.2 per cent iron extractable by acid ammonium oxylate, but this can rise to 15 per cent in some examples. After reaching its maximum amount of clay, the argic B horizon of Nitisols continues to considerable depth before the clay content declines (not more than 20 per cent reduction in the 150 cm from the soil surface is specified) (Fig. 12.5). The clays are usually kaolinitic (Plate B26).

Once it is decided that a soil belongs to the Nitisols, there are currently only three Soil Units within which a soil may be placed, although there are proposals for some additional units in the future (Fig. 12.6). Strongly humic soils with an umbric horizon and a base saturation of less than 50 per cent are **Humic Nitisols**; those soils with a dusky red argic B horizon (rubbed soil hue redder than 5YR and value less than 4) are **Rhodic Nitisols**; any remaining soils are **Haplic Nitisols.**

Fig. 12.5 Comparison of typical clay contents in Nitisols, Ferralsols, and Acrisols, Lixisols and Alisols.

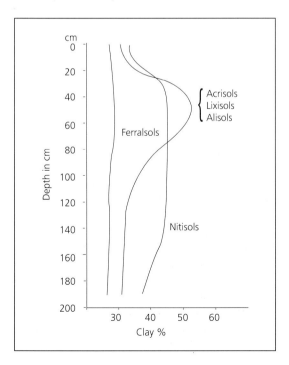

Profile of a Haplic Nitisol (Typic Hapludalf) from Guandong Province, China

ISRIC Profile CN 31
(Parent material: grey marble)
Diagnostic criteria: ochric A horizon; argic B horizon; nitic properties.

Ah	0–5 cm	Dark brown (10YR 3/3) slightly gravelly clay loam with fine subangular blocky structure; plastic, sticky; common pores; common roots; clear boundary
AB	5–24 cm	Yellowish-red (5YR 4/6) slightly gravelly clay with medium angular blocky structure; very sticky and plastic; common fine pores; common fine and medium roots; patchy thin cutans; gradual smooth boundary
Bt₁	24–51 cm	Dark reddish-brown (5YR 3/4) slightly stony clay with strong coarse angular blocky structure breaking easily to medium and fine angular blocky; very plastic and sticky; few fine pores; common fine roots; continuous thick cutans; few fresh marble fragments; gradual smooth boundary
Bt₂	51–120 cm	Dark reddish-brown (5YR 3/6) bouldery clay with strong angular blocky structure; very plastic and sticky; few pores; few fine roots; continuous thick cutans on ped faces
BC	120–165 cm	Dark yellowish-brown (5YR 3/6) bouldery clay; very sticky, very plastic; slightly porous; no roots

Selected analyses

Horizon	Ah	AB	Bt₁	Bt₂
Depth (cm)	0–5	5–24	24–51	51–120
Clay (%)	46	52	57	56
pH H₂O (1:2.5)	6.1	4.9	5.2	5.5
Org. C (%)	4.22	1.60	0.80	0.71
CEC	24.8	16.3	15.8	14.9
Base sat. (%)	86	49	51	68

Comment: deep, well-drained, dark reddish-brown clay soil derived from grey marble. There is a thin A horizon and the soil has a strongly developed subangular blocky structure throughout, with the shiny surfaces described as 'nitic'.

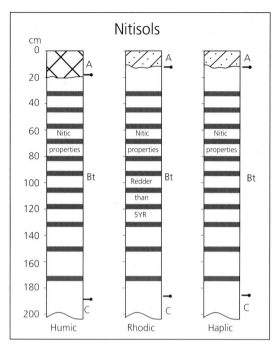

Fig. 12.6 Classification of Nitisols.

Plinthosols

The concept of the Plinthosols is of soils that have developed in a parent material which is under the influence of ground-water or stagnating surface water. These soils have formed in landscapes of low relief and high ground-water and are closely associated with geomorphologically old surfaces.

Two distinctly different phases of these soils can be identified: those in which the formation of plinthite is still taking place, and those where the process has ceased as a result of climate change or base-level change. At the present time, the process is observable in South America and Africa, where the majority of the world's 60 million hectares of Plinthosols occur. However, as a result of former climates and movements of the world's tectonic plates, the long-lasting effects of the process of plinthite formation may be seen widely distributed throughout the world, not just within the tropics (Plate B15).

Plinthosols are distinguished by the presence of **plinthite**, which is an iron-rich, humus-poor mixture of kaolinitic clay with quartz and only a few other minerals (Plate A24). Alternating wetting and drying cycles have segregated the iron compounds into iron-rich mottles set in a grey kaolinitic groundmass. When first exposed, the grey material has a cheese-like consistency and it may be dug easily with a spade, but on exposure to the air plinthite irreversibly hardens, a characteristic which gave it the name of 'Laterite' (from Latin *later*, brick). Thus, the current concept of plinthite includes many former ideas about Laterites. However, not all poorly drained, mottled tropical clay soils have plinthite; those which do not harden have been referred to as pseudoplinthite.

The iron-rich material may harden upon drying into concretionary forms or into a continuous mass of ironstone, when it becomes **petroplinthite** (Plate A25). Once formed, the ironstone is very resistant to further weathering. Consequently, when the base level of erosion changes, former Plinthosols may be found in the landscape capping residual tabular hills, the escarpment edges of which are reinforced by massive ironstone concretions. In semi-arid areas in particular, erosion of the soil above the ironstone reveals it at the surface, when hardening can take place. Slow redistribution of the ironstone occurs as the gradual break-up of the escarpment edge takes place. Fragments of the ironstone tumble to the foot of the slope and there become reincorporated by cementation into a secondary ironstone, especially where iron-rich seepage waters emerge. Hardening of plinthite may also occur along the banks of rivers incised below their floodplains. Former names of these soils were Ground-water Laterite, Low-level Laterite, *Sols Ferrugineux Tropicaux à Cuirasse* or Ironstone Soils.

Four Soil Units are recognized in the Plinthosols (Fig. 12.7). A soil is classified as a Plinthosol if it contains at least 25 per cent or more plinthite by volume and it is at least 15 cm thick and within 50 cm of the surface, except where there is an albic E horizon in which case it can be 125 cm below the soil surface. **Albic Plinthosols** have an albic E horizon. **Humic Plinthosols** have an umbric A horizon or a dystric H horizon. Where there is an ochric A horizon and a base saturation of less than 50 per cent throughout the upper 50 cm, the soil is a **Dystric Plinthosol**. Other Plinthosols with a base saturation over 50 per cent are **Eutric Plinthosols**.

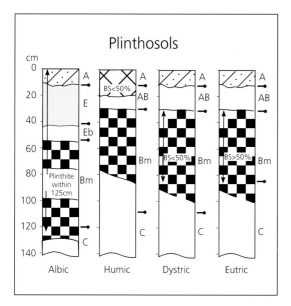

Fig. 12.7 Classification of Plinthosols.

Plinthosols are often restricted to grazing lands left under indigenous pastures as they have low natural fertility, are prone to waterlogging and may be subject to flooding. If hardening has occurred, root penetration is severely limited, which restricts the crops that can be grown. Although poor for agricultural purposes, the plinthite can be used as a building material: the temples at Ankor Wat in

Kampuchea are built of this material, and the ironstone is extensively used as a material for surfacing roads. Where the residual material is predominantly gibbsite, the possibility exists of using these materials as an ore from which aluminium may be smelted.

Profile of a Plinthosol from near York, Western Australia

(Parent material: gneiss)

0–150 cm	Ironstone crust. Yellowish-brown hard ironstone, becoming slightly softer towards the base
150–690 cm	Pallid zone. White and slightly pinkish clay with dark red patches. Quartz grains are bleached white in the clay and stained with iron oxide in red areas. Occasional mica flakes throughout
690+ cm	Pale brown and rusty mottled weathered gneiss

Comment: unlike the profile to the right, the ironstone has developed from the iron-rich layer of the plinthite. Ironstone-capped mesas are a feature of the landscape near York in Western Australia.

Profile of a Humic Plinthosol (Plinthaquept) from Goias Province, Brazil

ISRIC Profile BR 27
(Parent material: alluvium)
Diagnostic criteria: umbric A horizon; gleyic properties; presence of plinthite.

Ap	0–12 cm	Very dark grey (10YR 3/1) silty clay loam with weak fine to medium subangular blocky structure; slightly sticky, slightly plastic; very friable; many fine pores; common fine roots; abrupt smooth boundary
Ah	12–35 cm	Very dark greyish-brown (10YR 3/2) silty clay loam with massive structure; slightly sticky, slightly plastic; very friable; many fine pores; common fine roots; clear wavy boundary
E	35–75 cm	Dark yellowish-brown (10YR 4/4) clay loam with massive structure; slightly sticky, slightly plastic; common mottles (10YR5/6 and 10YR5/2); many pores; few fine roots; gradual smooth boundary
Bg₁	75–95 cm	Grey (10YR 6/1) clay with massive structure and prominent mottles (10YR5/6); few hard ferruginous concretions; gradual boundary
Bg₂	95–245 cm	Light grey (10YR 7/1) clay with massive structure and many prominent mottles (10YR5/8); many fine pores; few hard ferruginous concretions

Selected analyses

Horizon	Ap/Ah	E	Bg₁	Bg₂
Depth (cm)	0–35	35–75	75–95	95–245
Clay (%)	53	50	60	61
Bulk D	0.94	0.87	1.41	–
pH H₂O (1:2.5)	5.0	5.2	4.8	5.1
Org. C (%)	6.55	1.45	0.33	0.20
CEC	20.6	11.9	6.1	6.0
Base sat. (%)	28	9	2	13

Comment: very deep, poorly drained clay soil derived from kaolinitic sediments. Presence of gleyic properties and hardened outcrops of plinthite in nearby river bank confirms classification.

Acrisols, Alisols, Lixisols, Luvisols

After dealing with those soils having a ferralic (oxic) B horizon (the Ferralsols), soils with a deeply extended argic B horizon (the Nitisols), and soils with plinthite (the Plinthosols), there remains a further group of tropical soils in which there is also an argic B horizon. Unlike the Nitisols, with a deep, extended, clay-enriched B horizon, the amount of clay in these soils returns to background levels within a shallow depth (Fig. 12.5). Four Major Soil Groupings have been identified in this category: Alisols, Acrisols, Lixisols and Luvisols. The pattern of the clay increase with depth in all four soils is strongly suggestive of an accumulation through eluviation, rather than weathering and clay formation *in situ,* although this cannot be discounted. Differentiation of the four soils is achieved by use of chemical criteria: the CEC and the percentage base saturation, as shown in Fig. 12.8.

It is obvious that the separation of these soils is based entirely on properties determined in the laboratory, which makes their separation in the field difficult in a number of cases. In general, soil structure in Luvisols and Alisols is better developed, their pH is higher, and there is a greater content of weatherable minerals than in the Acrisols. Luvisols are more likely to be present on younger land-surfaces in the tropical regions, but their occurrence is mainly extra-tropical. The Lixisols are soils of the seasonally dry tropics.

Acrisols

The name of these soils is derived from Latin (*acer,* acid), and first appeared as a soil grouping on the FAO–Unesco *Soil Map of the World* legend in 1974.

Fig. 12.8 Chemical relationship between Acrisols, Lixisols, Alisols and Luvisols.

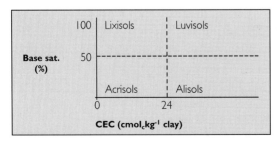

Formerly, these soils were known as Red-yellow Podzolic Soils, *Sols Ferrallitiques,* Red and Yellow Earths or Latosols. In *Soil Taxonomy* they are classed as oxic varieties of Alfisols and Ultisols.

Originally, an Acrisol was defined as a soil of humid tropical regions having an argic B horizon with a base saturation of less than 50 per cent. However, when the revised legend of the *Soil Map of the World* was published in 1988, an additional criterion was inserted, to separate clays with low activity from those with high activity. Low-activity clays form when the soil solution is very dilute and may include kaolinite, gibbsite and some of the

---

Profile of a Haplic Acrisol (Paleustult) from Mbala District, Northern Province, Zambia

ISRIC Profile ZM 03
(Parent material: coarse-grained intermediate igneous rock)
Diagnostic criteria: ochric A horizon; argic B horizon.

Ap	0–25 cm	Dark brown (8YR 4/4) loam with moderate subangular blocky structure; slightly hard; many pores; common fine and medium roots; termite activity; abrupt smooth boundary
AB	25–45 cm	Reddish-brown (5YR 4/4) clay with moderate coarse subangular blocky structure; extremely hard; many fine pores; few fine roots; gradual boundary
Bt$_1$	45–82 cm	Yellowish-red (5YR 4/8) clay with moderate coarse subangular blocky structure; soft; many fine pores; gradual smooth boundary
Bt$_2$	82–140 cm	Yellowish-red (5YR 4/8) clay loam; soft; many fine pores

Selected analyses

Horizon	Ap	AB	Bt$_1$	Bt$_2$
Depth (cm)	0–25	25–45	45–82	82–140
Clay (%)	22	41	45	39
pH H$_2$O (1:2.5)	5.8	6.0	5.8	6.1
Org. C (%)	0.9	0.49	0.23	0.15
CEC	8.1	8.4	8.6	6.8
Base sat. (%)	26	18	14	18

Comment: deep, well-drained, reddish-brown clay soil derived from intermediate igneous rock. The A horizon is hard setting and the profile is only slightly acid throughout. The B horizon does not qualify as a ferralic B horizon because CEC and silt:clay ratio are too high.

amorphous iron minerals. The threshold was set at $24\,cmol_c\,kg^{-1}$ clay which distinguished the Acrisols from a new group, the Alisols, with a CEC above this value. In simple terms, the Acrisols are acid soils with a sandy loam topsoil and an argic B horizon, containing low-activity clays. In the field, Acrisols are associated with Ferralsols, Cambisols, Arenosols or Nitisols, which develop on adjacent plateau surfaces or base-rich parent materials, and with Plinthosols and Gleysols downslope on level, poorly drained land.

Acrisols cover about 1000 million hectares and are extensive in the southeastern part of the USA, southeast Asia, areas peripheral to the Amazon lowlands in South America, and parts of West and East Africa. The profile of an Acrisol usually includes a thin ochric A horizon, a yellow eluvial horizon and a bright red and yellow coloured B horizon (Plate B28). The horizon sequence is more clearly developed than in the Nitisols but, unlike Nitisols, the Acrisols have weak structure, poor physical and chemical properties, a low nutrient-retention capacity, and the cation capacity is dominated by aluminium ions. These soils are liable to severe erosion when cleared, as the structure of the A and E horizons is weak and breaks down easily under heavy rain showers. The B horizon is more stable.

The diagnostic criteria for a soil to be classified as an Acrisol are that it should have an argic B horizon, at least part of which has a cation exchange capacity of less than $24\,cmol_c\,kg^{-1}$ clay. The base saturation of Acrisols is less than 50 per cent in some part of the soil horizons between 25 and 125 cm depth. Acrisols lack the properties for Ferralsols, Planosols or Nitisols, but they may have plinthite, ferric properties or an albic horizon.

Once it has been established that a soil is an Acrisol, it is possible to allocate the soil to one of five Soil Units (Fig. 12.9). If there is plinthite at a depth of less than 125 cm then the soil is a **Plinthic Acrisol**. If there are gleyic properties within 100 cm of the soil surface, the soil is a **Gleyic Acrisol**. Where the soil is strongly humic with a mollic or umbric horizon it is a **Humic Acrisol**. If there are ferric properties (mottles redder than 7.5YR), then it is a **Ferric Acrisol**. Any soils remaining after the elimination of those with the previously described characteristics are consigned to the **Haplic Acrisols**.

Lixisols

The Lixisols are soils of the seasonally dry tropical, sub-tropical and warm temperate regions.

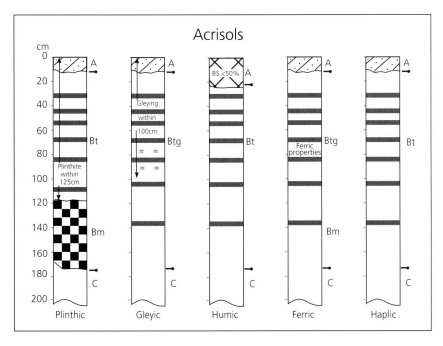

Fig. 12.9 Classification of Acrisols.

Profile of a Haplic Lixisol (Kanhaplustalf) from Itaguai, Rio de Janeiro, Brazil

ISRIC Profile BR 01
(Parent material: weathered gneiss)
Diagnostic criteria: ochric A horizon; argic B horizon.

Ap	0–14 cm	Dark greyish-brown (10YR 4/1) sandy clay loam with weak fine subangular blocky structure; slightly plastic, slightly sticky; many pores; many fine roots; abrupt boundary
E	14–38 cm	Yellowish-brown (10YR 5/4) sandy clay loam with massive structure; slightly plastic, slightly sticky; common pores; common fine roots; clear wavy boundary
Bt₁	38–50 cm	Red (2.5YR 4/6) clay with moderate subangular blocky structure; very plastic, very sticky; thick clay cutans; common pores; few roots; gradual wavy boundary
Bt₂	50–100 cm	Red (2.5YR 4/6) clay with moderate subangular blocky structure; very plastic, very sticky; moderately thick clay cutans; few strongly weathered rock fragments; gradual boundary
CB	100–150 cm	Yellowish-red (5YR 4/6) sandy clay loam with weak subangular blocky to massive structure; plastic, sticky; few strongly weathered rock fragments; gradual wavy boundary
C	150–180 cm	Reddish-yellow (7.5YR 6/6) sandy clay loam with massive structure; porous; slightly plastic, slightly sticky; frequent strongly weathered rock fragments

Selected analyses

| Horizon | Ap | E | Bt | CB/C |
Depth (cm)	0–14	14–38	38–100	100–180
Clay (%)	15	21	61	29
pH H₂O (1:2.5)	4.5	4.7	6.5	5.6
Org. C (%)	0.95	0.42	0.27	0.13
CEC	3.7	2.1	3.9	5.0
Base sat. (%)	49	67	85	46

Comment: deep, moderately well-drained red clay soil derived from gneiss. Clear grey and brown cutans coat structures in B horizon where increased clay content restricts drainage.

Previously these soils have been referred to as Red-yellow Podzolic Soils, Red and Yellow Earths, *Sols Ferrugineux Tropicaux Léssives*, *Sols Ferralitiques Faiblement Désaturés Appauvris* and Latosols. In *Soil Taxonomy*, these soils have been classified as oxic subgroups of the Alfisols using the term 'Kandic', which signifies the presence of a low exchange capacity and low-activity clays. The name 'Lixisol' was first introduced in the revised edition of the legend for the *Soil Map of the World*

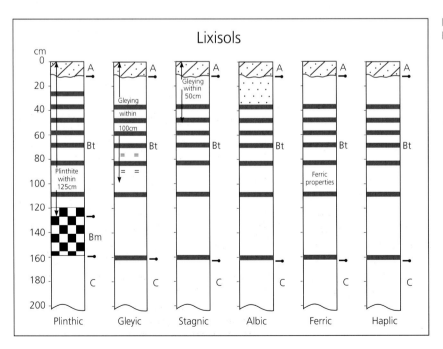

Fig. 12.10 Classification of Lixisols.

in 1988. It is estimated that there are 440 million hectares of these soils, with a distribution in eastern Brazil, India and west and southeast Africa.

The formation of Lixisols probably began in a wetter environment than that in which these soils are found today. It is suggested that although strong weathering occurred initially, giving the low exchange capacity, eluviation has enriched the argic B horizon, so that it has a base saturation of over 50 per cent. Aeolian contributions to these soils may have played a part in this process. The dry season is an important influence in the present soil-forming processes, the desiccation of the soil causing dehydration of iron compounds to give bright red (hematite) subsoil colours (Plate B30).

The definition of a Lixisol is that it should possess an argic B horizon with an exchange capacity of more than 24 cmol$_c$ kg^{-1} clay and that the base saturation should be 50 per cent or more throughout the B horizon to a depth of 125 cm.

If these criteria are satisfied, then the choice of Soil Units for these soils is as follows (Fig. 12.10). If there is plinthite within 125 cm of the surface, the soil is a **Plinthic Lixisol**. If there is gleying from ground-water within 100 cm of the surface it is a **Gleyic Lixisol**, but if the gleying results from slow permeability the soil is a **Stagnic Lixisol**. Where there is an albic E horizon the soil is an **Albic Lixisol**. If there are ferric properties (mottles redder than 7.5YR) it is a **Ferric Lixisol**. Any remaining soils are classified as **Haplic Lixisols**.

Alisols

The Major Soil Grouping of Alisols was introduced as a section in the classification to accommodate acid clayey soils of the humid tropical regions with high levels of aluminium cations. At the time of writing, it is not possible to give an estimate of the extent of the Alisols as they have not been mapped separately from the other acid, clayey soils of the warm humid regions of the world, the Acrisols. The Alisols were introduced as a separate grouping in the revision of the FAO–Unesco *Soil Map of the World* in 1988, but practical difficulties in separating them from the Acrisols have resulted in a suggestion by the World Reference Base panel that this Major Soil Grouping should be recombined with the Acrisols.

Alisols can develop on a wide range of parent materials associated with old landsurfaces with an undulating or hilly topography. They are common in southeast Asia, West Africa and South America. FAO is of the opinion that Alisols are probably more extensive than Acrisols in the southeastern USA.

Profile of a Haplic Alisol (Typic Paleudult) from Yurimaguas, Peru

ISRIC Profile PE 06
(Parent material: residium from claystone)
Diagnostic criteria: ochric A horizon; argic B horizon.

Ah	0–8 cm	Dark brown (10YR 3/3) loam with weak very fine granular structure; very friable; common fine and few medium roots; few krotovina and worm channels; abrupt wavy boundary
BA	8–25 cm	Yellowish-brown (10YR 5/6) silt loam with weak medium to coarse subangular blocky structure; friable; common fine and few medium roots; few krotovinas and worm channels; gradual wavy boundary
Bt$_1$	25–47 cm	Strong brown (7.5YR 5/6) clay loam; weak medium subangular blocky structure; friable; few fine and medium roots; few krotovina and worm channels; gradual wavy boundary
Bt$_2$	47–76 cm	Yellowish-red (5YR 5/8) clay with weak medium subangular blocky structure; firm; few fine roots; gradual smooth boundary
Bt$_3$	76–114 cm	Yellowish-red (5YR 5/8) clay with weak medium subangular blocky structure; firm; few fine roots; gradual smooth boundary
BC	114–150 cm	Red (2.5YR 5/8) clay with weakly coherent massive structure; very friable; few fine roots

Selected analyses

Horizon	Ah	BA	Bt1	Bt2+3	BC
Depth (cm)	0–8	8–25	25–47	47–114	114–150
Clay (%)	11	19	21	25	29
pH H$_2$O (1:2.5)	4.1	4.6	4.7	4.7	4.7
Org. C (%)	2.6	0.6	0.3	0.2	0.1
CEC	8.1	6.6	6.4	6.0	6.8
Exch. H$^+$ + Al^{3+}	3.2	4.4	4.8	5.4	5.7
Base sat. (%)	20	5	3	7	7

Comment: very deep, well-drained strong brown to red clay soil with a yellowish-brown topsoil and argic B horizon. Strongly acid with low nutrient reserves and a high content of exchangeable aluminium.

Alisols are defined as having an argic B horizon which has a CEC of more than $24\,cmol_c\,kg^{-1}$ clay and a base saturation of less than 50 per cent in at least some part of the B horizon within 125 cm of the surface. Unlike the Acrisols, the clays in Alisols are high-activity clays. Their formation is dominated by intense weathering of the parent material, producing kaolinitic clay, but with a high exchangeable aluminium content. The eluviation of clay takes place to form a dense argic B horizon.

Although Alisols have a high CEC, they are soils in which illitic and smectite clays are being broken down and replaced by kaolinite clay. As clay minerals are weathered, the aluminium released from the clay lattice is not removed and it comes to occupy a considerable part of the CEC of the clays. The prolonged but weak leaching makes these soils acid to very acid, and this allows a high level of aluminium toxicity. Physically, these soils are poorly structured and slake easily, resulting in reduced infiltration, reduced permeability and, in many cases, poor soil drainage (Plate B27).

Alisols characteristically have a relatively low biological activity because of their inherent infertility, and this keeps the organic matter content of the A horizon low and reduces the stability of the surface soil, which slakes easily. Slow permeability through the profile increases the likelihood of water flowing over the soil surface, hence erosion is a hazard.

Once it has been established that a soil is an Alisol, further classification is subject, in strict order, to the following criteria (Fig. 12.11): if there is plinthite within 125 cm of the soil surface the soil is a **Plinthic Alisol**; where gleyic properties occur within 100 cm of the surface the soil is a **Gleyic Alisol**; gleyic properties within 50 cm make it a **Stagnic Alisol**; if an umbric or mollic A horizon is present then the soil is a **Humic Alisol**; with ferric properties it is a **Ferric Alisol**; and any other soil meeting the basic criteria is a **Haplic Alisol**.

Associated soils

Luvisols have already been considered in Chapter 9, as they are more significant and extensive in extra-tropical areas. In the warm humid regions of the Earth's surface, these soils are of limited occurrence, being found in those areas with younger parent materials on landforms marginal to the old, stable continental masses. Histosols have been considered in Chapter 6. Limited areas of organic soils do occur in the tropical regions, but Andosols (Chapter 6) are more extensive although widely scattered.

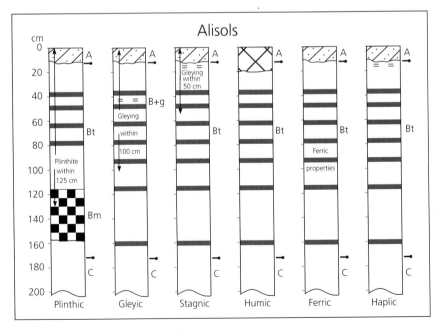

Fig. 12.11 Classification of Alisols.

Further reading

Ahmad, N. and Jones, R.L., 1969. A Plinthaquult of the Aripo Savannas, North Trinidad. I. Properties of the soil and chemical composition of the natural vegetation. II. Mineralogy and genesis. *Soil Science Society of America Proceedings* **33**:726–68.

Brinkman, R., 1979. *Ferrolysis: a Soil Forming Process in Hydromorphic Conditions*. Agricultural Research Report 887, Pudoc, Wageningen.

Buringh, P., 1979. *Introduction to the Study of Soils in Tropical and Subtropical Regions*. Pudoc, Wageningen.

Butler, B.E., 1959. *Periodic Phenomena in Landscapes as a Basis for Soil Studies*. Soil Publication No. 14, CSIRO, Melbourne.

Cunningham, R.K., 1963. The effect of clearing a tropical forest soil. *Journal of Soil Science* **3**:52–62.

Driessen, P.M. and Dudal, R., 1991. *The Major Soils of the World: Lecture Notes on Their Geography, Formation, Properties and Use*. Agricultural University, Wageningen and Katholieke Universiteit, Leuven.

Drosdoff, M., Daniels, R.B. and Nicholaides, J.J., 1978. *Diversity of Soils in the Tropics*. American Society of Agronomy, Soil Science Society of America, Madison.

McCaleb, S.G., 1959. The genesis of red-yellow podzolic soils. *Soil Science Society of America Proceedings* **23**:164–8.

Miller, B.J., 1983. Ultisols. In: Wilding, L.P., Smeck, N.E. and Hall, G.F. (eds.) *Pedogenesis and Soil Taxonomy. II. The Soil Orders*. Elsevier, Amsterdam, pp. 283–323.

Milne, G., 1935. Some suggested units of classification and mapping, particularly for East African Soils. *Soil Research* **4**:183–98.

Mohr, E.C.J., van Baren, F.A. and van Schuylenborgh, J., 1972. *Tropical Soils*. Mouton, Ichtiar Baru, van Hoeve. The Hague, Paris, Jakarta.

Mulcahy, M.J., 1960. Laterites and lateritic soils in south-western Australia. *Journal of Soil Science* **11**:206–25.

Nye, P.H., 1954. Some soil forming processes in the humid tropics. *Journal of Soil Science* **5**:7–21.

O'Brien, E.L. and Buol, S.W., 1984. Physical transformations in a vertical soil-saprolite sequence. *Soil Science Society of America Journal* **48**:354–7.

Sanchez, P.A., 1976. *Properties and Management of Soils in the Tropics*. John Wiley, New York.

Sanchez, P.A. and Buol, S.W., 1974. Properties of some soils of the upper Amazon basin of Peru. *Soil Science Society of America Proceedings* **38**: 117–21.

Van Wambeke, A., 1992. *Soils of the Tropics: Properties and Appraisal*. McGraw-Hill, New York.

Van Wambeke, A., Eswaran, H., Herbillon, A.J. and Comera, J., 1983. Oxisols. In: Wilding, L.P., Smeck, N.E. and Hall, G.F. (eds.) *Pedogenesis and Soil Taxonomy. II. The Soil Orders*. Elsevier, Amsterdam, pp. 325–54.

Watson, J.P., 1964. A soil catena on granite in Southern Rhodesia. 1. Field Observations. *Journal of Soil Science* **15**:238–50.

Young, A., 1976. *Tropical Soils and Soil Survey*. Cambridge University Press, Cambridge.

13 Soil mapping

As a natural resource, soils and their distribution are of national and international concern. The greater the knowledge of soil distribution and formation, as well as of the response of different soils to different forms of management, the greater is the chance that they will be used profitably for the individual, and on a sustainable basis for the community. Many countries of the world have a soil survey organization which is charged with mapping the distribution of soils and finding out about the genesis and properties of soils. Once this basic pedological knowledge has been acquired, a wide range of applications can be developed as outlined in Chapter 14.

The start of modern soil mapping

Modern soil mapping had an unprepossessing start towards the end of the 19th century, when Dokuchaev was asked to make a survey of soils in the Nizhni-Novgorod district of Russia 'to improve the basis for assessment and equalization of taxes'. In the USA, soil surveys began in 1898 when a trial map was compiled in the State of Maryland, to be followed by support from the Federal Government for mapping suitable 'tobacco lands'. Detailed soil surveys began in Australia in the 1920s to identify areas suitable for irrigation, and in Canada the first soil survey began in 1914, but later expanded rapidly to try to find the cause of farming failures by war veterans settled on crown lands, following the end of the First World War.

In Japan, between 1882 and 1894, a survey took place of soils based upon the surficial geology, and in China, soil surveys on the American pattern started in 1931. Although several soil surveys had taken place in England and Wales during the 1920s and 1930s, under the direction of G.W. Robinson, the Soil Survey of England and Wales was not inaugurated until 1939, when it was based at

Rothamsted with A. Muir as Director. In Scotland, surveys of soils have been part of the activities of the Macaulay Institute since it was established in 1930. In The Netherlands, following the 19th-century map of Staring, modern soil surveying was initiated somewhat surreptitiously by Edelman and some colleagues in 1943, when the country was still occupied during the closing years of the Second World War.

Scale and purpose of soil maps

The scale of a map and the use to which it is put are closely linked, and both are related to the type of mapping units employed to depict soil distribution on the map. Soil surveyors have developed a number of techniques to show the distribution of soils on the three-dimensional landscape. At the broadest scale, on world maps, the soil pattern depicted is generalized, eliminating all variations caused by local differences in the soil-forming processes. Earlier in the 20th century, world maps were largely deductive, based on climate and vegetation, which resulted in 'zonal' maps. During the second half of the 20th century, a great amount of information has been collected, providing a more accurate, but still patchy, picture. The scale of these maps is usually greater than 1:1,000,000 and the soil units employed in these world maps are the Great Soil Groups or Major Soil Groups. Such maps are produced by compilation rather than field mapping. The most detailed world map is the FAO–Unesco *Soil Map of the World*.

Maps to show national soil distributions or reconnaissance maps would normally be produced at a scale of between 1:1,000,000 and 1:100,000. These maps usually show the soil pattern in **associations** or **catenas** of related soils. An early attempt to map at this scale can be seen in the *Provisional Soil Map of East Africa* compiled by Milne and colleagues in 1936 using catenas. The 1:250,000 *National Soil Map* by the Soil Survey of England and Wales (now Soil Survey and Land Research Centre), published in 1983, is a modern, excellent example of this scale of map. It was produced by a combination of compilation from previous surveys and field observations made in every 100 km rectangle of the National Grid throughout the country. The map maintains a broad overview but still contains sufficient detail for use in research and planning. It uses composite mapping units called associations. Profile descriptions and analyses from this survey have formed the basis of the digital soil database of the Soil Survey and Land Research Centre, called 'Landis'.

Detailed maps range from 1:100,000 to 1:5000 or larger, depending upon the purpose of the investigation. Many routine soil maps have been produced at scales between 1:100,000 and 1:25,000, with the field work being done using maps at a scale of 1:10,000. At these scales, the **soil series** is employed as the main mapping unit, but in complex areas, associations or complexes may be used as well. A **soil association** is a term used to describe soils which occur together in a regular pattern on the landscape, as described for the catena, whereas the term **soil complex** implies an irregular distribution which cannot be deduced easily from the normal interactions of the basic soil-forming factors. At the 1:25,000 scale, it becomes possible to relate the soil pattern to field boundaries and greater detail can be shown. The density of observations may range from about 50 per km^2 to over 500 per km^2. Investigation of soil patterns at scales of less than 1:5000 would normally be for research purposes and would employ soil series with different phases to indicate local variations in texture, stoniness or organic matter content.

World maps

Because of a lack of pedological information, early world maps of soil distribution were based essentially on the prevailing environmental conditions, therefore they strongly reflected the patterns seen in climate and vegetation maps. They were based on the assumption that if the general conditions of soil formation were similar in two given areas,

then it was likely that the same soils would develop in both areas. Thus these maps did not show the actual soils but only the most probable zonal soil which might occur: tundra soils, Podzols, Chernozems, desert soils, etc.

World maps convenient for reproduction in atlases are usually at scales of about 1:80,000,000 and these were the only world maps that were available during the first half of the 20th century. Following the Second World War, a successful map of Africa was published in 1964, and this was followed in the period 1971–1981 by publication of the eleven sheets of the FAO–Unesco *Soil Map of the World*. This unique map has yet to be superseded, although parts of it are now being revised in the light of new information. A digital version of the FAO–Unesco *Soil Map of the World* has recently been made available, and using the rules by which it was compiled, it is possible to obtain a greater amount of information about world soil distributions than is apparent from the printed map. This information is now being utilized in global modelling exercises, such as soil moisture-holding capacity for crop yield prediction, the overall content of carbon in the soil, and the potential of soils to generate greenhouse gases such as methane and carbon dioxide. A simplified version of the *Soil Map of the World* is presented in Fig. 13.1.

Reconnaissance and national maps

Two groupings of soils have been used on maps of medium scale: the catena and the soil association. The **catena** was introduced by Milne for mapping soils in East Africa where he observed a regularly occurring relationship of soils with topographic features. In a paper presented to the Third International Congress of Soil Science in 1935, Milne noted that 'certain soils whose profiles and conditions of formation differ fundamentally, are found in association together, their boundaries forming a pattern which is repeated, with variations, over a considerable extent of country'. In another paper, in the journal *Soil Research*, Milne defined the catena as 'a unit of mapping convenience ... [which is] ... a grouping of soils which, while they fall wide apart in a natural system of

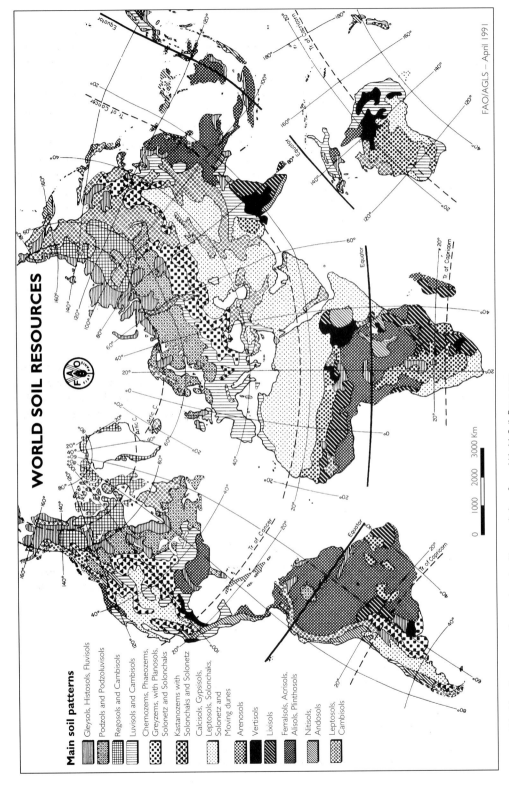

Fig.13.1 World soil resources (reproduced with permission from *World Soil Resources*, Report No. 66, 1991, Food and Agriculture Organization of the United Nations).

classification on account of fundamental genetic and morphological differences, are yet linked in their occurrence by conditions of topography and are repeated in the same relationships to each other wherever the same conditions are met with'.

As an example, Milne refers to 'the complex of soils encountered between the crest of a low hill and the floor of the adjacent swamp', a situation which is 'met with over a large part of the dissected peneplain of Uganda. Always', he states, 'the distribution of soils is a function of differences of level. For this type of association I have ... proposed the name catena. The word is intended by its derivation to serve as a mnemonic, the various soils included in a catena corresponding to the links in a hanging chain'.

Soils are not randomly distributed upon the landscape and at medium scales of mapping, soil variation can be correlated with the geomorphic patterns on the landscape. The northern and desertic parts of Australia, and Papua New Guinea, have been mapped using a **land systems** approach, developed in the 1950s, which is based upon aerial photograph analysis of landforms backed up with field work of a reconnaissance nature, which includes an assessment of the geology, geomorphology, vegetation, climate and water resources. The objective was to determine the most effective and sustainable use to which these lands could be put. In more recent years, FAO has been bringing up to date the *Soil Map of the World* and has chosen to use the physiographic units of the landscape in a similar manner to that used in the land systems approach.

Soil scientists in Canada and Scotland have grouped topographically related soils on similar parent materials into the **soil association** (Fig. 13.2). The concept of the soil association probably precedes that of the catena by a year or so, for Ellis in Canada used a mapping unit of soils linked by relief, which he called an association. It is uncertain if there was any contact between Ellis and Milne, or indeed if Milne even knew of Ellis's work, for there is no reference to it in his publications. It was emphasized by Ellis and colleagues that the factors controlling the soil-forming processes are temperature and moisture, vegetation, parent material, the position in which the soil is found in relation to the topography, internal drainage, length of time the soil has been under the influence of the soil-forming processes and the modifying effects of man. They stressed that the soil climate is modified by topographical position, thus a number of different soils may be found in association with each other on a given parent material: 'the knolls may be shallow black earth phase, while in the depressions black meadow soils may be surrounded either by a fringe of saline and alkalized soils or by degrading black earths'. Although parent materials may differ, the pattern of soils on the landscape had a similar expression and the individual soils were called 'soil associates' by these soil surveyors.

On the *National Soil Map* of England and Wales at 1:250,000, the main mapping unit displayed on the map sheets is the soil association. There are 296 of these geographic soil associations, which are identified by the most frequently occurring soil series and combinations of ancillary series. Two

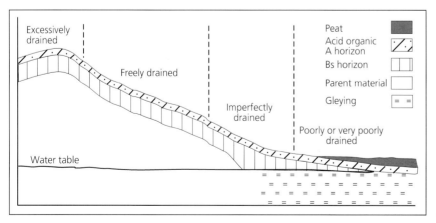

Fig. 13.2 A soil association on a permeable parent material.

types of association are described, one where a single extensive soil series dominates, covering more than 50 per cent of the area, and the other where there is no dominant soil series and the association is made from a larger number of component series.

Detailed maps

Detailed surveys published at scales of 1:50,000 and larger necessitate the examination of the soil at frequent intervals over the landscape, so that the profile characteristics are known and the boundaries between the recognized soil units can be drawn. The normal procedure is first to make a reconnaissance of the area to find the range of soils present. This can be systematically accomplished by an experienced soil surveyor taking a number of random traverses in flat country, or by making traverses across the grain of the country where there is pronounced relief. Once the framework of soil mapping units is established, it is possible for routine surveying to begin and for areas of defined soil mapping units to be depicted on a map. Such mapping units may be classified as established soil series, associations or complexes within the structure of the soil classification of the country being mapped.

Following the pattern of soil survey developed in the USA early in the 20th century, many countries adopted the concept of the **soil series** as the main unit for detailed soil maps. In Britain, the soil series was defined by Robinson as follows: 'soils with similar profiles derived from similar material under similar conditions of development are conveniently grouped together as a series'. In certain situations, minor variations of the profile character could be reflected in a **soil phase**. This distinction was used to show different topsoil texture in otherwise similar soils by surveyors in the USA, and in the UK to identify soils with a greater content of stones, or steepness of slope, than was typical of the modal soil series.

Where the pattern of soil series is too complicated and it is deemed uneconomic at a particular scale to delineate very small areas of each individual soil, an area can be mapped as a **soil complex**. This mapping unit can be employed on unsorted glacial tills or steep slopes where the variability of parent material and drainage can be considerable,

causing an extremely complicated soil pattern to develop.

Techniques of soil survey

Modern methods of soil mapping are based on the profile of soils; this presents a problem for the surveyor who can easily observe only the upper surface of the soil. Every opportunity must be taken to inspect roadside cuttings and other excavations or exposures, but in many cases the surveyor has to resort to extraction of samples using an auger. At intervals a small inspection hole is dug or, less frequently, a complete soil pit is excavated from which a full description can be made and representative samples obtained from the succession of horizons which constitute the soil profile. A selection of the tools of the soil surveyor is shown in Fig. 13.3.

Several approaches to soil mapping are possible, and the most suitable method is decided by the detail required, which in turn determines the scale to be used, and the purpose intended for the map when it is completed. The chief methods used in soil survey may be referred to as grid survey, free survey, boundary survey and remote sensing survey. Although these approaches may be identified separately, in reality it is incumbent upon the soil surveyor to integrate all the available information in the compilation of a soil map.

The first method, **grid survey**, involves observation of the soil at fixed points on a grid pattern imposed over the landscape. This is a method which is best used at either a very broad scale or a very detailed scale, for example when a field is being surveyed before an agricultural experiment is laid down. In the latter case, the soil would be examined at a close interval of 25 or 50 m using an auger and, based on the observations made, the boundaries would be drawn by interpolation. A similar, but less intense grid of observations is often adopted in densely wooded country when it is impossible to locate accurately the position of the soil observations being made. Surveys in West Africa followed topographic survey lines, cut through the forest 800 m apart, along which the soils were described and sampled at intervals of 200 m. This methodology was used to produce soil

Fig. 13.3 Field equipment of the soil surveyor: illustrated are two types of auger, spade, trowel and pick-axe. Tape measures are required for location and horizon depth. A map case, soil description card, field handbook, Munsell Colour Charts, pH kit, plastic bags and labels are required for description and sampling.

maps at a scale of 1:250,000 and the information gained was used to lay out plantations. The production of semi-detailed maps such as these often entails a certain amount of basic topographic survey as well as observations of hydrology, climate, vegetation and present land-use.

The second method, **free survey**, is a more interpretive approach in which the morphology of the landscape is used to elucidate the soil pattern. Depending upon the 'lie of the land', the soil is inspected with an auger or small inspection pits and the resulting information marked on a field map. Maps at a scale of 1:63,360 and 1:50,000 produced by the Soil Surveys of England and Wales and Scotland were compiled in this way using field maps of 1:10,560 or 1:10,000 (Fig. 13.4). A larger-scale field map enables additional relevant field information to be recorded on the map, which can be taken into consideration when the final map is drawn in preparation for reduction to the published scale. The free survey method assumes a close relationship between landforms and soils, and the surveyor is left free to make observations where appropriate and at a variable interval to suit the nature of the soil pattern.

Fig. 13.4 An example of detailed soil mapping.

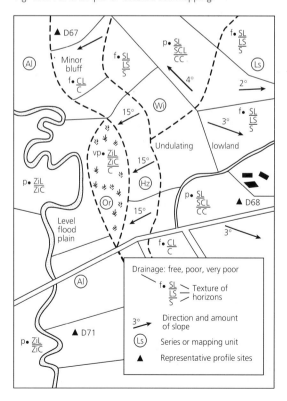

145

As the geomorphology often provides clues to the origin and nature of the parent material upon which the soil is developed, it follows that the soil produced will normally have a boundary which coincides with the physiographic boundary. A third method of mapping soils, **boundary survey**, is to locate a soil boundary and then to follow it, crossing and recrossing it until its position is known with accuracy. This is a time-consuming activity and the results are not materially better than those achieved by the interpretive methods of free survey. Fortunately, there are very few areas of the world which are featureless, so it is a method which is resorted to only when other features, such as relief or vegetation, cannot be interpreted.

A fourth method, also interpretive, uses information obtained by various types of **remote sensing**. Air photographs have been used in soil survey since the 1950s, when they first became widely available. They can be used simply in place of a topographic map, and this has proved invaluable in countries where there is inadequate map coverage. The additional information about vegetation boundaries, especially on colour air photographs, can be extremely helpful in a landscape covered by semi-natural and natural vegetation. The reaction of the plants to the underlying soil conditions is reflected in the tone and texture of the air photograph and this enables soil boundaries to be inferred in the laboratory. It does not absolve the surveyor from field work, but it can greatly economize on the time spent in the field. The availability of a stereoscopic three-dimensional image assists the accurate plotting of the extent of soils and the location of their boundaries. It also allows the soil surveyor to acquire information from otherwise inaccessible places and to gain some appreciation of catenary soil relationships without climbing every hillside.

The past two decades have seen rapid developments in the use of other techniques of remote sensing. Although satellite technology now permits accurate positioning of observations through global positioning systems, the poor definition of commercially available satellite images, conditioned by the large pixel size, combined with the limited ability of multispectral sensing apparatus to penetrate below the soil surface, has restricted the use which has been made of these techniques for soil survey. The use of less elevated platforms to carry the sensing apparatus, such as conventional aircraft, helicopters or balloons, does offer more scope for soil survey. The response of the soil and its different coverings of natural vegetation or crops, as recorded by up to a dozen different wavebands, can yield interesting information, particularly about soil moisture and chemical conditions, the state of erosion and the health of crops.

Reflectance data have been obtained for many minerals under laboratory conditions, but soils contain mixtures of minerals as well as organic matter, which lowers the discriminatory power of the airborne sensors. The roughness of the soil surface, its partial or complete cover by plants, and variable moisture conditions further reduce their effectiveness. Despite these limitations, soils with different albedo can be distinguished from each other. An increase in soil moisture results in an overall decrease in reflectance in both visible and near-infra-red spectra. Moisture contents can be observed in the $1.4\,\mu m$ and $1.9\,\mu m$ bands. A spectral response is obtained from different soil textures: the finer the soil particles, the higher the reflectance in the $0.43-0.47\,\mu m$ and $0.51-0.53\,\mu m$ bands; similarly, there is a response to different-sized soil aggregates. Soils with salt-encrusted surfaces have high reflectance values. Ferrous and ferric iron oxides have a response in the $0.4-2.5\,\mu m$ wavelength band. In the thermal band, soils can be observed to respond to solar warming during the day and cooling at night, but patterns may be disturbed by different moisture contents. With microwave, penetration of the surface is possible which may enable the detection of horizons strongly differing in texture or moisture content. Remote sensing of the environment has made great strides in many fields of study, but although useful for an overview of the landscape, its application in soil mapping remains problematic. Conventional soil survey does not normally provide much information about soil variation within map units. Remote sensing could perhaps provide some answers to this problem.

A skilled soil surveyor uses all the information which is available. This includes not only the soil observed underfoot, but the breaks and changes in the slope of the land, the origin of the soil parent materials, the natural vegetation, including the hedgerows in arable areas, as well as the present and potential land-use. However, in the latter case land utilization may be dictated by purely economic or personal considerations which are not always in the best interests of soil conservation and the sustainable use of the land.

The soil pit

Once the different soil units have been mapped, it is usual for the soil surveyor to select a suitable site for a representative profile description. A pit is dug, measuring approximately 1 m by 1.5 m, to a depth of 1 or 1.5 m unless limited by contact with underlying solid rock. Great care should be taken in the selection of the site in order to obtain a truly representative profile, and disturbance or pollution must be avoided (Fig. 13.5).

Profile description

The face of the profile is first cleaned of soil smeared during the excavation, then, with a scale in place, photographs are taken if required. The sequence of horizons is identified, and each one described in turn. Normally the profile description is entered on a field description sheet, where observations about site and soil are recorded systematically. These details may also be written out in a notebook or entered into a portable (laptop) computer using a code format suitable for data-handling equipment. Whichever method is used, observations are conveniently listed under the headings: A. General information; B. Site description; and C. Profile description.

The features listed are designed to give information about the area and immediate vicinity in which the pit is situated, so the different sections

Fig. 13.5 A soil pit, excavated for full description and sampling of a soil profile. A soil monolith is shown being prepared for removal to the laboratory.

A.	**General information:**
	Profile number
	Grid reference
	Locality, address
	Author
	Date
	Weather, before and at sampling.
B.	**Site description:**
	Elevation above sea level
	Geomorphology/macro-relief
	Micro-relief
	Soil erosion and deposition
	Flooding
	Rock outcrops
	Land-use and vegetation
	Soil surface characteristics.
C.	**Profile description:**
	Recognition of horizons
	Horizon designation
	Horizon depth and thickness
	Colour, background and mottling
	Texture
	Stoniness
	Structure
	Consistency
	Soil-moisture conditions
	Depth of ground-water table
	Organic matter, nature and amount
	Roots, size, nature and abundance
	Soil fauna
	Carbonates, gypsum
	Features of pedogenetic origin
	pH
	Nature of boundary to next horizon.

should be answered as fully as possible and amplified by notes or sketches where appropriate.

Once the various horizons of a profile have been recognized and identified, they may be referred to by a system of designation using capital letters and subscripts, as outlined in Chapter 1. Then details are given for each of the soil horizons found to occur in the profile. The full range of terminology is given in national soil survey field handbooks (e.g. that of Hodgson, 1976), but care should be taken to check the exact use of the terms employed, as slight variations occur from country to country. Measurements are made in the International System (SI) and the use of the Munsell Soil Colour Charts is widely accepted for the description of soil colours. An agreed international range of particle sizes exists and is incorporated into all soil survey systems, but again there is some variation in the way the particle sizes are grouped for soil textures.

Sampling

When description has been completed, a bulk sample from each horizon is taken for chemical and physical analysis. These bulk samples are placed in plastic bags, labelled and brought back to the laboratory, where analyses can be made to support decisions about classification made in the field. Small, undisturbed samples can be taken using 'Kubiena boxes' and used for resin impregnation and thin sectioning followed by micro-morphological study, or a 'soil monolith' of the whole soil profile may be collected in a galvanized iron trough or wooden box made specifically for that purpose. Like the small samples for thin sections, the monolith can also be impregnated with resin and prepared for display, together with supporting environmental information and the chemical and physical analyses. Many countries now have a national exhibition of representative soil profiles, and a collection of soil monoliths of the units of the FAO–Unesco *Soil Map of the World* is on permanent display at the International Soil Reference and Information Centre at Wageningen in The Netherlands and can be visited by arrangement

Soil variation

The concept of the soil profile, as representative of

an area of soil, was introduced in Chapter 1. Experience in the field has shown that variation is a significant property of soils, and may be found at different scales: micro-variation, variation within the profile, variation within mapping units, and the wider variations recognized by the major soil groupings of soil classifications. Soil variability is introduced by the nature of the parent material and the impact that other soil-forming factors have upon it. Human modification, through different land-use management practices, adds greatly to this inherent variability.

Soil micro-variation can be appreciated through studies of soil using microscopic methods. Different patterns of distribution of the soil constituents may be observed in thin sections of soils which show distributions of 'skeletal' mineral grains, fine-grained 'plasma' and 'voids' throughout the soil. Also to be seen are coatings, concentrations and depletions, which reflect differences in chemical and physical properties. These small-scale variations have an influence on the detailed moisture-holding capacity and indirectly on the composition of the soil biota within an otherwise uniform soil material.

Soil survey practice has been to assume that mapping units are uniform, but in fact most soil mapping units have at least 15 per cent 'other' soils as inclusions, and in many cases variability is such that there is only a 65 per cent chance of soils being the same throughout a mapping unit. Reference to the memoir accompanying the soil map often reveals the soil mapping units shown on the map to be an over-simplified picture of the true situation. Often this simplified picture is reinforced by the presentation of only one representative profile for a soil mapping unit, without any indication of the range of properties involved.

Some authors regard soils as members of a continuum, that is all soils are linked by a range of intermediate profiles from one to another. The boundaries which are placed upon them by soil classification and mapping are to some extent artificial and a construct which does not exist in nature. If the boundary between two soils (as mapped) is regarded more as a zone of rapid change of soil properties, then this approach becomes more acceptable.

Many soil properties may be predicted from the

landforms upon which they occur. This statement stems from the ideas of the catena, the nine-unit landsurface model, and catchment area conceptual models of the landscape, based on water movement through the Earth's superficial layers.

Certain soil properties are seen to be variable, but they are relatively stable soil characteristics, only subject to spatial changes (e.g. soil texture variation). Other properties are more dynamic in character and may vary rapidly in space and time (e.g. moisture relationships). In recent years it has become possible to study soil variation using pattern analysis and geostatistical techniques combined with soil databases, using techniques and information which was unavailable only a decade ago. Whilst much of this work is currently of a research nature, and often more closely resembles a mathematical investigation of soil properties, it is essential that a fuller understanding of soil variability is obtained in order to make sense of the patterns observed in the field. Variability at micro-, profile and macro-scales is an important soil characteristic and should not be overlooked in basic soil survey.

Further reading

Ball, D.F. and Williams, W.M., 1968. Variability of soil chemical properties in two uncultivated Brown Earths. *Journal of Soil Science* **19**:379–91.

Beckett, P.T.H. and Webster, R., 1971. Soil variability. *Soils and Fertilizers* **34**:1–15.

Bridges, E.M., 1982. Techniques of modern soil survey. In: Bridges, E.M. and Davidson, D.A. (eds.) *Principles and Applications of Soil Geography.* Longman, Harlow, pp. 28–57.

Carroll, D.M. and Evans, R., 1977. *Air Photo-interpretation for Soil Mapping.* Technical Monograph No. 8, Soil Survey of England and Wales, Harpenden.

Clayden, B., 1982. Soil classification. In: Bridges, E.M. and Davidson, D.A. (eds.) *Principles and Applications of Soil Geography.* Longman, Harlow, pp. 58–96.

Ellis, J.H., 1932. A field classification of soils for use in the Soil Survey. *Science in Agriculture* **12**:60–76.

FAO, 1990. *Guidelines for Soil Description.* 3rd edition, FAO, Rome.

FAO/Unesco, 1971–1981. *Soil Map of the World.* FAO, Rome.

Hodgson, J.M., 1976. *Soil Survey Field Handbook.* Soil Survey Technical Monograph No.5, Soil Survey of England and Wales, Harpenden.

Hodgson, J.M., 1991. *Soil Survey: a Basis for European Soil Protection.* EUR 13340EN, Council of the European Communities, Brussels.

Hodgson, J.M. and Whitfield, W.A.D., 1990. *Applied Soil Mapping for Planning, Development and Conservation: a Pilot Study.* HMSO, London.

Isbell, R.F., 1992. A brief history of National Soil Classification in Australia since the 1920s. *Australian Journal of Soil Research* **30**:825–42.

Jamagne, M. and King, D., 1991. Mapping methods for the 1990s and beyond. In: *Soil Survey: a Basis for European Soil Protection.* CEC, Brussels, pp. 181–96.

Landon, J.R. (ed.), 1991. *Booker Tropical Soil Manual.* Longman, Harlow.

Mausbach, M.J. and Wilding, L.P. (eds.), 1991. *Spatial Variabilities of Soils and Landforms.* Soil Science Society of America Special Publication No. 28, Madison.

McRae, S.G., 1988. *Practical Pedology.* Ellis Horwood, Chichester.

Milne, G., 1935. Composite units for the mapping of complex soil associations. *Transactions of the Third International Congress of Soil Science* **1**:345–7.

Milne, G., 1935. Some suggested units of classification and mapping, particularly for East African soils. *Soil Research* **4**:183–98.

Mulders, M.A., 1987. *Remote Sensing in Soil Science.* Elsevier, Amsterdam.

Nortcliff, S., 1978. Soil variation and reconnaissance soil mapping: a statistical study in Norfolk. *Journal of Soil Science* **29**:403–18.

Webster, R. and Oliver, M.A., 1990. *Statistical Methods in Soil and Land Resources Survey.* Oxford University Press, Oxford.

Zinck, J.A., 1992. *Soil Survey: Perspectives and Strategies for the 21st Century.* ITC Publication No. 21, Enschede.

14 Using soil information

In the past, knowledge about soils has been acquired slowly by experience, and only communicated by word of mouth. The best use of the soil has evolved by trial and error, controlled largely by tradition. However, in recent years the necessity for forward planning and sustainable use of the soil has become paramount. Before this can occur it is necessary to be in command of the right information. The sustainable use of the land, so strongly advocated by the United Nations Conference on Environment and Development (UNCED), held in Rio de Janeiro in 1992, is an important but poorly defined concept. At the centre of the concept, but rarely mentioned by non-soil scientists, lies the soil, a vital part of the intricate web of interactions between human beings and the natural environment. In order to understand these interactions and to be able to use land effectively on a sustainable basis, it is essential that maximum use is made of existing knowledge about soils. The existing distribution of different land-uses is shown in Fig. 14.1.

Fig. 14.1 World major land-use categories (compiled from FAO data).

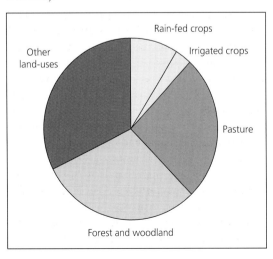

Soil distribution and utilization

The different soil groups are very unevenly distributed on the land masses of the Earth. This is seen readily from the world soil map (Fig. 13.1) and the approximate extent and percentage distribution of the Major Soil Groupings is given in Table 14.1. Unlike the older, climatically based systems of soil classification, the soil pattern resulting from a pedologically based classification does not completely reflect the pattern of climate on the Earth's surface. Ultimately, the world's ability to produce food for an ever-increasing population is limited by the climatic conditions, soils and the management of the land, and so there is a critical level of population which can be supported.

Any attempt to produce food beyond the capacity of the soil to grow it will result in soil degradation and reduced yields, as will attempts to cultivate additional areas of unsuitable soils to make up the short-fall. FAO has estimated that the total cultivated area of the world is 1400 million hectares (11 per

Table 14.1 World soil distribution according to Major Soil Groupings (after FAO, 1993)

Soil	Area (million ha)	Percentage
Leptosols	1655	12
Cambisols	1573	12
Acrisols	996	7
Arenosols	901	7
Calcisols	796	6
Ferralsols	742	6
Gleysols	718	5
Luvisols	648	5
Regosols	578	4
Podzols	487	4
Kastanozems	467	3
Others	–	28

cent of the land surface). An area of land twice this size could be brought under cultivation, but this would mean using soils which have serious limitations and which would therefore require greater capital inputs to obtain satisfactory crop yields. Twenty per cent of the Earth's surface is too cold, another 20 per cent is too shallow or steep for agriculture, 23 per cent is too dry, 5 per cent is too wet and 10 per cent too infertile (Fig. 14.2). In terms of 'spare capacity', there would seem to be additional land for arable cultivation in South America, but this would be at the expense of grazing land and woodland. In many parts of Africa, the provision of wood (charcoal) for domestic fuel presents as great a challenge as provision of food. Many developing countries lack the capacity to increase crop production and the infrastructure to deal with it. Regrettably, social and economic constraints result in inefficient and often unsustainable use of the soil.

Soil data handling

The rapid development of desk-top computer facilities has greatly increased the soil scientist's ability to handle large amounts of data. It has not always been appreciated that for each soil profile there may be a minimum of 250 separate attributes. An average map sheet may have 30 different soil mapping units, so if only one representative profile is taken from each one there is a great mass of

Fig. 14.2 Limitations on the use of the world's soils (compiled from FAO data).

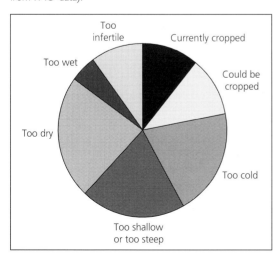

information to be handled. The modern desk-top computer has a capacity which can handle all these data.

At the International Soil Reference and Information Centre (ISRIC) in The Netherlands, FAO in Rome and the Soil Conservation Service of the United States (now Natural Resources Conservation Service, NRCS) and several other national soil survey institutes, considerable advances have been made in the techniques of storing and handling soil information. Storage of profile data in a database enables any soil description and supporting analytical data to be printed out directly. This enables a prompt response to any enquiry, and has made data more easily available.

During the last 10 years, with the co-operation of several international organizations including UNEP and FAO, ISRIC has developed a SOil and TERrain digital database (SOTER) to handle information on world soils at an equivalent scale of 1:1,000,000. The general approach in SOTER is to review all existing soil and terrain data in a georeferenced area and to supplement this with remotely sensed data for vegetation cover where appropriate. The data are then arranged according to the procedures of the SOTER manual. Individual facets of the land are grouped together into areas showing a distinctive and often repetitive pattern of landform, slope, parent material and soils. Areas so obtained are delineated as **SOTER units**. The area of each SOTER unit is georeferenced and considered to be unique with respect to its constituent soil and terrain characteristics (Fig. 14.3).

Areas of different lithology within SOTER units are separated as different **terrain units** which display similar patterns of surface form, slope, micro-relief and parent materials. The next step includes the delineation of **terrain components**, each of which will have within it a number of **major soils** (Fig. 14.4). Soil profiles (point data) of major soils are represented by actual soil profiles from an area and linked into the system (Fig. 14.5). At first only a few profiles may be available for inclusion, but the intention is to increase their number as rapidly as possible, as good quality information becomes available.

Individual terrain components are characterized in the database in terms of their major soils, but

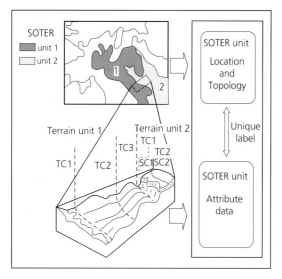

Fig. 14.3 SOTER units, their terrain components, attributes and location.

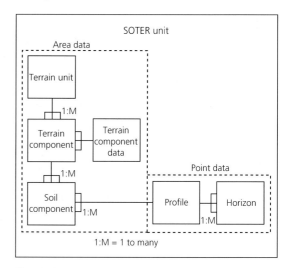

Fig. 14.5 Relationships of data within the SOTER system.

these cannot be shown on a 1:1,000,000 map. The morphological, chemical and physical attributes of these profiles are considered to be representative of the whole area covered by the soil under consideration. A list of the non-spatial attributes held by SOTER is given in Table 14.2. The attribute data stored in SOTER are handled by a relational database system which manages the files containing the data and enables manipulation of the data. The advantage of using this technology is that it can be linked to a Geographical Information System (GIS), so that the distribution of soil attributes can be rapidly assembled on screen, either singly or in multiple overlays, which enables the examination of relationships hitherto difficult to accomplish.

Interpretation of soil maps

It has been realized since the 1960s that, in order to gain wider acceptance of the value of soil surveys and to make full use of the information gathered, interpretation and presentation are required for the public outside soil science. Even within agriculture, where soils are most widely used, practical

Fig. 14.4 SOTER attribute database structure.

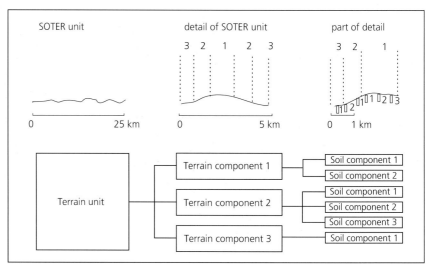

TERRAIN

1 SOTER unit ID
2 year of data collection
3 map ID
4 minimum elevation
5 maximum elevation
6 slope gradient
7 relief intensity
8 major landform
9 regional slope
10 hypsometry
11 dissection
12 general lithology
13 permanent water surface

TERRAIN COMPONENT

14 SOTER unit ID
15 terrain component number
16 proportion of SOTER unit
17 terrain component data ID

TERRAIN COMPONENT DATA

18 terrain component data ID
19 dominant slope
20 length of slope
21 form of slope
22 local surface form
23 average height
24 coverage
25 surface lithology
26 texture group non-consolidated parent material
27 depth to bedrock
28 surface drainage
29 depth to ground-water
30 frequency of flooding
31 duration of flooding
32 start of flooding

SOIL COMPONENT

33 SOTER unit ID

34 terrain component number
35 soil component number
36 proportion of SOTER unit
37 profile ID
38 number of reference profiles
39 position in terrain component
40 surface rockiness
41 surface stoniness
42 types of erosion/deposition
43 area affected
44 degree of erosion
45 sensitivity to capping
46 rootable depth
47 relation with other soil components

PROFILE

48 profile ID
49 profile database ID
50 latitude
51 longitude
52 elevation
53 sampling date
54 lab ID
55 drainage
56 infiltration rate
57 surface organic matter
58 classification FAO
59 classification version
60 national classification
61 *Soil Taxonomy*
62 phase

HORIZON (*mandatory)

63 profile ID*
64 horizon number*
65 diagnostic horizon*
66 diagnostic property*
67 horizon designation
68 lower depth*
69 distinctness of transition
70 moist colour*

71 dry colour
72 grade of structure
73 size of structure elements
74 type of structure*
75 abundance of coarse fragments*
76 size of coarse fragments
77 very coarse sand
78 coarse sand
79 medium sand
80 fine sand
81 very fine sand
82 total sand*
83 silt*
84 clay*
85 particle size class
86 bulk density*
87 moisture content at various tensions
88 hydraulic conductivity
89 infiltration rate
90 pH H_2O*
91 pH KCl
92 electrical conductivity
93 exchangeable Ca^{2+}
94 exchangeable Mg^{2+}
95 exchangeable Na^+
96 exchangeable K^+
97 exchangeable Al^{3+}
98 exchangeable acidity
99 CEC soil*
100 total carbonate equivalent
101 gypsum
102 total carbon*
103 total nitrogen
104 P_2O_5
105 phosphate retention
106 Fe dithionite
107 Al dithionite
108 Fe pyrophosphate
109 Al pyrophosphate
110 clay mineralogy

Table 14.2 Soil and terrain attributes held in the SOTER database (after van Engelen and Wen, 1993)

interpretations are required. In all cases it is necessary to ascertain what information is required and why. This must be followed by close collaboration between soil scientist and client in order to establish the data required to solve the problem. This may not always be straightforward as soil information is scattered, and non-soil information must also be considered. However, current developments in data-handling systems such as SOTER should make the task easier in the future. Once sufficient factual material has been assembled, soil survey interpretation attempts to predict soil performance for a particular activity under defined conditions of management.

Representation of soil data for other technical purposes has been taking place for the past 20 years at least, particularly in the USA, The Netherlands, Germany and the UK. In these countries, interpretations of soil surveys have been made for the selection of crops, yields of crops under varying management systems, measures for land reclamation, grazing practices on range lands, suitability of land for irrigation, the need for drainage, erosion hazard, choice of forest tree species and their growth rates, environmental impact studies, especially those concerning land and water, use of soil to treat wastes and to identify preferred sites for urban developments, and infrastructures such as roads and airfields. In The Netherlands, soil survey information has been used for decisions about urban expansion, the use of various geological deposits as soil substitutes and the suitability of soils for recreational areas and wildlife reserves.

Agriculture and forestry

Mapping units shown on soil survey maps are 'agriculturally significant because they are defined by properties that directly or indirectly affect crop production and management' (Mackney, 1974). The soil properties of direct importance to agriculture include soil colour, texture, structure, organic matter content, consistency and moisture regime. Several of these properties are interrelated, such as colour with organic matter and moisture content. Particle size is also closely linked with the hydrological properties of the soil, and the content and type of clay determines the mechanical and engineering properties. The physical condition of soils is of particular concern as intensive farming systems may reduce organic matter content to the point where soils become unstable and are easily eroded. The retention and release of soil moisture is of particular interest to the agronomist and, when balanced against demand by crops, areas of soil moisture deficit can be mapped and plans drawn up for irrigation. The relation between moisture content and physical condition of the soil determines when cultivation techniques can be applied. The workability of soils for farm implements at certain times of the year limits many farm operations.

The fertility of soils can be correlated broadly with texture as far as the availability of nitrogen and potassium responses are concerned; some soils have high reserves of non-exchangeable potassium which is released by weathering from the clay fraction. The ability of many soils, particularly in the humid tropics, to fix the phosphate added in fertilizers, so that it is unavailable for plants, is well known; if the distribution of these soils is known, appropriate action can be taken. In the UK it has been stated that a knowledge of the soil series can often be more useful than the analytical data from the laboratory for the interpretation of the results of experiments with potassium fertilizers. Trace element deficiencies, resulting in reduced crop yields, can also be related to soil series; again, if the distribution of the soils is known, appropriate amendments can be applied. At the other extreme, in a few soils the natural content of trace elements approaches the concentration which is a danger to human health. This is especially a problem in urban areas, where fallout of toxic metals from industrial activities is greater and can raise the content in the soil over the safe limit. Additions of sewage sludge containing metal pollutants could also push such soils over the safety limit.

The climate-based length of growing period and the seasonal rainfall characteristics of the FAO Agro-ecological Zones project have shown the physical limitations for the growth of certain crops, but when soil distribution is added to the climatic possibilities, a realistic picture emerges of the most appropriate areas for specific crops to be grown. In the case of Africa, land suitability for eleven crops has been considered and potential crop yields have been calculated. Accurate, soil-based information such as this is necessary to plan for sustainable soil use and food security in many developing countries.

Foresters are particularly concerned to plant trees in the most appropriate places, as once planted the crop takes between 75 and 250 years to come to maturity; in such circumstances, mistakes are expensive in both time and money. The information provided by a soil survey enables areas to be identified where organic soils render the trees liable to windthrow during gales, or where shallow soils limit the volume of soil the tree roots can exploit. The capability of soils to provide moisture and nutrients for the growing trees is a very significant factor, especially as many forest areas are in districts where growing conditions are not ideal. Combined with relief and climatic information, soil survey data can be used in planning drainage for wetter sites, and the correct tree species can be selected for planting on appropriate soils.

Over-production of farm crops in Europe and the USA has brought problems which the authorities have attempted to solve by setting land aside from 'productive' use. The problem lies in deciding which part of the land should be taken out of production. Interpretation of soil maps could provide valuable background information upon which rational decisions could be based; this can be done rapidly using databases and GIS.

Soil fertility

When dealing with soils, the agricultural aspect of their use naturally comes first to mind. A soil survey gives a basic knowledge of the distribution of soils and their chemical and physical properties. It enables more accurate advice to be given to the farmer regarding applications of fertilizers to amend plant nutritional deficiencies and the quantity of other amendments, such as lime, to correct acidity. Although individual farmers are well aware of the productivity of their own land, and the figures for national or regional areas are available, there is little available information about the productivity of individual soils (Fig. 14.6). The problem is that any field or group of fields includes several different soils with varied properties and fertility.

Fig. 14.6 A fertilizer trial with sugarbeet.

Elements are removed from the land when crops are harvested, pastures grazed or timber removed. At the same time soils lose constituents by the natural process of leaching. Figures for these losses are given in the following example:

	Annual losses (kg ha^{-1})					
	N	P	K	Ca	Mg	S
Leached from a representative silt loam	22.4	trace	28.0	112	22.4	11.2
Removed by an average rotation crop	134.5	24.6	112	44.8	33.6	22.4

Soil fertility has been defined as *the ability of the soil to supply enough nutrients and water to allow the crop to make the most of the site.* Although the supply of plant nutrients is a chemical phenomenon, the physical condition of the soil is also important, especially the ability of the soil to supply water, the medium through which nutrients reach the growing plant. Plant nutrients are present in two forms: available and unavailable. Available nutrients are present in readily assimilable forms which plants can absorb. They are usually present in the soil solution as ions or are adsorbed onto the exchange positions of the clay–humus colloids. Two examples of unavailable plant nutrients are nitrogen, which may be locked up in undecomposed plant remains, and phosphates, which become immobilized as insoluble forms of calcium, iron or aluminium phosphate. The majority of soils do not contain sufficient plant nutrients for regular cropping to be continued without their replacement, so if sustained yields are to be obtained, these mineral elements must be replaced. Any form of sustainable land-use must work towards the most efficient use of available plant nutrients.

There are about seventeen elements which are essential for satisfactory plant growth. Carbon, hydrogen and oxygen are obtained directly from the atmosphere and the remainder of the major and minor nutrients are obtained from the soil. Average amounts of major plant nutrients found when surface soils of temperate regions are analysed are 0.2 to 0.5 per cent nitrogen, 0.01 to 0.2 per cent phosphorus, and 0.17 to 3.3 per cent potassium. The amounts of other elements which are utilized by plants include 0.70 to 3.60 per cent calcium, 0.12 to 1.50 per cent magnesium, and 0.10 to 0.20 per cent sulphur. Other elements are required in very small amounts, but without them plant growth is unsatisfactory. These 'trace elements' include zinc, in the range of 0.001 to 0.025 per cent, boron and copper, 0.0005 to 0.015 per cent, and molybdenum, 0.00002 to 0.00005 per cent. Although necessary in very small amounts, these metallic elements can be toxic to plants if present in larger quantities. From these figures it is clear that plants need nutrient elements in widely differing amounts.

For many years the supply of **nitrogen** to plants was a mystery, as plants cannot obtain nitrogen themselves from the atmosphere. It was not until the end of the 19th century that microbiologists in Germany showed that nitrogen was 'fixed' by micro-organisms living symbiotically in root nodules of leguminous plants, such as beans, peas, vetches and clovers, or living free in the soil. Before the invention of artificial nitrogenous fertilizers, nitrogen was obtained for crops by the decomposition of animal and vegetable material by bacterial attack in the soils to release ammonia, which breaks down further to nitrites and nitrates in the well-known nitrogen cycle. Only in the form of nitrate is the nitrogen available to plants.

Nitrogen is closely linked to the amount of vegetative growth, so additions of nitrogenous fertilizer increase the bulk of forage crops, but can delay ripening in cereals and leave the crop susceptible to fungal attack. Shortage of nitrogen in plants can be seen by a yellowish colour in the foliage, combined with a lack of growth.

Phosphorus also occurs naturally in breakdown products of plant or animal matter and in this form is most readily available for crops. Inorganic calcium phosphate, such as the mineral apatite, occurs in many localities throughout the world. When finely ground and spread on the soil it is referred to as 'rock phosphate' from which phosphate is slowly released as it weathers. Bones were used by J.B. Lawes when he ran out of local naturally occurring phosphate deposits in his early attempts to make 'superphosphate' fertilizer with sulphuric acid. Commercial production of phosphate fertilizer now takes place by the action of orthophosphoric acid on rock phosphate, yielding about 50 per cent soluble P_2O_5. Unfortunately, when it is added to the soil, much of the phosphate may be immobilized as insoluble compounds of iron, calcium and aluminium and so is unavailable for the growing plants.

Root crops, particularly swedes, turnips and potatoes, are sensitive to a lack of phosphorus. More rapid growth in the early stages and better tillering is obtained in cereal crops by the application of phosphate. This element is involved in the formation of cell nucleoproteins as well as in the metabolism of carbohydrates.

The third major plant nutrient, **potassium**, occurs in silicate minerals, such as orthoclase and mica, as well as in evaporite deposited as inland seas dried out in past geological times. The common name 'potash' derives from the concentrated leachate of wood ash, chiefly potassium carbonate, from which this element was formerly derived. Although potassium salts readily dissolve in water, not all the potassium applied in fertilizer is immediately available, as some becomes adsorbed on the clay–humus complex. The process of base exchange then allows a steady release over a period of time and potassium can be taken up by plants or lost to the drainage waters (thus the cation exchange capacity can be used as an indirect indication of soil fertility). Potassium is utilized by plants in their metabolic processes, particularly in the building of amino acids and proteins. When a deficiency occurs, leaf tips and margins are seen to be dying prematurely and plants are small with low yields.

Although it is necessary to have these major plant nutrients available for good crop growth, it is essential that they are in the right proportions. It is essential also that the soil is neither too acid nor too alkaline, because the availability of nutrients and trace elements is limited at extremes of pH value. It is also important for the soil to have good physical condition, as without stable soil structure drainage is impaired and the diffusion of oxygen into, and carbon dioxide out of, the soil is restricted. Modern intensive forms of agriculture with monocultures tends to return limited amounts of organic matter to the soil and structure has become weaker. At the same time, agricultural machinery has become heavier, compressing and compacting the soil. Clearly, these problems must all be kept in focus, otherwise the optimum yields will not be obtained, even where plant nutrients are present in the correct proportions.

All farming systems attempt to utilize the soil for crop production on a continuing, sustainable basis but they may use different approaches to achieve this end. A simple system, such as shifting cultivation or bush fallow, allows a natural regeneration of fertility under wild vegetation. Burning then releases the combined plant nutrients which fertilize the succeeding crop. Unfortunately, through leaching and combustion, there are always losses and fertility rapidly declines, particularly in soils of the humid tropical regions.

Over-use of fertilizers can be harmful as it leads to eutrophication of rivers and lakes, a process whereby rapid aquatic plant growth can lead to deoxygenation and death of all aerobic life in those bodies of water. Drinking water supplies can be affected by nitrates leached from the soil; these are particularly harmful to very young children, and strategies are available for reducing losses from fields. For reasons of both health and economy, fertilizers should not be applied at rates in excess of those found by experimentation to be justified by economic returns.

Land reclamation

Many 19th- and 20th-century land-uses have left a legacy of derelict land, so badly damaged that in the worst cases it cannot be rectified without the expenditure of considerable sums of money. Derelict land is defined as *land so damaged by industrial and other development that it is incapable of use without treatment*. Some of this land is also badly polluted and this adds to the costs of reclamation. Recognition of such sites depends upon definitions decreed by politicians and administrators and so conflicting figures are given for the extent, depending upon the author's views. For example in the UK, official figures of 300 sites covering about 10,000 hectares contrast with a report by the House of Commons Committee of 50,000–100,000 sites covering up to 100,000 hectares.

The contaminants may affect the solid, liquid or gaseous phases of the soil. The most common culprits are toxic metals and their compounds, asbestos, various organic chemicals, oils, tars, pesticides, explosive and asphyxiant gases, radioactive materials, combustible materials, biologically active materials and other hazardous minerals. Commonly, these occur on restricted sites, some designated as official landfills, but leakages and unofficial dumping can affect other areas. Contaminants may also be dispersed widely, as with radioactive fallout or acid deposition, and toxic metals have been spread by the use of contaminants in fertilizers and organic manures.

Polluted sites occupying restricted areas can be contained by barriers, capping and undersealing (Fig. 14.7) to keep the pollutants from affecting the surrounding areas; alternatively, techniques exist to stabilize polluted soils, setting them in a solid, insoluble mass. Reclamation by thermal techniques is expensive as it is necessary for complete removal to take place, followed by combustion at very high temperatures, and finally the return of the lifeless soil material to the site. Claims are being made for the efficacy of micro-biological soil-cleaning techniques, especially where organic chemicals are involved. A few sites may be cleaned by simple physical or chemical means, but most sites have a multiple contamination problem and reclamation has to involve a range of techniques.

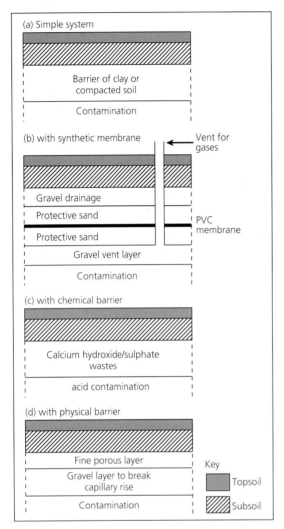

Fig. 14.7 Cover systems for isolating polluted soils (reproduced from *Soil Use and Management* **7**:151–8, with permission of CAB International).

Former gravel pits and old quarries have been used for the dumping of household wastes; in the better examples they have been covered over and soil material spread on the surface. These sites are capable of producing methane and other gases for up to 15 years after burial. If such areas are scheduled for amenity planting or cropping, failures must be expected where soil air is displaced by non-life-supporting gases. Toxic drainage waters can also emanate from landfills, affecting riparian soils and life. The selection of sites and the choice of materials used to form intermediate and final cover of

landfills can be influenced by the nature of the soil present. An input of information about their suitability for the desired use from the pedological point of view should be of obvious value, but advantage is rarely taken of it.

Areas mined by the opencast (open pit) method for coal, lignite, ironstone, gravel, and many other minerals, can be restored to a productive capability. Soil scientists, in collaboration with ecologists, agriculturalists and foresters, can help accelerate the natural processes of soil formation and revegetation to return the area to usefulness (Figs 14.8 and 14.9). In land reclamation, and on large civil engineering projects, soil is handled by heavy earth-moving equipment. It is first stripped and placed into stockpiles, where it remains until it is required. Some soils are resilient to this treatment, but others are very vulnerable to damage whilst handling. Information about the soil moisture content at which they can safely be moved can make all the difference between a successful reclamation and a disaster. A poor restoration is not a good advertisement for civil engineering firms and, if the restoration phase has to be done again, extra costs are incurred.

Soil conservation

Only a few years ago, the topic of soil conservation was synonymous with measures to prevent or contain soil erosion. In the last few years the scope of soil conservation has widened to include protection against chemical and physical damage. Forward-looking countries have legislation to protect their soil resources against exhaustive exploitation. Whilst each episode of soil erosion is a unique event, some general conclusions may be drawn. Certain particle-size classes are more at risk than others, for example silt loam, sand, sandy loam and sandy silt loam, particularly if the sand is fine-grained or has a low content of organic matter. The occurrence of intense rainfall events and periods when the soil is left bare after cultivation are other contributory factors to the risk of soil erosion.

Considerable effort has been made to develop a model for determining the risk of soil erosion. These models require input of basic soil data which is then linked to climate and slope of landforms to arrive at an answer. Models have been developed in

Fig. 14.8 Removal of coal from an opencast site.

the USA (Universal Soil Loss Equation, USLE) and in southern Africa (Soil Loss Estimation Model of South Africa, SLEMSA), and a facility now exists (Soil Water Erosion Assessment Program, SWEAP) for these models to interface with databases such as those developed at ISRIC under the SOTER project. SWEAP enables assessments to be made using monthly steps and taking into account seasonal dynamics of crop cover and rainfall erosivity. Results are obtained in abstract erosion hazard units rather than as quantified estimates of soil losses.

The wider problems of human impact and the need for soil conservation are discussed in Chapter 8, where the twelve clauses of the *European Soil Charter* are presented.

Soil quality

Whether a soil is 'good' or 'poor' is a somewhat subjective assessment, depending upon the observer's experience, the nature of the surrounding soils and the desired use for the soil. Traditionally, the quality of a soil has depended upon its ability, with appropriate management, to produce crops, to

Fig. 14.9 Opencast site restored to productive use.

support a building, to form a building material, to filter sewage, or to fulfil whatever other need is envisaged. Farmers and horticulturalists have been well aware that certain soils possess qualities which identify them as good for certain crops or plants. Similarly, civil engineers have particular criteria for the use of soils in construction activities.

Physical soil quality depends upon the volume (depth) of soil which the plant roots can exploit, the water-holding capacity and the moisture release potential. The soil's physical response to deformation by the growing roots of plants or the weight of traffic is significant, for if roots cannot penetrate the soil the plant will suffer, and if the soil cannot support vehicular traffic it may be difficult to harvest the crop. Such properties will vary according to the season. Successful road building in many parts of the world is completely dependent upon the physical quality of the soil materials available.

Chemical qualities which mark a good soil include the content of organic matter and of available plant nutrients. Management practices can have a large effect on soil chemical properties and advantage should be taken of these to improve soil quality. Some soils have disadvantages, such as the ability to 'fix' added phosphate fertilizers so that they are unavailable for plants. In other cases, the presence of soluble salts can severely inhibit the growth of crops, as well as causing physical damage to buildings and roads.

Biological constraints of soils are often related to previous misuse which has allowed a pathogen or disease to flourish. The build-up of eelworm in soils where successive potato crops have been grown can form a severe limitation to land-use. Soils used for sewage disposal can accumulate pathogens, in addition to substantial quantities of toxic metals, which decrease their quality.

Quantification of soil quality has proved difficult, even though in most cases the soil properties which constitute soil quality are known and quantifiable, so it is theoretically possible to use forms of scoring to amalgamate the different effects in an assessment of soil quality. These soil properties can also be used to monitor how soils are standing up to the pressures imposed upon them by increasing demands for crop production. Soil monitoring has been proposed for the surveillance of soils against contamination and degradation. The tasks of soil monitoring are seen as early detection of any potentially hazardous impact on the soil, the anticipation of as yet unidentified dangers, the assessment of the current health of soils and diagnosis of trends.

Despite the difficulties, it is almost inevitable that, in the future, soil knowledge will play an increasingly important part in the valuation of land. Obviously the soil already figures in a prospective buyer's assessment of a market price, although the assessment is usually based upon instinct and local knowledge rather than on accurate scientific knowledge of the soils concerned.

Capability and suitability

Several attempts have been made to classify land with its soils from the standpoint of land-use capability. Some of the difficulties in this procedure will be evident from the previous comments on soil quality, so although it might seem to be a simple and straightforward geographical exercise, it is fraught with many difficulties because of the many combinations of site, soil and current economic conditions. Maps of land-use are an essential part of the environmental assessment, but such maps are not based upon the fundamental properties of the

Table 14.3 The land-use capability classes of the Soil Survey of England and Wales

I	Land with very minor or no physical limitations to use
II	Land with minor limitations that reduce the choice of crops and interfere with cultivations
III	Land with moderate limitations that restrict the choice of crops and/or demand careful management
IV	Land with moderately severe limitations that restrict the choice of crop and/or require very careful management practices
V	Land with severe limitations that restrict its use to pasture, forestry and recreation
VI	Land with very severe limitations that restrict its use to rough grazing, forestry and recreation
VII	Land with extremely severe limitations that cannot be rectified.

land and soils. In extreme cases, land-use is dependent upon the landowner's whim rather than on what is the best use or the use which is sustainable in the long term.

However, if an evaluation system is based upon the properties or actual limitations imposed by the environment, parameters which are not so easily changed, the resulting classification can be interpreted in the light of current economic conditions. The limitations included in this type of soil and landscape assessment include wetness caused by impermeable or slowly permeable soil horizons, flooding, shallowness, extremes of soil texture and structure, the inherent low fertility of some soils, gradient of the land, complexity of the soil pattern, liability for erosion, altitude above sea level, and high rainfall amounts.

Consideration of these limiting factors enables land to be classified on a scale of eight classes in the USA or seven classes in the UK (Table 14.3) and Canada. In both schemes, arable land with decreasing versatility constitutes classes I to IV (Fig. 14.10). The remaining classes are concerned with land most suitable for grazing, forests or nature reserves.

Within each class, subclasses can be identified according to the limiting factor or factors which detract from the ideal, and these subclasses are given an appropriate symbol. In the UK system, five are used: wetness (w), soil (s), gradient (g),

climate (c) and erosion (e). Similar subclasses are used in the original USDA version of the land capability classification. The system is primarily for use with agricultural land, and the land capability is assessed assuming a moderately high level of management. It does not attempt to state the suitability of soils for particular crops, nor does it attempt to forecast yields of crops. Such factors as the distance to markets, availability of capital, mechanization or farm structure are not taken into account, even though these will influence decisions about land-use. Minor improvement schemes, liable to deteriorate with time, will not affect the classification, but major schemes, such as lowering the regional water table, will necessitate a change in classification. Finally, it must be appreciated that land and soils may be grouped together within classes and subclasses for very different reasons, and will require individual management, fertilizer and cropping programmes.

It has been suggested that the land-use capability classification stresses the negative features, whereas it would be preferable to stress the good points of the land. A system which attempted this was proposed

Fig. 14.10 A landscape with land-use capability classes and subclasses indicated. Well-drained shallow chalky loams (2s), wet clay lowlands (3w) and steep slopes (4g) occur related to the pattern of topography and soils.

by an American author (Storie, 1933) who used the product of an assessment of four profile characteristics to give a capability classification; this parametric scheme was subsequently expanded by FAO staff to include eight profile characters (Riquier, 1974). Each parameter is rated as a percentage and the product of these gives an index of productivity. When these are adjusted for optimum management, a potentiality index is obtained, thus land can be classified on both potential and productivity.

FAO continued its interest in land classification with the 1970 *Framework for Land Evaluation*. Central to this approach is a land suitability classification, in which suitability is defined as *the fitness for a given type of land for a specified purpose*. In this system, land is classified first as suitable or not suitable. Suitable land is then subdivided into up to five classes (S1, S2, S3 etc.) on a scale corresponding to highly, moderately and marginally suitable, respectively (Table 14.4 and Fig. 4.11). Subclasses indicate the potential limitations, drawing attention to specific limitations which affect the land. A land suitability unit is the lowest tier in the system, used to identify areas which require different management at a farm level. However, what is suitable is not necessarily always sustainable. Consequently, FAO has recently published *An International Framework for Evaluating Sustainable Land Management* (FESLM), a methodology for the analysis of land-use sustainability.

By nominating a particular crop (e.g. maize, cotton) and taking into account the biophysical requirements which have to be met (temperature, day length, water, nutrients), the soil requirements (resilience against erosion, compaction, etc.) and the management requirements (motive power, equipment, costs, pesticides, markets, etc.), it is possible to compile a table of ratings for the suitability of land for that crop.

The suitability of land for a defined agricultural use is often conditioned by relatively few significant factors. Once chosen and given values, these parameters may be used to give estimates of soil productivity which lie between a qualitative 'expert' judgement and estimates produced by mathematical models.

Individual parameters of soils, when multiplied together, can provide an index of productivity. One example developed at the ICRISAT Centre in India is the use of an equation to predict the consequences of soil erosion:

$$PI_{soil} = (A_i C_i D_i G_i WF_i)$$

where PI_{soil} = soil productivity index; A_i = available water capacity of layer i; C_i = bulk density of layer i; D_i = pH of layer i; G_i = gravel content

Table 14.4 Land suitability classes (after FAO, 1976)

Class	Definition
S1 Highly suitable	Land having no significant limitations to sustained application of the defined use, or only minor limitations that will not significantly reduce productivity or benefits and will not raise input requirements above an acceptable level.
S2 Moderately suitable	Land having limitations that in aggregate are moderately severe for sustained application of the defined use; the limitations reduce productivity or benefits, or increase required inputs to the extent that the general advantage to be gained from the use, although still attractive, will be appreciably inferior to that expected from class S1.
S3 Marginally suitable	Land having limitations that in aggregate are severe for sustained application of the defined use and will reduce productivity or benefits, or increase required inputs to the extent that the defined use will be only marginally justified.
N1 Currently not suitable	Land having limitations that may be surmountable in time but that cannot be corrected with existing knowledge at a currently acceptable cost; the limitations are so severe as to preclude the defined land-use at present.
N2 Permanently not suitable	Land having limitations that appear so severe as to preclude any possibility of successful sustained application of the defined land-use.

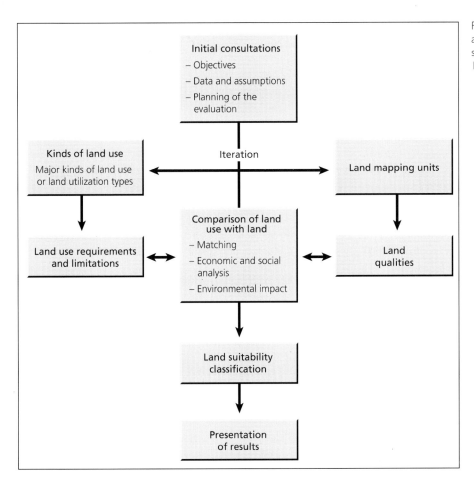

Fig. 14.11 Schematic approach to land suitability (after FAO, 1976).

of layer i; WF_i = weighting factor for layer i; i = a serial number 1,2...n; n = number of layers.

In countries which have large areas still under-developed or at a low level of production, the apportionment or reapportionment of land could be an important sequel to natural resource surveys. Perhaps the best-known surveys of the type are those done by the Land Research Division of CSIRO in Australasia. These surveys are carried out at a reconnaissance scale, and subsequently detailed soil surveys can be used when specific development project areas have been identified, such as an irrigation scheme, pasture improvement areas, or areas for forest planting.

In other countries of the British Common-wealth, similar surveys were carried out by the Directorate of Overseas Surveys. In The Netherlands, an important part of the development of the land-use plans for Flevoland, the last large polder reclaimed from the IJsselmeer, was based on soil surveys carried out during the final stages of the draining process.

Conclusions

Pedology is a correlative science, bringing together the many facets of the environment which are involved in the formation and maintenance of soils. It is a young science and has within it room for many different scientific approaches. Unfortunately, new approaches are not always met with an enthusiastic reception, but current aware-ness of the need for soil science to take a more cen-tral role in the environmental sciences is a hopeful sign, and the acceptance of a more holistic approach should help ensure that the results of soil research reach the people for whom it is taking place. Soil scientists are urged by the International

Society of Soil Science to take a more positive and broadly based approach towards soil care, and to raise the awareness of a wider public, particularly administrators and governments, about the need to fully integrate soil science with policies of sustainable land management. It is hoped that this book will help to mould opinion about soils amongst the coming generation and so go some way towards reaching this goal.

The sustainable use of soils can be achieved by the adoption of appropriate systems of management. In western Europe, throughout the medieval period and culminating with the English 'agricultural revolution', mixed systems of arable and pastoral husbandry were developed. Although these systems minimized soil degradation in the European environment, when taken to other places, notably the United States, South America and Australia, they were not always successful and resulted in soil losses through erosion and chemical degradation. Mechanization of agriculture in the 20th century has also changed the balance, producing systems with a high input–high output type of economy which cannot be replicated easily, other than in the economic framework of the developed countries.

Important aspects of soil management include the enhancement of organic matter content and with it, the maintenance of the diversity of the soil's biological population. This will improve the stability of soil structure and minimize losses of soil through erosion. Additionally, a higher organic matter content will improve the nutrient- and moisture-holding capability of the soil. These concepts for soil management are not new; they have been known in principle for the last century. What is desperately needed is that they should be put into practice before degradation of the world's soils proceeds beyond the point at which they are irreversibly damaged.

Some soils have high stability and resilience to mismanagement, while others are vulnerable and require more careful use. The distribution of resilient and vulnerable soils in the landscape is known in general terms, but more quantitative statements are required from soil scientists to convince other disciplines that soil knowledge has a vital part to play in global resource management. It is possible to manage soils for maximizing profit, for reduction of soil degradation risk, for reduction of emissions which risk global warming, or reduction of the risk of water pollution. In each of these approaches, techniques are known and available for achieving the desired objective. However, in the end it is the actual soil, with its particular attributes, which should dictate the most appropriate methods of management.

As an important factor in the life of all ecosystems and mankind, soils can filter harmful pollutants from downward-percolating waters, thus keeping the aquifers clean. The buffering function, responsible for holding and releasing plant nutrients, also acts to adsorb and hold many pollutants, such as radionuclides from atomic fallout. The soil, with its wide range of faunal and floral inhabitants, transforms organic pollutants, such as urine, faeces, pesticides and other organic wastes, into harmless compounds. Soils are indeed one of the most important environmental factors in our lives.

Further reading

Alloway, B.J. (ed.), 1990. *Heavy Metals in Soils*. Blackie, Glasgow.

Anon., 1985. *Erosion and Soil Productivity. Proceedings of the National Symposium on Erosion and Soil Productivity*, American Society of Agricultural Engineers, St Joseph, Michigan.

Batjes, N.H. and Bridges, E.M., 1993. Soil vulnerability to pollution in Europe. *Soil Use and Management* **9**:25–9.

Bibby, J.S. and Mackney, D., 1969. *Land Use Capability Classification*. Technical Monograph No. 1, Soil Survey of England and Wales, Harpenden.

Blum, W.E.H., 1990. *Soil Pollution by Heavy Metals*. Council of Europe, Strasbourg.

Boels, D., Davies, D.B. and Johnston, A.E. (eds.), 1982. *Soil Degradation*. Balkema, Rotterdam.

Bouma, J., 1994. Sustainable land use as a future focus for pedology. *Soil Science Society of America Journal* **58**:645–6.

Bridges, E.M., 1991. Dealing with contaminated soils. *Soil Use and Management* **7**:151–8.

Cattle, S.R., McBratney, A.B. and Yates, D.B., 1995. The soil stack: an interactive computer program describing basic soil science and soil degradation. *Journal of Natural Resources and Life Sciences Education* **24**:33–6.

Davidson, D.A., 1980. *Soils and Land Use Planning*. Longman, London.

Driessen, P.M. and Konijn, N.T., 1992. *Land Use Systems Analysis*. Department of Soil Science and Geology, Wageningen Agricultural University.

FAO, 1976. *A Framework for Land Evaluation*. Soils Bulletin No. 32, FAO, Rome.

FAO, 1993. *FESLM, an International Framework for Evaluating Sustainable Land Management*. World Soil Resources Report No. 73, FAO, Rome.

FAO, 1994. *Cherish the Earth: Soil Management for Sustainable Agriculture and Environmental Protection in the Tropics*. FAO, Rome.

Greenland, D.J. and Szabolcs, I. (eds.), 1994. *Soil Resilience and Sustainable Land Use*. CAB International, Wallingford.

Hillel, D., 1991. *Out of the Earth: Civilization and the Life of the Soil*. University of California Press, Berkeley, California.

Ineson, P. (ed.), 1986. *Pollution in Cumbria*. ITE Symposium No. 16, Grange over Sands, Cumbria.

Jarvis, M.G. and Mackney, D., 1979. *Soil Survey Applications*. Technical Monograph No. 13, Soil Survey of England and Wales, Harpenden.

Klingebiel, A.A. and Montgomery, P.H., 1966. *Land Capability Classification*. USDA Agriculture Handbook 210, Washington.

Lal, R., 1994. *Soil Erosion: Research Methods*. Soil and Water Conservation Society, Delay Beach, Florida.

Lal, R. and Stewart, B.A. (eds.), 1990. *Soil Degradation*. Advances in Soil Science, Volume 11, Springer-Verlag, New York.

Lal, R., Kimble, J.M. and Levine, E. (eds.), 1994. *Soil Processes and Greenhouse Effect*. USDA Soil Conservation Service, National Soil Survey Centre, Lincoln.

Mackney, D., 1974. Soil survey in agriculture. In: Mackney, D. (ed.) *Soil Type and Land Capability*. Technical Monograph No. 4, Soil Survey of England and Wales, Harpenden.

MAFF, 1993. *Code of Good Agricultural Practice for the Protection of the Soil*. MAFF Environment, London.

McRae, S.G. and Burnham, C.P., 1981. *Land Evaluation*. Clarendon Press, Oxford.

Miller, F.P., 1993. Soil Science: a scope broader than its identity. *Soil Science Society of America Journal* **57**:299, 564.

Olson, G.W., 1981. *Soils and the Environment*. Chapman and Hall, New York and London.

Pierce, F.J. and Lal, R., 1991. Soil management in the 21st century. In: *Soil Management for Sustainability*. Soil and Water Conservation Society, pp. 175–9.

Riquier, J., 1974. A summary of parametric methods of soil and land evaluation. *FAO Soils Bulletin* **22**:47–53.

Simonson, R.W. (ed.), 1974. *Non-agricultural Applications of Soil Surveys*. Elsevier, Amsterdam.

Storie, R.E., 1933. *An Index for Rating the Agricultural Value of Soils*. California Agricultural Experimental Station Bulletin 556.

Syers, K. and Rimmer, D. (eds.), 1994. *Soil Science and Sustainable Land Management in the Tropics*. CAB International, Wallingford.

Tiedje, O. and Tapkenhinrichs, M., 1993. Evaluation of pedo-transfer functions. *Soil Science Society of America Journal* **57**:1088–95.

van Engelen, V.W.P. and Wen, T.T. (eds.), 1993. *Global and National Soils and Terrain Digital Databases (SOTER): Procedures manual*. ISRIC, Wageningen.

van Keulen, H. and Wolf, J. (eds.), 1986. *Modelling of Agricultural Production, Weather, Soils and Crops*. Pudoc, Wageningen.

Webster, R., 1985. *Quantitative analysis of soil in the field*. Advances in Soil Science 3, Springer-Verlag, New York.

Wild, A., 1992. *Soils and the Environment: an Introduction*. Cambridge University Press, Cambridge.

Wösten, J.H.M., Bouma, J. and Stoffelsen, G.H., 1985. The use of soil survey data for regional soil water simulation. *Soil Science Society of America Journal* **49**:1238–45.

Index

Plates A1–A32 are between pages 58 and 59; Plates B1–B32 are between pages 122 and 123. Italic page numbers refer to figures and tables.